THE UNITED STATES AND EUROPE
IN THE GLOBAL ARENA

Also by Frances G. Burwell

PARTNERS FOR PEACE? The United States and Europe in the Global Arena

Also by Ivo H. Daalder

GETTING TO DAYTON: The Making of America's Bosnia Policy

RETHINKING THE UNTHINKABLE: New Directions for Nuclear Arms Control

NATO IN THE 21st CENTURY: What Purpose? What Mission?

THE NATURE AND PRACTICE OF FLEXIBLE RESPONSE: NATO Strategy and Theater Nuclear Forces since 1967

THE SDI CHALLENGE TO EUROPE STRATEGIC DEFENCES IN THE 1990s: Criteria for Deployment

The United States and Europe in the Global Arena

Edited by

Frances G. Burwell
Executive Director
Center for International and Security Studies in Maryland
School of Public Affairs
University of Maryland

and

Ivo H. Daalder
Director of Research
Center for International and Security Studies in Maryland, and
Associate Professor
School of Public Affairs
University of Maryland

D
1065
.U5
U55
1999

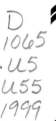

First published in Great Britain 1999 by
MACMILLAN PRESS LTD
Houndmills, Basingstoke, Hampshire RG21 6XS and London
Companies and representatives throughout the world

A catalogue record for this book is available from the British Library.

ISBN 0–333–74081–5

First published in the United States of America 1999 by
ST. MARTIN'S PRESS, INC.,
Scholarly and Reference Division,
175 Fifth Avenue, New York, N.Y. 10010

ISBN 0–312–22188–6

Library of Congress Cataloging-in-Publication Data
The United States and Europe in the global arena / edited by Frances
G. Burwell and Ivo H. Daalder.
p.   cm.
Includes bibliographical references and index.
ISBN 0–312–22188–6 (cloth)
1. Europe—Foreign relations—United States.   2. United States–
–Foreign relations—Europe.   3. United States—Foreign
relations—1989–   I. Burwell, Frances G. (Frances Gale)
II. Daalder, Ivo H.
D1065.U5U56   1999
327.7304—dc21   99–11219
                                                             CIP

Selection and editorial matter © Frances G. Burwell and Ivo H. Daalder 1999
Chapters 1 and 11 © Frances G. Burwell 1999
Chapter 2 © Michael E. Brown 1999
Chapter 5 © Philip H. Gordon 1999
Chapter 9 © Richard H. Steinberg 1999
Chapters 3, 4, 6–8, 10 © Macmillan Press Ltd 1999

This book is printed on paper suitable for recycling and made from fully managed and
sustained forest sources.

10   9   8   7   6   5   4   3   2   1
08   07   06   05   04   03   02   01   00   99

Printed and bound in Great Britain by
Antony Rowe Ltd, Chippenham, Wiltshire

Contents

Acknowledgements

This volume is a product of the Project on a New US–European Dialogue of the Center for International and Security Studies at the University of Maryland (CISSM). The Project seeks to examine the assumptions, institutions and processes of the transatlantic relationship as it recasts itself in the wake of the Cold War. It particularly seeks to cross two borders: first, the division between policy and academe; and second, that between security and economic issues. It does this by bringing together policymakers and scholars to debate current issues and collaborate on policy-oriented research, and by involving analysts who work across the entire gamut of transatlantic issues in its projects.

This book has its roots in a December 1994 conference which applied that approach to the subject of US–European cooperation and conflict on a range of security, political and economic issues. In particular, it focused on those issues that went beyond the narrow confines of the traditional transatlantic relationship, to address the roles of the United States and Europe (usually, but not always, the European Union) in dealing with the new challenges of the post-Cold War era. That conference led to a brief monograph – *Partners for Peace? The United States and Europe in the Global Arena* – and to a desire to explore transatlantic behaviour on these issues in greater depth. Thanks to the generosity and patience of our funders, we were able to launch the idea of this volume. An authors' workshop allowed us not only to review chapters under way but also to pull together some common threads and key themes. The result is this book, which we hope will enhance understanding on both sides of the Atlantic of both the importance of transatlantic cooperation and the difficulties in achieving it.

Such an undertaking inevitably requires the support and efforts of many individuals and institutions along the way. Our biggest debt is to our colleagues at CISSM, particularly the director, Mac Destler, who provided both encouragement and insights as we developed this project and pushed it toward fruition. Naledi Saul, Parin Shah, and Andrea White provided invaluable administrative assistance, without which running the initial conference and finishing the manuscript would have been even bigger challenges. Along with all the chapter authors, we owe a special debt to Ellen Frost and Steven Miller. They played key roles at the authors' workshop, critiquing all the papers, and making vital contributions to our identification of cross-cutting themes and common conclusions. Jane M.O. Sharp also enlivened our gatherings with her forthright observations and her insights into transatlantic cooperation – or the the lack of it – on the former Yugoslavia.

Finally, neither the Project on a New US–European Dialogue nor this book would exist without our funders. The Washington office of the Friedrich Ebert Stiftung, directed by Dieter Dettke, co-sponsored the initial conference at which the idea for this book was born. Support from the German Marshall Fund of the United States made it possible for our European colleagues to participate in that meeting. Last, but certainly not least, our major funder, the European Commission, provided esential and generous support throughout the project. In a very real sense, this book is not only about transatlantic cooperation, but the product of it as well.

FRANCES G. BURWELL
IVO H. DAALDER

Notes on the Contributors

Michael E. Brown teaches in and is Director of Research for the National Security Studies Program, Edmund A. Walsh School of Foreign Service, Georgetown University. He is the author of *European Security: The Defining Debates* (1998) and *Flying Blind: The Politics of the US Strategic Bomber Program* (1992), which won the Edgar Furniss National Security Book Award.

Frances G. Burwell is the Executive Director of the Center for International and Security Studies at Maryland (CISSM), where she is also co-director of the Project on a New US–European Dialogue. She is the author of the project's conference report, *Partners for Peace? The United States and Europe in the Global Arena* (July 1995). Prior to joining CISSM in July 1992, Ms Burwell was Executive Director of Women in International Security. Ms Burwell has also worked as senior editor at the *Foreign Service Journal*, and as a consultant to the John D. and Catherine T. MacArthur Foundation, the Ford Foundation, and the Aspen Institute.

Ivo H. Daalder is a Visiting Fellow at the Brookings Institution on leave from the University of Maryland where he is Associate Professor at its School of Public Affairs and Director of Research at the Center for International and Security Studies. He is co-director of CISSM's Project on a New US–European Dialogue. From 1995 until 1997, he served on President Clinton's National Security Council staff, where he was responsible for US policy towards Bosnia. Dr Daalder received his PhD in Political Science from the Massachusetts Institute of Technology and has been a fellow at Harvard University's Center for Science and International Affairs and the International Institute for Strategic Studies in London. His most recent publications include 'Bosnia after SFOR: Options for Continued US Engagement', *Survival* (1997–98), *NATO in the 21st Century: What Purpose? What Missions?* (1999), and *Getting to Dayton: The Making of America's Bosnia Policy* (1999).

Renée de Nevers is a Program Officer in arms reduction and security, in the Program on Global Security and Sustainability at the John D. and Catherine T. MacArthur Foundation. She has been a fellow at the Belfer Center for Science and International Affairs at Harvard University, Stanford University's Center for International Security and Arms Control and the Hoover Institution, and has worked at the International Institute for Strategic Studies in London. She has published articles and monographs on Russian foreign policy, European security, and Western efforts to assist democratization in former communist states.

Lily Gardner Feldman is currently Senior Scholar in Residence at Georgetown University's Center for German and European Studies. From 1991 until 1995, she was Research Director of the American Institute for Contemporary German Studies/ The Johns Hopkins University. From 1978 until 1991 she was a professor in the Political Science Department at Tufts University. During her time in Boston, Dr Gardner Feldman was a Research Associate at the Center for European Studies and the Center for International Affairs at Harvard University. Dr Gardner Feldman's research and writing have focused on the European Union (particularly the role of Germany and the EU's international activities), on German foreign policy, and on federalism in international relations. Her current research involves critical evaluation of the concept of 'reconciliation' in international affairs, drawing on Germany's relations with France, the United States and Israel after 1949, and Poland and the Czech Republic after 1989.

Philip H. Gordon was, from 1994 to 1998, the Carol Deane Senior Fellow for US Strategic Studies and the Editor of *Survival* at the International Institute for Strategic Studies in London. He has previously held posts at the Johns Hopkins University School of Advanced International Studies (SAIS) in Washington, DC; the European Institute for Business Administration (INSEAD) outside Paris; the RAND Corporation in Santa Monica; and the German Society for Foreign Affairs in Bonn. The author of several books on European security, his most recent publications include *The Transatlantic Allies and the Changing Middle East* Adelphi Paper 322 (1998); *NATO's Transformation: The Changing Shape of the Atlantic Alliance* (editor 1997); 'Europe's Uncommon Foreign

Policy', *International Security* (Winter 1997–98); 'The European Union and the United States: Looking Toward 2010', *SAIS Review* (Summer/Fall 1997); 'Does the WEU Have a Role?', *Washington Quarterly* (Winter 1997); and 'NATO's Grey Zone', *Prospect* (March 1996). After this chapter was completed Dr Gordon joined the National Security Council staff, where he holds the position of Director for European Affairs. The views expressed are his own, and do not necessarily reflect those of the NSC, US government or any other organization.

Harald Müller has been Director of the Peace Research Institute Frankfurt (PRIF) since 1996. He received his PhD in political science at the Johann Wolfgang Goethe University, Frankfurt, in 1981. A researcher at PRIF (1976–84) and the Center of European Policy Studies in Brussels (1984–1986), he has been directing PRIF's non-proliferation project since 1986. Dr Müller teaches international relations at the Technical University Darmstadt (Germany) and the Johns Hopkins University Center for International Relations in Bologna (Italy). In 1995, he was a member of the German delegation to the NPT Review and Extension Conference.

Brad Roberts is a member of the research staff of the Institute for Defense Analyses in Alexandria, Virginia. From 1986 to 1995 he served as editor of *The Washington Quarterly* and as a research fellow at the Center for Strategic and International Studies (CSIS). He is also chairman of the research advisory council of the Chemical and Biological Arms Control Institute (CBACI), an adjunct professor at George Washington University, and a consultant to the Los Alamos National Laboratory. His recent publications include: *Weapons Proliferation and World Order after the Cold War* (1996); (editor) *Terrorism with Chemical and Biological Weapons: Calibrating Risks and Responses* (1996); 'Rethinking How Wars Must End: NBC War Termination Issues and Major Regional Contingencies', *IDA Report* (May 1996); 'World Order in the Post-Post Cold War Era', *IDA Report* (September 1996); 'Arms Control in the Emerging Strategic Era', *IDA Report* (December 1996); and 'Technology Diffusion and International Politics' in James Brown, ed., *Arms Control in a Multipolar World* (1996).

Beth Simmons is a Professor of Political Science at the University of California, Berkeley, specializing in international political economy and international law and institutions. She has also been a Senior Fellow at the United States Institute of Peace in Washington. Formerly on the faculty of Duke University, she spent 1995–96 working in the Capital Markets and Financial Studies Division of the International Monetary Fund as an International Affairs Fellow, sponsored by the Council on Foreign Relations. Her work has been published in *International Organization* and *World Politics*, and her book, *Who Adjusts? Domestic Sources of Foreign Economic Policy During the Interwar Years, 1923–1938* (1994) was awarded the American Political Science Association's Woodrow Wilson Award for the best book published in the US on government, politics or international affairs, and APSA's Section on Political Economy Award for the best book or article published in the past three years. Professor Simmons received her PhD from Harvard University.

Richard H. Steinberg is Acting Professor of Law at the University of California, Los Angeles, and is also Senior Research Fellow at the Berkeley Roundtable on the International Economy (BRIE) at the University of California, Berkeley. Dr Steinberg was Assistant General Counsel to the United States Trade Representative (USTR) from 1989 to 1991. At USTR, Dr Steinberg worked on the negotiation of the GATT Uruguay Round trade agreements, the North American Free Trade Agreement (NAFTA), and industrial and agricultual trade disputes and accords with foreign governments. In addition, he served as acting chairman of the inter-agency 301 Committee, represented USTR on interagency committees pertaining to trade matters, and represented the Administration's position on legislation concerning specified aspects of trade policy. From 1991–93, Dr Steinberg practiced law at the international firm of Morrison & Foerster. From 1993–96, he was Project Director for International Trade Studies at BRIE, where he directed collaborative projects between BRIE, the Council on Foreign Relations, and other organizations and trade policy experts, to develop a post-Uruguay Round trade agenda. Dr Steinberg received a JD degree from Stanford Law School (1986), as well as a PhD degree in International Politics from Stanford (1992).

Stephen Woolcock is currently Senior Research Fellow at the European Institute, London School of Economics. He was previously with the LSE's Centre for Research on the United States and the European Programme at the Royal Institute of International Affairs (Chatham House). His publications include *Market Access Issues in EC–US Relations: Trading Partners or Trading Blows* (1991); 'European and American Approaches to Regulation: Continued Convergence?' in Jens von Scherpenberg, *Towards Rival Regionalism? US and EU Regional Economic Integration Policies and the Risk of a Transatlantic Regulatory Rift* (1997).

1 Introduction: The United States and Europe in the Global Arena

Frances G. Burwell

For forty years, the partnership between the United States and Western Europe was central to the preservation of peace in the postwar era. Together, they rebuilt Western Europe economically and politically. Together, they created a military alliance that protected Western Europe and reinforced the postwar order. And, together, they constructed an international economic system that brought unprecedented prosperity to the industrialized West.

This cooperation was predicated on two fundamental conditions. First, the overwhelming priority of the Cold War era was to deter Soviet aggression in Western Europe. Any disagreements that threatened to divide the transatlantic partners would be moderated so as not to endanger the cooperation needed to achieve that fundamental goal. Second, it was not a partnership of equals – throughout this period, the United States was the predominant partner and assumed a leadership role. This was fitting, given that only the United States could provide the military power required to deter the Soviet Union. Even when Western Europe began to challenge that preeminence in the economic arena, there was little real questioning of the basic relationship. And when European citizenry seemed on the verge of defying Washington, as with the extensive protests against the deployment of intermediate range nuclear missiles, in the end, Washington's leadership remained a central fact of the Alliance.

The end of the Cold War, however, brought both of these conditions into question. The collapse of the Soviet Union fundamentally altered the environment in which the transatlantic relationship had been formed, and removed the threat that had so effectively encouraged unity within the Alliance. Instead, the United States and Europe faced a proliferation of challenges

1

from around the world – political and economic turmoil in the emerging democracies; regional conflicts from the Gulf area to the southern Russian republics and the Balkans; civil wars in Africa and elsewhere; instabilities fostered by particular rogue regimes; the spread of weapons of mass destruction; and financial crises and trade disputes in an increasingly interconnected global economy. The transatlantic Alliance could no longer simply focus on deterring Soviet aggression; instead it faced a multitude of challenges around the world. Few of these challenges could be resolved by either the United States or Europe working alone; instead they required the active cooperation of both Alliance partners.

Given this shift in the nature and location of threats, the transatlantic partnership at first seemed unlikely to persist in its Cold War form. Under the new circumstances, it was no longer clear that the United States would – or should – retain its preeminent role in the Alliance. As the Warsaw Pact disintegrated, US military power did not seem so essential; in fact, many problems were best addressed by social, political and economic reform. At the same time, the West European states belonging to the European Community embarked on an ambitious agenda towards political union, including the creation of a common foreign and security policy. For a brief time at the beginning of the 1990s, it looked as though the transatlantic relationship might evolve into a true partnership of equals, working to preserve peace and stability, not just in Europe, but throughout the world.

By the late 1990s, however, the United States and Europe seemed no closer to this new form of partnership than they were the day the Berlin Wall fell. Although there had been much discussion about the new post-Cold War threats and the changing role of the Alliance, in fact, as the end of the decade neared, old patterns of transatlantic relations reemerged. The early attention to global issues gave way to a renewed focus on peace and stability in Europe. This remained the priority for the transatlantic partners, while rivalry and disagreements seemed – at least at first glance – to dominate approaches to issues outside Europe. Moreover, the US role as preeminent leader in this partnership had been reasserted, as witnessed by the rejuvenation of NATO as the premier security organization on the continent. And in the wake of the Bosnia crisis, the need for US involvement and leadership in managing such conflicts seemed reestablished in both Europe and Washington.

But if the transatlantic Alliance is to remain truly relevant to the challenges and opportunities of a new century, it must move beyond this focus on military security issues. There will be increasing pressure for the United States and Europe to respond to the broader realities of the post-Cold War era, including its diverse threats and global interdependencies. A key element in their ability to respond to these challenges effectively will be their capacity for cooperation on a range of global issues, not simply on preserving peace and security in Europe. If the transatlantic partnership is to be relevant in resolving or managing conflicts outside Europe – including issues in which the United States and Europe have significant stakes – they must find the incentives and mechanisms for effective cooperation. Such cooperation can reinforce the importance of the relationship and demonstrate its ability to adapt to a new environment. It may require Alliance members to develop new capabilities, and new patterns of leadership may need to be explored. Without this cooperation, however, the focus of the relationship will remain on traditional European security concerns. The transatlantic partnership will have only limited relevance for many of issues of great importance, and, as a result, will itself become less relevant as non-European issues take centre stage.

Of course, cooperation on these new challenges will not be easy. The United States and Europe may have differing interests on some, or even many, of the new issues before them. Even when their interests are similar, the pressure of domestic politics may lead them to neglect the relationship, at least until a crisis arises. The constant statements of support for the Alliance by high-level officials on both sides of the Atlantic – for there is no doubt that the rhetorical commitment to transatlanticism is strong – can blind policymakers to the need for adaptation. Even if the United States and Europe were to agree on new priorities for the transatlantic relationship, a thousand details of implementation could well scuttle the very best intentioned efforts. Recasting an international relationship, especially one with as many components, both formal and informal, as the transatlantic one, is an undeniably complex process. Yet tracing the ability of the United States and Europe to cooperate in addressing the new challenges before them should provide significant insights into the present and future health of the transatlantic relationship.

This volume examines US–European cooperation across three critical issues: restructuring relations with the East, addressing global security concerns, and managing the global economy. These issues involve many of the new threats that must be faced in the post-Cold War world: including social and economic instability, 'rogue states', weapons and technology transfer, and political upheaval. These issues extend beyond the usual limited parameters of US–European relations and test the ability of the transatlantic partnership to cope with global issues.

RESTRUCTURING RELATIONS WITH THE EAST

Without doubt, one of the most critical issues facing the United States and Europe today is the restructuring of relations with their neighbours to the East. The former Eastern-bloc countries, including the East European states, Russia and the other newly-independent states remain in transition from communism to democracy, and from command economies to market capitalism. That this dual transition will be successful is far from assured; yet the costs of failure will be high for both the United States and Western Europe – reinforcing both the need for and importance of cooperation.

As it happens, the challenge of restructuring relations with the East proved to be the clearest instance of the reemergence of traditional patterns of transatlanticism. After the initial fall of communism, it seemed for a time that the Western European states, particularly the European Community, would take the lead in integrating their eastern neighbours into the western political and economic system. The Europe agreements, identifying membership in the EC as an eventual goal, the Stability Pact, the early EC involvement in the former Yugoslavia – all seemed to indicate that Western Europe would assume the leading role in assuring the transition of these new societies, while the United States focused on the Gulf region and its own domestic imperatives. Eight years later, it is NATO – led by Washington – that has firmly tied the Central and East European countries to the West, attaching them to the established European security structure.

In this volume, Michael Brown examines the process through which NATO became the instrument of choice for stabilizing Central and Eastern Europe, with US leadership playing a key role. But stabilizing this region will not be accomplished solely through military means; thus, Lily Gardner Feldman considers the efforts of the transatlantic partners to bolster political and economic stability in the CEE countries through various assistance programmes and an expansion of the European Union. Not to be ignored or forgotten, however, is Russia, which could become an enormously destabilizing influence in Central Europe if it turns away from democracy or looks beyond its borders to relieve its internal problems. Renée de Nevers examines US and European efforts to assist the Russian reform process and to ameliorate some of the potentially serious international effects.

ADDRESSING GLOBAL SECURITY ISSUES

The end of the Cold War has brought a variety of global security issues to the forefront of world attention, and the transatlantic allies have responded with varying degrees of cooperation and effectiveness. Perhaps the most prominent issue has been that of ethnic and regional conflict, and, particularly for its impact on the US–European relationship, the dissolution of the former Yugoslavia. That conflict exemplifies the reemergence of traditional patterns of transatlantic relations: initially, the Europeans assumed an active leadership role, with the United Nations managing the peacekeeping operations. As the conflict escalated, however, US involvement and leadership became essential to any viable peace settlement, as did NATO management of the military operation. The Yugoslav experience demonstrated the importance of the United States and Europe working together, but also highlighted the difficulties of doing so and the dangers of failing.[1]

Less prominent than the example of the former Yugoslavia, but perhaps even more instructive in terms of understanding transatlantic cooperation on global security questions, are the issues of the so-called 'rogue states' and non-proliferation. These cases illustrate, on the one hand, a case in which no real cooperation exists, and on the other, an example of modest but effective coordination. Intra-Alliance disputes over 'rogue states' such as Iran and Cuba have threatened to disrupt the Alliance considerably. Despite some compromises, neither partner has shown much willingness to shift its position. As a result, cooperation remains negligible and the United States and Europe continue to base their approaches to these regimes on very different assumptions. In his chapter, Philip Gordon examines the issue of rogue states, and particularly US–European differences over the nature of these outlaws and the best means for dealing with them.

The second global security issue examined here – proliferation of weapons of mass destruction – has received considerable attention in recent years, with the revelations about Iraq's weapons programmes, the crisis over North Korean capabilities, nuclear testing by India and Pakistan, and concerns about the security of Soviet (and later Russian) weapons systems and materials. Moreover, debates over the nuclear Non-Proliferation Treaty and the Chemical Weapons Convention provided opportunities for transatlantic cooperation on these issues, while intra-Alliance quarrels over fuel-cycle matters and counter-proliferation policy demonstrated the need for such collaboration. In his chapter, Brad Roberts examines recent transatlantic cooperation on proliferation, especially the work of NATO's Defense Group on Proliferation, as well as efforts to use economic and political tools to reduce the risk of proliferation. Harald Müller examines the state of the US–European transatlantic community on such issues as the nuclear inheritance of the Soviet Union, the renewal of the US–Euratom agreement, improving the IAEA safeguards system, and extension of the NPT.

MANAGING THE GLOBAL ECONOMY

Finally, the management of the global economy has been a transatlantic responsibility for many years. Of all the issues examined in this volume, it is the one least affected by the end of the Cold War. Yet, on this matter too, the United States and Europe must deal with a changed environment: the end of the Uruguay Round and establishment of the World Trade Organization (WTO); the development of the European Single Market and European Monetary Union; the growing spillover between the international and domestic economies; and the ever-increasing speed with which events move through the global economy. In his chapter, Stephen Woolcock examines the New Transatlantic Agenda (NTA) and its relationship to the global economy, as well as the increased importance of 'beyond the border' issues as international tariffs continue to fall. Richard Steinberg considers transatlantic cooperation as the basis for management of the global economy, and examines various proposals to foster such cooperation. Finally, Beth Simmons considers an area of growing importance – financial regulation – and reviews US and European cooperation (and sometimes lack of cooperation) in creating a global regulatory environment.

OPPORTUNITIES AND CHALLENGES OF TRANSATLANTIC COOPERATION

These examples provide an opportunity to examine the mechanisms of cooperation, and perhaps draw some conclusions about what works and what does not. As Thomas Frellesen and Roy Ginsberg point out, the opportunities for transatlantic cooperation, in terms of meetings and other consultations, are extensive.[2] But opportunities by themselves do not equal cooperation. Thus, in evaluating cooperation, we have looked for a few minimum conditions: (1) a shared recognition that a particular issue must be addressed; (2) a basic consensus about the means, even if the parties differ over the nature of the problem's origin and the requirements for its eventual resolution; and (3) sufficient communication between the cooperating parties that they can keep each other informed as to their view of the situation (including criticisms and praise of the other's efforts). Even with these basic conditions, cooperation is likely to take many forms, depending on the issue and the available resources. In her chapter, Lily Gardner Feldman makes a useful distinction between three forms of cooperation: parallelism, division of labour, and joint coordination.[3] In *parallelism*, the governments involved work to achieve similar goals or resolve the same problem, but they do so with little or no communication between them. If their actions reinforce each other, it is perhaps due to happenstance. One could argue that this is not cooperation, but only coincidence; however, parallelism often does reflect shared interests, in the sense that both respond to a particular threat or situation.

In *division of labour*, there is a more or less explicit agreement on the objectives to be pursued and the threats to be countered. And, because of differing perspectives and capabilities, there is at least an implicit agreement that the cooperating countries will apply different resources to an issue – for example, one might supply military forces, while the other provides financial and technical assistance. Once this agreement is struck, there can be only a limited need for communication between the cooperating parties, each of which is busy focusing on their own particular set of objectives and tasks.

In *joint coordination*, however, there is not only agreement on objectives and tasks, but also frequent communication between the cooperating parties. Although there may be some division of labour, reflecting the variety of strengths and weaknesses among the partners, the entire effort is conducted with a sense of jointness. That is, the partners are more likely to collaborate on specific tasks, rather than splitting them up; and they are likely to be in frequent – if not constant – consultation as the situation changes. Coordination thus requires a high degree of commitment to working with the other cooperating parties on a daily basis, which can be time-consuming and institutionally difficult.

Finally, in assessing the capacity of the United States and Europe to cooperate across these issues, the many different identities of Europe add a real measure of complexity. 'Europe' today has almost as many definitions as there are individuals who use the term. In this volume, we have not limited our case studies to those that would allow all the authors to use a single conception of Europe, but instead have let each author use the one most suited to the particular issue. Thus, when the discussion focuses on NATO and military security issues,

'Europe' usually refers to the West European allies in NATO, and when the discussion turns to international economic policy, the relevant 'Europe' is usually the European Union. On many issues, however, 'Europe' refers to a still-evolving international actor in which the EU provides a forum for discussion and coordination – and may even be the implementing institution – but the member states remain the primary decision-makers. To complicate matters further, which Europe is predominant may change as the issue evolves. In the case of the former Yugoslavia, the EU initially assumed a leading role, but as the need for effective military force and US leadership became apparent, 'Europe' came to be synonymous with the European allies in NATO. The multiple meanings of 'Europe' used in this volume may at times be confusing; but it is an accurate reflection of the real complexities facing the evolving transatlantic partnership.

These issues are far from exhaustive, yet they provide important indicators of how effective the transatlantic partners are likely to be in addressing key issues outside of the European security framework – issues that will demand responses from the United States and Europe. To date, the United States and Western Europe have simply allowed old patterns of behaviour to re-emerge, without grappling with the fundamental changes in their environment. For the most part, they have proceeded in an *ad hoc* manner, addressing each issue separately as it arises. Whether this is an effective recipe for long-term management of global issues remains to be seen. Clearly, however, the ability of the United States and Europe to collaborate effectively on global issues will do much to determine their success in coping with the post-Cold War era. This volume seeks to shed light on the progress – or lack of progress – the transatlantic partners have made so far.

Notes

1. The US and European experiences in the former Yugoslavia have been treated extensively elsewhere. See, in particular, James Gow, *Triumph of the Lack of Will: International Diplomacy and the Yugoslav War*

(New York: Columbia University Press, 1997); and Richard H. Ullman (ed.), *The World and Yugoslavia's Wars* (New York: Council on Foreign Relations Press, 1996).

2. Thomas Frellesen and Roy H. Ginsberg, *EU–US Foreign Policy Cooperation in the 1990s: Elements of Partnership*, CEPS Paper no. 58 (Brussels: Centre for European Policy Studies, 1994). This valuable monograph examines the foreign policy relations of the United States and the European Union (omitting the security and economic aspects of their bilateral relations) and lists numerous specific instances of 'coordinated actions' or 'complementary actions', ranging from diplomatic statements to agreements to impose sanctions.

3. See Lily Gardner Feldman's chapter in this volume.

2 The United States, Western Europe and NATO Enlargement

Michael E. Brown[1]

The revolutions of 1989 brought down the iron curtain that had divided Europe for over four decades, and raised the curtain on new sets of questions: What kinds of ties would Western Europe and the United States be willing to form with members of the soon-to-be defunct Warsaw Pact as well as with states, such as Austria and Finland, that had been caught between the two blocs? In the security arena, would new ties translate into full membership in NATO? If so, when? And what states would be invited to join?

The evolution of NATO policy on enlargement went through three distinct phases between November 1989, when the Berlin Wall was torn down, and July 1997, when NATO's leaders invited the Czech Republic, Hungary and Poland to begin accession negotiations.

In phase one, 1989–92, NATO's members proclaimed their deep and abiding interest in forging new links with Central and Eastern Europe, but they were slow to move beyond rhetorical pronouncements. In November 1991, NATO's leaders announced that the Alliance would form the North Atlantic Cooperation Council (NACC), a forum for multilateral discussions on security questions, with former members of the Warsaw Pact. Although NATO's members tried to portray the creation of the NACC as a bold step forward, it would be more accurate to describe it as a holding action.

In phase two, 1993–95, NATO's members finally began to focus on the question of bringing Central and Eastern European states into the Alliance. Central and Eastern European leaders stepped up their campaign for membership in NATO in 1993, and Germany's leaders were receptive to the idea of moving forward – provided that a way could be found to enlarge NATO without enraging Russia. At the Brussels

11

Summit in January 1994, NATO's members invited the other states in Europe to join the Alliance's new Partnership for Peace (PfP) programme. Although this initiative was also intended to serve as a holding action, NATO's leaders affirmed in Brussels that they were willing to welcome new members. US President Bill Clinton stated even more forcefully that NATO would be enlarged, and the United States pushed this issue energetically in the second half of 1994. By the end of the year, the Alliance was firmly committed to enlargement. In 1995, it conducted a study on enlargement questions that produced comparatively easy criteria for membership. The only thing that kept NATO from pressing ahead and opening accession discussions with Central and Eastern European states soon thereafter was the Russian presidential election scheduled for mid-1996: the Alliance's leaders worried that NATO expansion would hurt Russian President Boris Yeltsin's chances of winning re-election.

In phase three, 1996–97, NATO's leaders took several steps to move the enlargement process along. Once the Russian election was over and Yeltsin's victory sealed, NATO's leaders engaged in a whirlwind of diplomatic activity to lay the groundwork for an enlargement announcement. At the Madrid summit in July 1997, NATO's leaders invited the Czech Republic, Hungary and Poland to begin accession talks. Accession agreements were completed in just a few months and signed in December 1997, with the expectation that these three states would formally join the Alliance by the time of the Washington Summit in April 1999 – the fiftieth anniversary of the signing of the North Atlantic Treaty.

This chapter examines the evolution of NATO policy on enlargement, analysing each of these three phases in turn. It concludes with a discussion of why NATO's members – in contrast to their EU counterparts – facilitated enlargement. I argue that NATO moved forward on enlargement for three main reasons. First, NATO enlargement was championed by the United States, and none of NATO's Western European members wanted to antagonize Washington on this issue when it moved to the top of the Alliance's agenda in 1994–95. Second, NATO enlargement was supported by Germany, and France – in particular – was keen to maintain close relations with its most important partner in the European Union. Third,

NATO enlargement was supported by many of the Alliance's Western European members because it was a cheap and easy alternative to EU enlargement.

QUIET AND DISQUIET ON THE EASTERN FRONT, 1989–92

Promises, Promises

NATO's leaders began to issue solemn declarations about their intentions to build new, constructive ties with the erst-while members of the Warsaw Pact in December 1989 – just weeks after the Berlin Wall was breached. When they met in Brussels in mid-December, NATO's foreign ministers declared: 'We want the reforms in Central and Eastern Europe to succeed peacefully and democratically. We are determined to facilitate and promote them without seeking one-sided advantage'.[2] They promised to play 'a constructive role' in overcoming Europe's divisions, but they did not launch any major policy initiatives with respect to Central and Eastern Europe at this juncture.

The dust began to settle in Central and Eastern Europe in 1990, and NATO's leaders began to make more elaborate declarations about developing links with states in the region. At the London Summit in July 1990, they stated that NATO would 'reach out' to its former adversaries and 'extend to them the hand of friendship'.

NATO moved quickly to implement the policy initiatives it announced at the London Summit: by the end of the year, Central and Eastern European governments had established diplomatic liaisons at NATO headquarters, and political and military leaders from the region had visited NATO.[3] These were modest steps, however. NATO's leaders had talked in grandiose terms in London about building 'new partnerships with all the nations of Europe' and 'the structures of a more united continent', but the steps it took in the second half of 1990 did not fulfill these sweeping rhetorical commitments.[4] There were three main reasons for this.

First, NATO's July 1990 proclamations were designed to reassure Moscow about the Alliance's intentions and to get

Moscow to go along with the idea of unified Germany being in NATO; they were not motivated by a deep desire to form close ties with Czechoslovakia, Hungary, Poland and other erstwhile members of the Warsaw Pact. The London declaration was successful in that Mikhail Gorbachev subsequently acquiesced on the German question: the Federal Republic retained its membership in NATO when it absorbed the German Democratic Republic in October 1990. Once this happened, NATO's incentives to launch new policy ventures in Central and Eastern Europe declined.

Second, NATO's leaders were preoccupied in the second half of 1990 with more urgent security problems: completing the negotiations on the terms of German unification and on the Conventional Forces in Europe (CFE) Treaty; and orchestrating the allied military response to the Iraqi invasion of Kuwait. As the build-up in the Gulf region continued and war became increasingly likely, the issue of developing new institutional ties with states in Central and Eastern Europe faded into the background.

Third, NATO's leaders were worried that former members of the Warsaw Pact would begin to push not just for diplomatic liaisons with NATO, but full membership in the Alliance. NATO's leaders were not inclined to start bringing former members of the Warsaw Pact into the fold in 1990: many of these countries were still in turmoil, and NATO's leaders were worried about antagonizing the Soviet leadership at a critical juncture in Soviet history. NATO's leaders wanted Soviet domestic and foreign policy to evolve in benign directions, and they recognized that bold moves to develop close ties with Moscow's former allies could be counter-productive.

The good news for NATO was that Central and Eastern European leaders were not campaigning aggressively for NATO membership in 1990; most governments were preoccupied with compelling domestic problems. Their main foreign policy concerns were establishing trade and investment relationships with their western brethren and, in the longer term, forging closer economic and political ties with Western Europe by joining the European Community (EC). Central and Eastern European leaders were keen to reintegrate with Western Europe, but they initially saw the EC as the main institutional vehicle for bringing this about. Indeed, in 1990 many Central and Eastern European leaders thought that NATO's days might be numbered, given that its counterpart – the Warsaw Pact – had disintegrated.

In any event, there was no pressing need for Central and Eastern European states to seek security guarantees from the West in 1990. Mikhail Gorbachev, the man who had endorsed the Central and Eastern European reforms that led to the revolutions of 1989, was still in charge in Moscow, where, in addition, political and economic reforms were still the order of the day. As long as the process of reform in Moscow stayed on course, there were reasons for being hopeful about the Soviet Union's political evolution and the future of Moscow's relations with its neighbours to the west.

Holding Actions

Central and Eastern European attitudes towards NATO began to change in 1991. The EC moved slowly on the enlargement question, and came to be seen in a more critical light. The Soviet Union lurched in unpredictable ways before disintegrating, and Moscow therefore came to be more of a worry. NATO came to be seen as increasingly important.

The EC's leadership was almost totally absorbed in 1991 with internal matters – the negotiations on economic and political union that continued through the year and culminated in the signing of the Treaty of European Union in Maastricht in December. The completion of the treaty was, in important respects, discouraging to Central and Eastern European leaders. Although the treaty provided that any European state with a democratic system of government could apply to join the Union, the creation of a more tightly integrated economic and political Union made accession more difficult.[5] Carrying out the economic and political reforms needed to join the 'old' EC would have been hard enough; laying the necessary groundwork to join the 'new' EU would be even more difficult. As Poland's president, Lech Walesa, remarked just after the Maastricht treaty was signed, 'The bar was raised...at Maastricht'.[6] By the end of 1991, therefore, it was starting to become clear to Central and

Eastern European leaders that membership in the new Union was probably a decade or more away.

At the same time, developments in the Soviet Union began to raise security concerns in Central and Eastern Europe. In January 1991, Moscow cracked down on moves towards independence in Latvia and Lithuania. The violent repression of reformers in the Baltics sent shock waves through the eastern half of the continent. The failed coup in Moscow in August 1991 was even more unsettling to Central and Eastern European leaders: they could no longer assume that Moscow would continue to embrace democratic and economic reforms. This pushed the issue of Western security guarantees and NATO enlargement closer to the top of Central and Eastern Europe's agenda. It was not a coincidence that Czechoslovak President Vaclav Havel and Lech Walesa traveled to Brussels and called for a 'partnership' with NATO in March and July 1991, respectively, or that Czechoslovakia, Hungary and Poland called for 'close and institutionalized' cooperation with NATO in October 1991.[7]

NATO's leaders were in fact starting to develop ideas for strengthening ties with Central and Eastern European states. In October 1991, US Secretary of State James Baker and German Foreign Minister Hans-Dietrich Genscher proposed that NATO sponsor the creation of a multilateral forum that would include all NATO states as well as former members of the Warsaw Pact.[8] The creation of what became known as the North Atlantic Cooperation Council was announced, over French objections, at the NATO summit held in Rome the following month.[9] Although the NACC included Moscow and did not involve security guarantees, its formation constituted a small step in the direction of developing institutional ties with Central and Eastern European states. The first meeting of the NACC took place in Brussels in December 1991.[10] Although NATO's leaders tried to portray the creation of the NACC as a momentous development, it was designed to pacify Central and Eastern European leaders and keep them from pressing forward with demands for full membership in NATO.

The most momentous development of late 1991 was, of course, the break-up of the Soviet Union in December. This had mixed implications for those with national security responsibilities in Central and Eastern Europe. On the positive side of the ledger, the break-up of the Soviet Union ravaged Moscow's conventional military capabilities and, therefore, its ability to threaten states to the west. It also created important buffers, Belarus and Ukraine, between Moscow and its former Warsaw Pact allies. At the same time, the political turmoil in the former Soviet Union, including Mikhail Gorbachev's passing from the political scene, was unnerving. The fact that Moscow persuaded many former Soviet republics to join a new umbrella organization, the Commonwealth of Independent States (CIS), in December was also disquieting. Many feared that Russian nationalists and imperialists would use the Commonwealth as the framework for creating a new Russian empire.

Busy Signals

The same broad pattern of events repeated itself in 1992. The EC's members concentrated almost all of their energies on the problems associated with keeping monetary and political union on track. Ratification of the Maastricht treaty stalled when Danish voters rejected the treaty in a June 1992 referendum, and exchange-rate crises added to the confusion in the second half of the year. The EC's main foreign policy concern was the growing horror in the former Yugoslavia. Membership in the EC appeared to be an increasingly distant prospect as far as former members of the Warsaw Pact were concerned.

Unfortunately, all was not quiet on the eastern front. Russia sparked and fueled civil wars in Moldova and Georgia, two of the former Soviet republics that had refused to join the Commonwealth of Independent States, and thereby brought them to heel.[11] In the spring of 1992, Russian military forces still stationed in Moldova threw their support behind Russian nationals who sought to secede from Moldova and remain affiliated with Moscow. A civil war ensued. To bring fighting to an end, the Moldovan government agreed in July to join the CIS and form a closer economic and security relationship with Russia. A similar chain of events unfolded in Georgia, where Russian military forces provided Abkhaz separatists with arms, equipment, training and direct military support in the form of air strikes against the Georgian military. Georgia, one of the most fiercely independent of the former Soviet republics, ultimately capitulated, agreeing to join the CIS and to allow Russian military forces to be stationed on Georgian territory indefinitely. These actions indicated to many Central and Eastern Europeans that Russia's imperialist inclinations were still strong, that Russia was not adverse to using military force to get its way, and that their national security could not be taken for granted.

NATO, however, made no moves to develop closer ties with Central and Eastern European states in 1992. The creation of the NACC was supposed to have convinced Central and Eastern European leaders that they had a special relationship with NATO, but the NACC became a much less exclusive club in 1992: after the Soviet Union disintegrated, all 15 republics of the former Soviet Union were invited to join. The NACC met on multiple occasions in 1992, but as its membership soared, its appeal to Central and Eastern European leaders plummeted.

At the NATO foreign ministers meeting in June, US Deputy Secretary of State Lawrence Eagleburger suggested in a carefully qualified way that bringing new members into the Alliance might be a possibility in the future: 'Indeed, even the very composition of the Alliance may need to expand, at the appropriate time, taking full account of our rigorous democratic standards and the need to preserve the strong fibre of common defense'.[12] The Bush administration did not develop this idea in any significant way in the second half of 1992. Its main concerns were the US presidential election campaign and, in the foreign policy arena, the disposition of nuclear weapons in the former Soviet Union. NATO enlargement did not make its way onto the short list of the administration's political concerns, and none of NATO's other members pressed the case for bringing new members into the Alliance.

NATO MOVES FORWARD, 1993–95

NATO's leaders finally began to focus on the question of bringing former members of the Warsaw Pact into NATO in

1993: their initial response was another holding action – the creation of the Partnership for Peace programme. The next year, however, NATO's leadership expressed a willingness to bring new states into the alliance, and NATO began to move forward on enlargement. In 1995, NATO established comparatively easy criteria for membership and began to move quickly to bring new members into the fold.

NATO Focuses on the Enlargement Question

Czech, Hungarian and Polish leaders began to campaign more aggressively for membership in NATO in the spring and summer of 1993. They were motivated by two sets of developments: first, it was becoming increasingly clear that the EU's members were dragging their feet on enlargement – at least as far as former members of the Warsaw Pact were concerned; and, second, Russian nationalists were becoming more vocal and therefore more worrying.[13] The NACC was seen by most Central and Eastern European policy-makers as a forum for discussion, not an institution that could safeguard their security. NATO membership, therefore, became a high priority. Czech President Vaclav Havel and Polish President Lech Walesa both pressed the case for NATO enlargement when they met Bill Clinton at the opening of the Holocaust Museum in Washington in April 1993.[14]

Russian government officials were generally critical of the possibility of NATO expansion, characterizing it as a provocative move that would pose a threat to Russian national security and thereby strengthen the hands of nationalists and communists in Russian domestic politics. However, mixed signals from the Russian leadership confused the situation. During a visit to Warsaw in August 1993, Russian President Boris Yeltsin and Polish President Walesa signed a joint statement that noted Poland's 'intention' to join NATO and Yeltsin's 'understanding' of the Polish position. The joint statement went on to observe that Polish membership in NATO 'does not go against the interests of other states, including the interests of Russia'.[15] When asked about Czech membership in NATO the next day in Prague, Yeltsin replied, 'Russia does not have the right to prevent a sovereign state from joining a European organization'.[16]

Within a matter of weeks, the Russian leadership was back-tracking from Yeltsin's pronouncements in Warsaw and Prague, and expressing opposition to NATO expansion. In mid-September, Yeltsin himself wrote to the head of each NATO government and expressed his reservations about enlargement of the alliance: 'It is important to take into account how our public opinion may react to such a step. Not only the opposition, but the moderates, too, would no doubt see this as a sort of neo-isolation' of Russia.[17] Yeltsin's warnings about Russian domestic politics could not be taken lightly in the West. By the end of September, Yeltsin would dissolve the parliament and order troops to surround the parliament building, where opposition leaders had formed a rump parliament and voted to impeach the president. On 3 October, Yeltsin declared a state of emergency and ordered the military to attack and seize the parliament building.[18]

For understandable reasons, Germany was the first NATO member to favour expansion of the Alliance. Germany was anxious to stabilize the region to its east, and in the event that a new confrontation developed with Russia, it did not want to serve as NATO's first line of defense. The German Defense Minister, Volker Rühe, began to campaign publicly for enlarging the Alliance as early as May 1993.[19] In October, after Yeltsin's crackdown in Moscow, Rühe pushed even harder for NATO expansion:

> Preventive crisis management means for us Germans above all extending the zone of stability in the west as far as possible to the east. Germany has no interest in remaining the eastern frontier state of the western zone of prosperity. We are the ones who feel the effects of instability to the east most immediately.[20]

At the same time, he noted, 'We must take into account the extremely difficult situation of the forces for reform in Russia'. With this in mind, Rühe called for the development of a 'strategic partnership' between NATO and Moscow, which he hoped would take the sting out of NATO expansion.

Although the idea of bringing Poland and the Czech Republic into NATO received strong support from most German elites and German public opinion, some worried that proceeding too quickly would produce a backlash in Russia that would have adverse implications for German national security. German Foreign Minister Klaus Kinkel explicitly supported NATO expansion in early September: 'The historical task of Europe is to incorporate the countries of Eastern Europe' into NATO and 'other Euro-Atlantic organizations'.[21] In late October, after weeks of turmoil in Moscow, he was more cautious:

> NATO will...have to respond to the desire of East European governments to join the Alliance. But enlargement raises serious issues...We cannot risk reviving East–West strategic rivalry. It would be tragic if, in reassuring some countries, we alarmed others.[22]

Chancellor Kohl was also sensitive to the impact NATO enlargement might have on Russia. In September, he insisted that he would push this issue at the upcoming NATO summit: 'At these talks in January, I will raise the question of how we can give these countries not only the feeling but also a guarantee that they have a security umbrella'.[23] After the clash between Yeltsin and his opponents in Moscow in early October, Kohl observed that expansion of the Alliance belonged in 'a farther-off future'.[24]

France, the United Kingdom, Italy and other Western European members of NATO were generally cooler than Germany to the idea of inviting Central and Eastern European states to join the Alliance. Although the most intense phase of France's institutional debate with NATO had passed by the autumn of 1993, Paris still opposed expansion of NATO's area of responsibility in either functional or geographical terms. It also worried that NATO expansion would shift the centre of gravity in European affairs even more in Germany's direction: Germany would move from the outer edge to the centre of the Alliance in geographical terms, and it would undoubtedly play a key role in integrating new members into Alliance activities. At the same time, France did not want to alienate Germany, its most important partner in the effort to create a European monetary and political union and, therefore, the most important celestial body in its universe.

The net effect of these conflicting pressures was that France could neither support nor strongly oppose NATO expansion: it could only urge its allies to slow down and proceed cautiously. In September, French Defense Minister François Léotard offered a lukewarm endorsement of enlargement initiatives: 'The process has started and we on the French side will certainly not raise any obstacle in this expansion'.[25] In October, the French Foreign Minister, Alain Juppé, urged Western leaders to explore other institutional options before proceeding with NATO expansion: 'Before entering into the process of enlargement, let us make the existing institutions work. For that we have the North Atlantic Cooperation Council'.[26] The irony is that France had opposed creation of the NACC in late 1991; now that the NACC was a fact of life, Juppé hoped to use it to keep what were, from his perspective, even worse institutional developments from taking place.

The British were also unenthusiastic about NATO expansion, but they could afford to be more open about their reservations because they were less worried about annoying Germany. In October, British Defence Secretary Malcolm Rifkind insisted, 'Membership of NATO involves responsibility as well as rights and cannot be seen as a political statement'.[27] The British Foreign Secretary, Douglas Hurd, put it more bluntly a few months later: 'A decision to extend NATO's territory and commit our troops to the defense of new borders cannot be taken lightly. We are not talking about the membership of a social club'. He continued, 'Any hasty decision about who does and does not belong to NATO risks creating a new division in Europe. We do not want to set Russia's teeth dangerously on edge'.[28] In addition, British and other Western European officials worried that the risks of becoming involved in ethnic and territorial disputes, such as those raging in the former Yugoslavia, would increase if new Central and Eastern European members were brought into the Alliance. Even if this did not happen, the Alliance would inevitably find it harder to reach a consensus and make decisions if more members were part of the equation.

In Washington the debate on the expansion question was initially three-sided. In October 1993, Undersecretary of State Lynn Davis sent a memo to Secretary of State Warren Christopher, in which she recommended that NATO offer associate membership to the Czech Republic, Hungary, Poland and Slovakia in 'the near future'.[29] She also recommended establishing a timetable and criteria for making associate members full and regular members of the Alliance. Her concern was that political and economic reforms in Central and Eastern Europe might falter if these countries were denied membership in both the EU and NATO; since the EU was unlikely to offer membership to any of these countries in the near term, NATO should fill the void and do so. The president's National Security Advisor, Anthony Lake, also favoured enlargement of the Alliance.

The Chairman of the Joint Chiefs of Staff, General John Shalikashvili, feared that rapid expansion might weaken an Alliance that had served US and European security well for decades. He was also concerned about the strategic and military implications of extending security guarantees to new states as well as the cost implications of these new undertakings. As an alternative to rapid expansion, he proposed that NATO establish bilateral military cooperation programmes with Central and Eastern European countries interested in forging stronger ties with the Alliance. This came to be known as the Partnership for Peace (PfP) initiative.[30]

Strobe Talbott, the senior State Department official in charge of coordinating US policy towards the former Soviet Union, agreed with Shalikashvili but for different reasons. In a 17 October memo of his own to Christopher, Talbott wrote that rapid expansion of NATO would be 'provocative and badly timed' with respect to Russia.[31] He supported Shalikashvili's Partnership for Peace proposal, and recommended making it the centrepiece of NATO's efforts to address Central and Eastern European concerns.

The Partnership for Peace initiative was adopted by the Clinton administration at a White House meeting on 18 October. It had the great virtue of being ambiguous enough to satisfy all of the participants in the bureaucratic debate about US policy towards Central and Eastern Europe.[32] Advocates of rapid expansion saw it as a step in the right direction; Pentagon officials saw it as a programme that would strengthen military-to-military ties with these states and lay the groundwork for enlargement of the Alliance – should that become appropriate in the future; and opponents of NATO enlargement saw the Partnership for Peace programme as a holding action. As one opponent of NATO expansion later maintained, 'The partnership was deliberately designed to enable member states to put off questions of formal enlargement and of NATO's ultimate disposition in post-Cold War Europe'.[33] The US proposal was presented by the Secretary of Defense, Les Aspin, at a meeting of NATO defense ministers on 20–21 October in Travemünde, Germany. It received unanimous support from the Alliance's other members.[34]

The Partnership for Peace programme was formally adopted at the NATO summit in Brussels in January 1994. Invitations to participate in the programme were extended to all non-NATO members of the NACC and the Conference on Security and Cooperation in Europe (CSCE). Over two dozen states (including Russia) signed PfP agreements in subsequent months. At an operational level, the PfP programme was designed to create bilateral relationships between NATO and partner countries, each individually tailored to the needs and capabilities of the country in question. The expectation was that, over time, joint planning activities, joint training exercises and extensive consultations would close the gap that existed between NATO and non-NATO forces in doctrine, force-structure, organization and training. It was expected that in many cases, close working relationships would develop and a foundation for joint military operations would be created. Military obstacles to NATO expansion would gradually disappear.

Some Central and Eastern European leaders worried that the PfP programme was a holding-action designed to postpone accession discussions – and, indeed, many American and Western European leaders hoped that it would serve this purpose. Publicly, however, NATO officials insisted that enhancing military interoperability was a prerequisite to expansion. In this respect, they argued, the Partnership for Peace programme would facilitate expansion of the alliance.[35]

NATO Moves Forward on the Enlargement Question

NATO leaders also affirmed at the Brussels Summit that the alliance was open to new members: 'We expect and would welcome NATO expansion that would reach to democratic states to our East, as part of an evolutionary process, taking into account political and security developments in the whole of Europe'.[36] While visiting Prague in the aftermath of the Brussels meeting, US President Clinton was even more explicit about NATO's intentions, insisting, 'The question is no longer whether NATO will take on new members, but when and how'.[37] Clinton reiterated his commitment to NATO expansion during his trip to Warsaw in July, stating that a 'timetable should be developed' for bringing in new members.[38]

The president's declarations galvanized advocates of rapid expansion within the Clinton administration, and led to a US push on the expansion question in the last few months of 1994. Given the president's public pronouncements on this question, those within the government who had reservations about NATO enlargement were forced to fall into line.[39] The campaign to forge ahead was led by Assistant Secretary of State Richard Holbrooke, who had returned to Washington in September after serving as US ambassador to Germany. The goal was to transform the general commitment to expansion enunciated in Brussels into a more formal process that would lead to new members being brought into the Alliance. More specifically, it was hoped that NATO's foreign ministers, who were scheduled to meet in Brussels in December, would approve a quick study of the expansion question, which would then lead to accession decisions.

Many Western European officials, however, were uneasy about pushing ahead quickly. Their main concern was that the political situation in Russia was still precarious, especially after communists and ultra-nationalists captured over 40 per cent of the vote in the country's December 1993 parliamentary elections. NATO expansion, they feared, could spark a Russian backlash that could tip the balance against Boris Yeltsin and his reform-minded colleagues. A more aggressively nationalist government, in turn, could pose problems for Ukraine and the Baltic states. In the worst case, this could lead to a confrontation between Russia and the West. Even if Yeltsin and company managed to stay in power, they would be obliged to adopt a harder line in their dealings with their neighbours and the West. With this in mind, Germany and France successfully argued in favour of a longer study of the expansion question. The fact that Germany was anxious about going too fast shows that Washington was far in front of its allies on this issue in late 1994.[40]

At the same time, NATO's Western European members did not want to pick a fight with the United States over this issue. Intra-Alliance relations had been stretched to the breaking point in 1993–94 by bitter disagreements over western policy in Bosnia. The Clinton administration wanted to lift the UN arms embargo that had been placed on the Bosnian government (along with the other combatants) and launch air-strikes against Bosnian Serb targets. Britain and France, which had troops on the ground, did not want to take such aggressive actions. This dispute came to a head in November 1994, when the United States announced that it would no longer enforce the arms embargo with respect to the Bosnian government. This astounded and enraged Washington's allies. Many Western Europeans wondered if this split would lead to US disengagement from Europe and the end of NATO, which was something that Britain, France, Germany and NATO's other Western European members were keen to avoid. Under the circumstances, they were not inclined to oppose Washington when it was pushing a comparatively constructive initiative and, indeed, when it was calling for *additional* US engagement in European security affairs. Once the Clinton administration assured its allies that NATO expansion would proceed slowly until after the Russian presidential election scheduled for 1996, and that a concerted effort would be made to maintain good relations with Russia, Western European support for enlargement solidified.

When the Alliance's foreign ministers met in December, they reaffirmed NATO's expectation that expansion would take place – this would subsequently become a ritualistic declaration at NATO meetings and in NATO communiqués – and they announced that a study of what US officials billed as the 'why and how' of NATO expansion would be conducted in 1995. Decisions about 'who and when' – who would be asked to join and when this might take place – would follow at some unspecified point in the future. NATO's foreign ministers maintained that it would be 'premature to discuss the timeframe for enlargement or which particular countries would be invited to join the Alliance'.[41] NATO's ambiguity on the 'who and when' questions was driven mainly by external considerations: NATO's leaders wanted to maximize Boris Yeltsin's chances of winning re-election in 1996.

From this point on, the NATO allies spoke with one voice on the question of inviting Central and Eastern European states to join the Alliance. A strong consensus emerged that NATO expansion would take place, that different states might be asked to join the Alliance at different times, and that every effort would be made to reassure Moscow about NATO's intentions and to build a close and cordial relationship with Russia.

The NATO enlargement study, which was publicly released in September 1995, developed the rationale for expansion, and it outlined the criteria for membership. Enlargement of the Alliance, it was argued, would enhance stability and security by: encouraging and supporting democratic reforms in Central and Eastern Europe, including civilian control of the military; fostering patterns and habits of cooperation, consultation and consensus-building; promoting good relations between and among Central and Eastern European states by increasing transparency in defense planning and military budgets; curbing ethnic conflict and secessionism; strengthening NATO's ability to undertake peacekeeping operations on behalf of the Organization for Security and Cooperation in Europe (OSCE) and the United Nations; and strengthening and broadening the transatlantic partnership.[42] Significantly, NATO's members did not develop extremely demanding criteria for membership.[43]

- *Politically*, new members would have to embrace democracy, the rule of law and individual liberty; demonstrate 'a commitment' to the peaceful resolution of ethnic and territorial disputes; and establish 'appropriate democratic and civilian control' over their military forces.
- *Militarily*, new members would have to be able to 'share' the burdens of common security and collective defense and 'contribute' to the Alliance's military undertakings. This would involve making a 'good faith' effort towards military standardization and interoperability through an 'evolutionary' process.
- *Organizationally*, new members would have to commit themselves to 'good faith efforts to build consensus within the Alliance', establish permanent representation at NATO offices and commands, and accept NATO's 'open-door' policy with respect to other applicants.

The NATO enlargement study was endorsed at the December 1995 meeting of the Alliance's foreign ministers.[44] However, the Alliance's leaders maintained their ambiguous stance on the 'who and when' aspects of enlargement, as the Russian election was still pending.

NATO AND THE ROAD TO MADRID, 1996–97

NATO's leaders deliberately downplayed their plans for enlargement in the first half of 1996, seeking to minimize the problems Boris Yeltsin would have in the Russian presidential election scheduled for June. After Yeltsin won re-election, Clinton and the other leaders of the Alliance were less constrained about moving forward publicly on expansion plans. In September, Secretary of State Christopher announced that a NATO summit would be held in the spring or early summer of 1997, and that a first round of invitations to join the Alliance would be issued at that time.[45] In October, Clinton stated that his goal was to extend full-fledged membership to a first group of countries by 1999, and in November, after he won re-election, he was in a position to act on these plans.[46] In December, NATO's foreign ministers announced that one or more countries would be invited to begin accession negotiations at the NATO summit that would be held in Madrid in July 1997.[47] It was widely assumed that the Czech Republic, Hungary and Poland were at the front of the membership queue.

Little took place on the diplomatic front until February 1997, after Clinton was inaugurated for his second term and his new foreign policy team, headed by Secretary of State Madeleine Albright, was installed. The next five months witnessed a whirlwind of bilateral and multilateral activity, as US and NATO officials sought to lay the groundwork for the decisions that would be made in Madrid. NATO's leaders did three things over the course of this diplomatic campaign: first, they tried to pacify Russia; second, they decided on which states would be invited to join the Alliance; and third, they tried to mollify those who would not be invited in Madrid to begin accession discussions.

Pacifying Russia

From the time NATO's leaders opened the door to enlargement in 1994, the Russian leadership was steadfast in its
opposition to the idea.[48] Russian opposition intensified in late
1996 and early 1997, as NATO's plans to bring new members
into the alliance moved forward. In November 1996, President
Yeltsin stated that 'Russia's stance on NATO expansion
remains unchanged, that is, negative...NATO expansion will
lead to new divisions in Europe'.[49] In December, Russia's
Defence Minister Igor Rodionov warned that NATO expansion would 'upset the strategic balance on the continent and
restore a Cold War situation in Europe that would force
Russia to take countermeasures'.[50] In February 1997, Prime
Minister Viktor Chernomyrdin worried about the impact of
NATO expansion on Russia: 'Developments in Russia could
take an ominous turn'. Ultranationalists, he maintained, 'will
accuse the president and the government of doing nothing to
prevent this development'. Western efforts 'to comfort us', he
said, have been inadequate.[51]

NATO's members – individually and collectively –
launched four main initiatives to placate the Russian leadership. First, to address Russian concerns about the changing
balance of conventional forces in Europe and NATO 'infrastructure' being moved eastward, the Alliance's leaders proposed sweeping changes in the 1990 CFE Treaty.[52] NATO's
leaders proposed that the treaty's bloc and zonal limits, which
had been overtaken by events with the demise of the Warsaw
Pact and the break-up of the Soviet Union, be replaced
by country-by-country ceilings for tanks, artillery and
armoured combat vehicles. Countries would have 'national
ceilings' on their own forces and 'territorial ceilings' that
would limit allied forces deployed on the territory of the state
in question. NATO's leaders also proposed lower ceilings for
forces throughout the CFE area. This would 'significantly'
lower NATO force levels, according to NATO officials.
Moreover, NATO proposed creating a 'stability zone' – con-
sisting of Belarus, the Czech Republic, Hungary, Poland,
Slovakia, western Ukraine, and the Kaliningrad *oblast* of
the Russian Federation – where special limits on ground
forces would apply. This zone would include the states most

likely to be invited to join NATO. The fact that a revised CFE Treaty would be legally binding was especially appealing to the Russian leadership, which sought formal constraints on NATO activities on the territories of new member states.

Second, to address Russian concerns about NATO nuclear forces, NATO's leaders declared that they had 'no intention, no plan, and no reason' to deploy nuclear weapons on the territories of new member states. This declaration was first made by NATO's foreign ministers in December 1996, repeated by NATO officials throughout early 1997, and incorporated in the NATO–Russia accord signed in May 1997.[53] Russian leaders had hoped for a formal, legally-binding commitment from NATO on these questions, but the Alliance's leaders were unwilling to limit their options in the event of a crisis or to create two classes of NATO membership, with new members being consigned to second-class status.

Third, to address Russian concerns about the future of the strategic nuclear balance, the United States developed and presented new arms-control proposals.[54] The START II Treaty, which was signed in January 1993 but not ratified by the Russian Duma, obligates the United States and Russia to reduce the number of nuclear warheads deployed on long-range missiles and bombers to 3000–3500 by the year 2003. Russian critics of START II worry that, because of economic constraints and cutbacks in military production, Russia might have only 2500 warheads in service at that time; Russia would be at a disadvantage unless it developed and built a new missile that would be allowed under the terms of the treaty. With this in mind, US officials proposed extending the implementation period for START II an additional year – to the end of 2003. They also outlined a START III framework that called for each side to reduce the number of deployed strategic nuclear weapons in its arsenal to 2000–2500 by the end of 2007. Formal talks on a START III treaty, however, would begin only after the Duma ratified START II. At the Helsinki summit in March 1997, Yeltsin and Clinton agreed to proceed on this basis, and Yeltsin promised to push the Duma to ratify START II.

Fourth, to address Russian concerns about becoming estranged from NATO, the Alliance's leaders proposed that

NATO and Russia sign a joint accord and create a joint council that would provide a forum for consultations. Russian leaders pushed for a formal treaty that would be signed by all 16 NATO members and a council that would give Russia a veto over NATO decisions and actions. NATO's leaders refused to concede on either point and, in the end, they got what they wanted. The Founding Act gave Russia a more elaborate and permanent institutional platform in Brussels: a permanent Russian mission would be established at NATO headquarters, and a NATO–Russia Permanent Joint Council would be formed. The council would provide 'a mechanism for consultations, coordination and, to the maximum extent possible, where appropriate, for joint decisions and joint action with respect to security issues of common concern'.[55] However, according to the Founding Act, the 'provisions of this Act do not provide NATO or Russia, in any way, with a right of veto over the actions of the other'.

In the end, the Russian leadership recognized that it could not stop NATO expansion, so it struck the best deal available under the circumstances. This included signing the Founding Act and agreeing to form the NATO–Russia Permanent Joint Council. The Alliance's leaders took this as a sign that Russian objections to NATO expansion had been overcome.

Deciding on New Members

Although it had widely been assumed since 1995 that the leading candidates to join NATO were the Czech Republic, Hungary and Poland, the Alliance's leaders did an admirable job of declining to speculate on the record about specific countries. They also wanted to wait until the last minute to make their decision on new members: this would make it difficult for those not on the list to try to get NATO's leadership to change its collective mind. As a result, the intra-Alliance debate over new members did not come to a head until the NATO foreign ministers meeting held in Sintra, Portugal, in late May 1997.

At Sintra, nine of NATO's 16 members – Belgium, Canada, France, Greece, Italy, Luxembourg, Portugal, Spain and Turkey – came out in favour of extending membership to Romania and Slovenia, in addition to the three well-established front runners.[56] Some favoured Romania and Slovenia simply because they met the criteria the Alliance itself had established for membership. Others were keen to extend the Alliance's presence into south-eastern Europe. Italy, for example, favoured Slovenia and Turkey favoured Romania for this reason. France was keen to keep Germany from becoming the Alliance's geographical and political pivot.

Others – led by the United States, but including Britain, Germany and Norway – favoured limiting membership to the Czech Republic, Hungary and Poland. They argued that integrating three states into the Alliance would be easier militarily and cost less financially, and that ratification of accession protocols would therefore be more likely. In addition, keeping the invitation list small would pacify Russia and strengthen the Alliance's claim that more invitations would be extended in the future; the latter, they said, would help to mollify those who failed to make the cut this time around. Those who favoured limiting expansion to three states also argued that Slovenia could contribute little to NATO's military capacities because its armed forces were small, and that Romania's commitment to democratic forms of governance extended only to the very recent past.

Here things stood until 12 June, when US Secretary of Defense William Cohen announced at the semi-annual meeting of NATO's defense ministers that the United States would support the admission of only three new members to the alliance – the Czech Republic, Hungary and Poland.[57] This infuriated many – the French leadership, in particular – who felt that the United States was imposing a diktat on the alliance. French and Italian leaders tried to persuade Clinton to change his mind at the G-7 summit held in Denver at the end of the month. They failed. The debate continued at Madrid in July 1997, with French President Jacques Chirac making what was described as a 'spirited' case for inviting Romania and Slovenia, but the United States continued to stick to its position.[58]

The US handling of the enlargement decision left a bitter taste in the mouths of many Western European members of the Alliance. French Prime Minister Lionel Jospin commented that the United States was demonstrating 'a certain tendency toward hegemony' within the Alliance.[59] French President

Jacques Chirac warned, 'We take the risk of breaking the allies' cohesion and hurting the credibility of the Alliance by excluding today two countries who comply with the criteria we set ourselves.'[60] British and German officials, whose governments supported the US position on substantive grounds, nonetheless were underwhelmed by US diplomacy on the membership question. According to one senior German official, 'everyone seemed to agree that if this [US arrogance] gets out of hand, it could lead to some serious problems for the Alliance'.[61]

In the end, the United States got what it wanted, simply because any member of the Alliance could veto any candidate for membership; expansion therefore had to be limited to states that were supported by all 16 NATO members. That said, the Clinton administration's imperious attitude and inept diplomacy earned very low marks from its allies. Indeed, one could argue that the Clinton administration failed to respect one of NATO's criteria for membership – a commitment to 'good faith efforts to build consensus within the alliance'.[62]

Mollifying the Rest

NATO's leaders also took preemptive steps in the first half of 1997 to pacify those who wanted to join the Alliance, but who would not be invited at Madrid to begin accession negotiations. The Alliance's leadership did three main things. First, it stated and re-stated that NATO would 'maintain an open door' as far as additional members were concerned.[63] As US National Security Advisor Samuel Berger put it, 'The first shall not be the last'.[64] President Clinton insisted that 'NATO's doors will remain open to all those willing and able to shoulder the responsibilities of membership'.[65] A special effort was made to assuage Romania, Slovenia and the Baltic states, which ultimately did not receive an invitation to enter into accession talks. These states were singled out for favourable mention in the communiqué issued at the Madrid summit, and NATO's leaders pledged to revisit the membership question at the Washington Summit 1999.

Second, NATO transformed the NACC into the Euro-Atlantic Partnership Council which, it was said, would 'raise to a qualitatively new level' the political and military interactions between the Alliance and the countries in the Partnership for Peace programme. Specifically, the Council would involve regular and expanded consultations and a 'more operational' role. This would 'allow partner countries to draw closer to the Alliance'.[66] The Council would meet monthly at the ambassadorial level, four times a year at the ministerial level, and occasionally at the level of heads of state and government.

Third, NATO's leaders signed a special charter with Ukraine, which would be particularly vulnerable if Russia embarked on a campaign to regain control over territories located between the Russian Federation and the expanding NATO alliance. Although this charter called for the creation of yet another multilateral body – the NATO–Ukraine Commission – it would not afford Ukraine any real protection in the face of a resurgent, revanchist Russia.[67]

Although these diplomatic overtures were not unwelcome, many of the states that were not invited at Madrid to begin accession negotiations – the Baltic states, Romania and Slovenia, in particular – remained determined to become full members of NATO. Leaders in these states will continue to put pressure on NATO's leadership to follow through on the Alliance's self-proclaimed 'open-door' policy on membership.

NATO Moves Forward after Madrid

NATO's members maintained their brisk pace after Madrid. Accession talks with the Czech Republic, Hungary and Poland began in September 1997 and were concluded in less than three months. Accession protocols were signed when NATO's foreign ministers gathered for their semi-annual meeting on 16 December 1997.[68] The fact that these negotiations took only three months was one clear indication that NATO's membership criteria were designed to facilitate accession, and that NATO's leaders were determined to translate their rhetorical commitments to enlargement into reality. Their plan was to complete the ratification process in 1998 and bring these three states into the Alliance in April 1999 – the fiftieth anniversary of the signing of the North Atlantic Treaty.

WHY NATO FACILITATED ENLARGEMENT

Compared to their EU counterparts, NATO's members moved quickly on the enlargement question: they agreed in late 1994 to translate their rhetorical commitments to enlargement into a process that would bring this about; they adopted membership criteria in 1995 that facilitated enlargement; and they completed accession negotiations with the Czech Republic, Hungary and Poland in a matter of months in the last half of 1997. Why did NATO's members adopt policies that facilitated enlargement? Three factors stand out.

First, although the EU's and NATO's membership lists overlap, they are not identical: the United States is in NATO, and Washington pushed to bring new members into NATO quickly. The Clinton administration seized the initiative on this issue in 1994, and Western European members of the Alliance did not want to alienate the United States. This begs the question of why the Clinton administration decided to begin pushing for NATO enlargement. A combination of regional, domestic and bureaucratic developments came together at that time to shape US policy.

At the regional level, President Clinton was moved by the pleas made by Vaclav Havel, Lech Walesa and other Central and Eastern European officials for closer ties with western institutions.[69] The Clinton administration was also acutely aware of Germany's desire to promote stability in the Czech Republic, Poland and the rest of the region through associations with western institutions. In addition, the administration was keen to undo the damage its flawed Bosnia policies had inflicted on transatlantic relations and America's standing in Europe. Taking the lead on NATO enlargement was seen as a way of convincing NATO's Western European members that the United States could play a constructive role on European security issues, and that it could be counted on over the long haul: the United States, the Clinton administration was trying to say, was not going to disengage from Europe. It is not a coincidence that the Clinton administration began to push on the enlargement issue in the last few months of 1994, when the transatlantic debate over Bosnia was extremely bitter and Western European doubts about the United States were growing. The fact that the EU was dragging its feet over enlargement gave Washington an added incentive to push NATO to bring in new members: this would strengthen NATO's position in Europe *vis-à-vis* the EU, which in turn would strengthen America's position in European affairs.

At the domestic level, Clinton administration officials were worried that if they did not adopt an aggressive policy in favour of NATO enlargement, their Republican opponents would have another issue to use against them in the 1994 and 1996 elections. Prominent officials from previous Republican administrations, such as James Baker and Henry Kissinger, started attacking the Clinton administration on this issue in late 1993, and the Republican leadership in the Congress supported NATO enlargement in its 1994 platform – 'Contract with America'.[70] This was an issue, moreover, to which Czech-American, Hungarian-American, and Polish-American voters attached great importance – a political fact that Clinton administration operatives duly noted. It was not a coincidence that presidential speeches in favour of NATO expansion tended to be given in cities with large blocs of Hungarian-American and Polish-American voters.[71]

At the bureaucratic level, enlargement advocates within the Clinton administration gained the upper hand in 1994. Clinton's National Security Advisor, Anthony Lake, favoured NATO expansion, and Lake attracted to the National Security Council (NSC) staff people who shared his views. Richard Holbrooke's transfer from the ambassador's residence in Bonn to the State Department brought a forceful advocate for expansion to Washington. Strobe Talbott's elevation to Deputy Secretary of State gave him a different perspective on the enlargement question; he subsequently overcame his reservations about enlargement, and became a supporter of it.[72] With both the NSC and the State Department lining up behind enlargement, the main source of resistence to the idea was the Department of Defense. After the president spoke out publicly in favour of enlargement in January and July 1994, enlargement advocates within the administration were able to neutralize the Pentagon's opposition and push forward.

Although many Western European officials had reservations about Washington's efforts in late 1994 to accelerate the enlargement process, they did not want to place further strain on a transatlantic relationship that had already been battered over Bosnia. The main concern in Western Europe in 1993–94 was getting the United States to play an active and constructive role in the Balkans and in European security affairs more generally. There was considerable anxiety about Washington's lack of involvement in Western efforts to deal with the carnage in the Balkans: this was the first time since 1945 that the United States had not been deeply involved in a European security crisis. The fear in Western Europe was that this might be a portent of the future. Therefore, Western European officials were not about to undercut Washington in an area where it was active and, indeed, pushing for additional US engagement in Europe. They consequently shied away from public debate with the United States on the expansion question, even when Washington pushed to bring new members into the alliance very quickly.

Second, Germany was committed to NATO enlargement – it was concerned about instability in Central and Eastern Europe for legitimate and understandable national security reasons – and neither the United States nor France wanted to alienate Germany. The United States recognized that Germany would be the most important power in post-Cold War Europe for years to come, and it was keen to build on the strong post-Cold War relationship forged in the struggle for German unification (when the United States and Germany faced opposition from both France and the United Kingdom, not to mention the former Soviet Union). Washington saw a strong German–American relationship as one of the keys to reinforcing the US role in European affairs in general. The United States was therefore aggressive in pushing what it saw as the German agenda on expansion, even to the point of getting out in front of Germany in late 1994.

France, for its part, saw the Franco-German relationship as nothing less than pivotal. From France's perspective, the Franco-German relationship was the key to economic and political integration in Europe, and it would constitute the main pillar of a more united Europe. Germany was therefore central to France's national security, its economic prosperity, and, indeed, its political identity. At the same time, Paris was uneasy about NATO expansion because it would make both Germany and NATO more central in European security affairs. Paris, however, could not and did not protest strongly in the enlargement debate: it reconciled its conflicting impulses by urging the alliance to go slow.

Third, the EU's members saw NATO enlargement as a cheap and easy alternative to EU enlargement, and therefore as a way of putting off enlargement of the Union. The EU's leaders argued that there were practical obstacles to bringing Central and Eastern European states into the EU that could only be overcome in the fullness of time. This was certainly true, but it was mainly an excuse: the critical point was that bringing Central and Eastern European states into the EU on an accelerated schedule would have been politically difficult and economically expensive.

One implication of this line of reasoning was that trade policies and agricultural subsidies were held to be more important than security guarantees and defense commitments – from the standpoint of Western European domestic politics, perhaps they were. It was never explained, though, why commitments to go to war to uphold solemn mutual defense pledges should be treated in such a cavalier fashion – as consolation prizes in Europe's institutional raffle.

CONCLUSIONS

Plus ça change, plus c'est la même chose – the more things change, the more they stay the same. Although the strategic landscape in Europe has changed dramatically since 1989, US–European security relations have thus far followed a familiar pattern. First, as we have seen in the Gulf region in 1990–91, in Bosnia in 1995, and with respect to NATO enlargement, US leadership is one of the keys to getting the allies to take concerted action in the security arena. Setting aside the merits of the decision to bring new members into NATO – and, indeed, many commentators believe NATO enlargement will prove to be a colossal blunder[73] – there is no doubt that the US government was the driving force behind both the pace of the enlargement process and the composition of the new membership list. Second, many Western European leaders disagreed with US enlargement initiatives and resented the Clinton administration's arrogant and maladroit diplomacy, but they nonetheless went along with Washington because they were unable to forge a united, alternative front and they did not want to antagonize their American counterparts. Western European leaders are still keen to keep American policy-makers happy – not because the West needs to maintain a united front against Moscow, but because Western Europeans worry that the United States might pull out of Europe. In short, the United States continues to lead – in its heavy-handed way – and Western Europeans continue to follow – grumbling amongst themselves and about Washington as they trudge along.

Although the first decade of the post-Cold War era has seen more continuity than change in US–European security relations, one should not assume that this state of affairs will continue indefinitely. If the European Union develops into a political entity capable of forging a common foreign and security policy, or if the United States shows signs of disengaging from European security affairs, the nature of US–European security relations will change in fundamental ways. Neither development has yet taken place. US–European security cooperation therefore continues to be defined by US leadership and Western European follower-ship.

Notes

1. This chapter is based on Michael E. Brown, *European Security: The Defining Debates* (Cambridge, Mass.: MIT Press, 1999), chap. 4.
2. North Atlantic Council, Ministerial Meeting, *Final Communiqué*, Brussels, 14–15 December 1989.
3. North Atlantic Council, Ministerial Meeting, *Final Communiqué*, Brussels, 17–18 December 1990.
4. North Atlantic Council, *London Declaration on a Transformed North Atlantic Alliance*, London, 5–6 July 1990.
5. See European Council, *Presidency Conclusions*, Maastricht, 9–10 December 1991.
6. Walesa quoted in David Buchan, *Europe: The Strange Superpower* (Aldershot, UK: Dartmouth, 1993), p. 99.
7. Quoted in Alfred A. Reisch, 'Central Europe's Disappointments and Hopes', *RFE/RL Research Report*, vol. 3, no. 12 (25 March 1994), p. 20.
8. Catherine McArdle Kelleher, *The Future of European Security: An Interim Assessment* (Washington, DC: The Brookings Institution, 1995), p. 92.
9. North Atlantic Council, *Rome Declaration on Peace and Cooperation*, Brussels, 8 November 1991.

10.   See North Atlantic Council, *North Atlantic Cooperation Council Statement on Dialogue, Partnership, and Cooperation*, Brussels, 20 December 1991.

11.   See Matthew Evangelista, 'Historical Legacies and the Politics of Intervention in the Former Soviet Union', in Michael E. Brown (ed.), *The International Dimensions of Internal Conflict* (Cambridge, Mass.: MIT Press, 1996), pp. 107–40.

12.   Eagleburger quoted in Jonathan Dean, *Ending Europe's Wars: The Continuing Search for Peace and Security* (New York: Twentieth Century Fund Press, 1994), p. 252.

13.   See Kelleher, *The Future of European Security, op. cit.*, p. 95.

14.   See James M. Goldgeier, 'NATO Expansion: The Anatomy of a Decision', *Washington Quarterly*, vol. 21, no. 1 (Winter 1998), pp. 85–102.

15.   Quoted in Michael Mihalka, 'Squaring the Circle: NATO's Offer to the East', *RFE/RL Research Report*, vol. 3, no. 12 (25 March 1994), pp. 1–9 at p. 2. See also Jane Perlez, 'Yeltsin Endorses Polish NATO Bid', *International Herald Tribune*, 28 August 1993.

16.   Yeltsin quoted in Mihalka, 'Squaring the Circle', p. 3.

17.   'Russian President Boris Yeltsin's Letter to US President Bill Clinton', 15 September 1993; reprinted in Stockholm International Peace Research Institute (SIPRI), *SIPRI Yearbook 1994* (Oxford: Oxford University Press, 1994), pp. 249–50.

18.   See International Institute for Strategic Studies (IISS), *Strategic Survey, 1993–1994* (London: IISS, 1994), pp. 81–9; Brian D. Taylor, 'Russian Civil–Military Relations After the October Uprising', *Survival*, vol. 36, no. 1 (Spring 1994), pp. 3–29.

19.   See Mihalka, 'Squaring the Circle', *op. cit.*, p. 7.

20.   Rühe quoted in Quentin Peel, 'Rühe Call for Partnership with Moscow', *Financial Times*, 8 October 1993.

21.   Kinkel quoted in Mihalka, 'Squaring the Circle', *op. cit.*, p. 7.

22.   Klaus Kinkel, 'NATO Requires a Bold but Balanced Response to the East', *International Herald Tribune*, 21 October 1993.

23.   Kohl quoted in Andrew Marshall, 'NATO Moves to Include Former Enemies', *Independent* (London), 7 September 1993.

24.   Kohl quoted in Mihalka, 'Squaring the Circle', *op. cit.*, p. 8.

25.   Léotard quoted in *ibid.*, p. 7. See also Philip H. Gordon, *A Certain Idea of France: French Security Policy and the Gaullist Legacy* (Princeton, N.J.: Princeton University Press, 1993), pp. 170–2; and Robert P. Grant, 'France's New Relationship with NATO', *Survival*, vol. 38, no. 1 (Spring 1996), pp. 58–80 at p. 67.

26.   Juppé quoted in Mihalka, 'Squaring the Circle', *op. cit.*, p. 7.

27.   Rifkind quoted in David White, 'Caution Urged on NATO Expansion', *Financial Times*, 23 September 1993.

28.   Hurd quoted in Mihalka, 'Squaring the Circle', *op. cit.*, p. 6.

29.   Davis quoted in Michael Dobbs, 'With Cold War Over, U. S. Policy Debate Flared', *Washington Post*, 5 July 1995. For a good overview and analysis of the debate in Washington over NATO enlargement, see Goldgeier, 'NATO Expansion', *op. cit.*

30.   See *ibid.*

31. Talbott quoted in Dobbs, 'With Cold War Over', *op. cit.*
32. This argument is developed in Goldgeier, 'NATO Expansion', *op. cit.*, pp. 91–2.
33. Charles A. Kupchan, 'Strategic Visions', *World Policy Journal*, vol. 11, no. 3 (Fall 1994), pp. 112–22 at p. 113.
34. See *ibid.*; David White, 'US Defers Prospect of NATO Enlargement', *Financial Times*, 21 October 1993. Peter Almond, 'NATO Offers a Welcome to 25 More Countries', *Daily Telegraph* (London), 22 October 1993.
35. For more discussion of the Partnership for Peace programme, see William T. Johnsen and Thomas-Durell Young, *Partnership for Peace: Discerning Fact from Fiction* (Carlisle Barracks, Penn.: U.S. Army War College, Strategic Studies Institute, August 1994); Nick Williams, 'Partnership for Peace: Permanent Fixture or Declining Asset?' *Survival*, vol. 38, no. 1 (Spring 1996), pp. 98–110; Kupchan, 'Strategic Visions', *op.cit.*, pp. 112–22. For more on Central and Eastern European reactions to the PfP proposal, see Reisch, 'Central Europe's Disappointments and Hopes', *op. cit.*, pp. 21–34.
36. North Atlantic Council, *Declaration of the Heads of State and Government*, Brussels, 11 January 1994.
37. Clinton quoted in 'Clinton Hints NATO Would Defend East Against Attack', *International Herald Tribune*, 13 January 1994.
38. Clinton quoted in Dobbs, 'With Cold War Over', *op. cit.*, See also The White House, *A National Security Strategy of Engagement and Enlargement*, Washington, DC., July 1994, p. 22.
39. See Dobbs, 'With Cold War Over', *op. cit.*, See also Bruce Clark, 'NATO Rallies to Call of "Expand or Die",' *Financial Times*, 29 September 1994.
40. See Elaine Sciolino, 'U.S. and NATO Say Dispute on Bosnia is Resolved', *New York Times*, 2 December 1994; Craig R. Whitney, 'Adversarial Allies: Sparring Over Bosnia and NATO Membership', *New York Times*, 2 December 1994; Rowland Evans and Robert Novak, 'Yeltsin Victorious', *Washington Post*, 12 December 1994.
41. North Atlantic Council, Ministerial Meeting, *Final Communiqué*, Brussels, 1 December 1994. See also Richard Holbrooke, 'America: A European Power', *Foreign Affairs*, vol. 74, no. 2 (March–April 1995), pp. 38–51.
42. See NATO, *Study on NATO Enlargement*, Brussels, September 1995, pp. 1–2. For a contrary view, see Michael E. Brown, 'The Flawed Logic of NATO Expansion', *Survival*, vol. 37, no. 1 (Spring 1995), pp. 34–52.
43. See *Study on NATO Enlargement*, pp. 23–6.
44. See North Atlantic Council, Ministerial Meeting, *Final Communiqué*, Brussels, 5 December 1995.
45. See Norman Kempster, 'Christopher Calls For a Charter Linking Russia With NATO', *Boston Globe*, 7 September 1996.
46. See John F. Harris, 'Clinton Vows Wider NATO in 3 Years', *Washington Post*, 23 October 1996; Alison Mitchell, 'Clinton Urges NATO Expansion in 1999', *New York Times*, 23 October 1996.
47. North Atlantic Council, Ministerial Meeting, *Final Communiqué*, Brussels, 10 December 1996.

48. Writing in mid-1997, Michael McFaul observed, 'No political actor of importance in Russia today, including even unabashed pro-Western liberals such as First Deputy Prime Minister Anatoly Chubais, has supported NATO expansion'. See Michael McFaul, 'A Precarious Peace: Domestic Politics in the Making of Russian Foreign Policy', *International Security*, vol. 22, no. 3 (Winter 1997–98), pp. 5–35 at p. 26.

49. Yeltsin quoted in 'Yeltsin Reiterates "Nyet" to NATO', *Washington Times*, 30 November 1996.

50. Rodionov quoted in William Drozdiak, 'Russian Defense Chief Blasts NATO's Plans', *Washington Post*, 19 December 1996.

51. Chernomyrdin quoted in Jim Hoagland and David Hoffman, 'NATO Plans Worry Russia's Premier', *Washington Post*, 4 February 1997.

52. See Joseph Fitchett, 'Tank Cuts for Central Europe', *International Herald Tribune*, 21 February 1997; Michael R. Gordon, 'Albright Offers Russia Plan to Ease Fears Over NATO', *New York Times*, 21 February 1997; US State Department, 'NATO Proposal on Adaptation of the CFE Treaty', February 1997; 'NATO Enlargement and the CFE Treaty', *Strategic Comments*, vol. 3, no. 2 (March 1997).

53. See *Final Communiqué*, 10 December 1996; *Founding Act on Mutual Relations, Cooperation, and Security between NATO and the Russian Federation*, Paris, 27 May 1997.

54. See David Filipov, 'US, Russia Agree on Arms, Split on NATO', *Boston Globe*, 22 March 1997; Thomas W. Lippman, 'Clinton, Yeltsin Agree on Broad Arms Cuts', *Washington Post*, 22 March 1997.

55. *Founding Act, op. cit.*

56. See Steven Lee Myers, 'US Now at Odds with NATO Allies on New Members', *New York Times*, 30 May 1997.

57. See Philip Shenon, 'US, Defying Allies, Insists NATO Limit Expansion to 3', *New York Times*, 13 June 1997.

58. See William Drozdiak and John F. Harris, 'NATO Invites 3 Former Foes to Join', *Washington Post*, 9 July 1997.

59. Jospin quoted in William Drozdiak, 'Europeans Charge US Arrogance on Issues from NATO to Jobs', *Washington Post*, 27 June 1997.

60. Chirac quoted in Brian McGrory and Elizabeth Neuffer, 'NATO Votes to Admit 3 Nations', *Boston Globe*, 9 July 1997.

61. Quoted in Drozdiak, 'Europeans Charge US Arrogance', *op. cit.*

62. NATO, *Study on NATO Enlargement, op. cit.*, p. 23.

63. North Atlantic Council, *Madrid Declaration on Euro-Atlantic Security and Cooperation*, Madrid, 8 July 1997.

64. Berger quoted in Brian McGrory, 'Battle Lines Forming Over NATO Expansion', *Boston Globe*, 5 July 1997.

65. Clinton quoted in Peter Baker, 'NATO Plan Draws Some Salutes at West Point', *Washington Post*, 1 June 1997.

66. See *Basic Document of the Euro-Atlantic Partnership Council*, Sintra, 30 May 1997. See also North Atlantic Council, Ministerial Meeting, *Final Communiqué*, 29 May 1997.

67. See *Charter on a Distinctive Partnership between the North Atlantic Treaty Organization and Ukraine*, Madrid, 8 July 1997.

68.   See North Atlantic Council, Ministerial Meeting, *Final Communiqué*, Brussels, 16 December 1997.
69.   See Goldgeier, 'NATO Expansion', *op. cit.*, pp. 86–7.
70.   See Henry Kissinger, 'Not this Partnership', *Washington Post*, 24 November 1993; Kissinger, 'It's an Alliance, Not a Relic', *Washington Post*, 16 August 1994; Kissinger, 'Expand NATO Now', *Washington Post*, 19 December 1994; Baker quoted in Michael Kramer, 'The Case for a Bigger NATO', *Time*, 10 January 1994; Proposed Republican Legislation, 'NATO Revitalization and Expansion Act of 1995', 23 September 1994. For more discussion, see Goldgeier, 'NATO Expansion', *op. cit.*, pp. 92–3; Dobbs, 'With Cold War Over', *op. cit.*
71.   See Goldgeier, 'NATO Expansion', *op. cit.*, pp. 94–5; Michael Dobbs, 'Balancing Domestic Political Costs After the Rhetoric is Spent', *Washington Post*, 7 July 1995.
72.   See Goldgeier, 'NATO Expansion', *op. cit.*, pp. 87–99; Dobbs, 'With Cold War Over', *op. cit.*
73.   See George F. Kennan, 'A Fateful Error', *New York Times*, 5 February 1997; Brown, 'The Flawed Logic of NATO Expansion', *op. cit.*

3 The European Union's Enlargement Project and US–EU Cooperation in Central and Eastern Europe

Lily Gardner Feldman

This evaluation of EU–US cooperation in Central and Eastern Europe (CEE) focuses on four dimensions: (1) the overall goals and methods of the EU and the US in their efforts to integrate the East into Europe; (2) the purpose, nature and implications of EU enlargement towards the East, which constitutes a common focal point of EU and US integration strategies in the political and economic arenas; (3) the existing attempts at linking US and EU activities towards Central and Eastern European countries (CEEC);[1] and (4) the consequences of enlargement for future US–EU partnership in the region and for transatlantic relations more generally. In all four areas, mixed assessments and contradictory signals prevail. Crystalline conclusions are further hampered by the reality of all three actors – the United States, the EU and Central and Eastern Europe – confronting profound change with respect to both their self-definition and their respective international roles. Cooperation does occur but the rhetoric of commitment to work together has outstripped the reality of continued discord. The shortfall in results suggests neither hollow commitment nor inadequate effort, but rather the tenacity of bureaucratic obstacles and structural differences.

EU AND US INTEGRATION STRATEGIES FOR CENTRAL AND EASTERN EUROPE

Before detailing the potential and reality of US–EU cooperation in Central and Eastern Europe, we must recognize first the stylistic and structural differences between the two actors. The basic interest of the EU and the US is similar: to encourage the development of a stable Central and Eastern Europe that can become an integral part of the European and transatlantic systems through a process of political and economic reform. Yet, the principal strategies for including Central and Eastern Europe are different, reflecting the reality of the EU as a regional, middle power, and the United States as a global superpower.

Moreover, after 1994 the relationship of the two actors toward the region changed, accentuating the geographic attributes of US distance and EU proximity. While agendas were never identical in the immediate post-Cold War period, they were highly connected until 1995 when the elaboration of the EU's pre-accession strategy underscored an inevitable divergence. Since then, the EU has been cementing ties in the CEE with potential equals and co-members in a significantly supranational enterprise, whereas the US has been working towards 'moving [the CEEC] relationship with the United States beyond that of assistance recipient to full partnership in the world community' through a process of political independence and economic autonomy.[2] There is further asymmetry in the fact that the US is formally excluded from the EU, and therefore has no direct role in the process of EU enlargement, whereas many EU members do participate formally in the inter-governmental NATO and, hence, in its enlargement project.

How do these structural differences manifest themselves? Based on a broad conception of the sources of stability and security, the EU has identified the CEEC integration challenge as one of political inclusion. Leon Brittan, the Commissioner overseeing US–EU relations, has noted that enlargement to the east 'is first and foremost a political process'.[3] Hans van den Broek, the Commissioner responsible for the EU's strategy of Eastern enlargement, has recognized that the outcome of the process will affect the EU as a political actor:

Either the Union will be enlarged as a genuinely integrated structure ... speaking with one voice in world affairs; or a wider Union will become a kind of United Nations of Europe, with little internal coherence and, consequently, little external clout in world affairs; [an]...organisation...unable to compete on an equal basis with the United States, Japan and the world's other major powers.[4]

Success of the enlargement process will depend on the political will of the EU member-states and institutions, and the political acumen of national leaders to sell the idea to skeptical publics.[5]

The US has hardly ignored the political aspects of integration, as US government documents readily attest,[6] but its ultimate goal is CEE military integration into the new Europe through NATO enlargement, as Secretary Christopher concluded in June 1995, and Secretary Albright reaffirmed in October 1997.[7] The debate over NATO enlargement's political acceptability by the US. Congress and the American public increasingly turned to issues of its future military benefits and its capacity to repeat, in a new environment, its 'successful Cold War military mission'.[8]

Both the EU and the United States have emphasized economic instruments for CEE integration, but the approaches vary, mirroring the actors' different institutional natures and differing policy strengths and experiences. Key economic instruments have included economic assistance, trade and investment – but in each area the approaches and overall commitment have differed.

In the initial stage, economic aid represented a common effort to mount and implement international assistance through the G-24 process (which the European Community chaired). In the second stage, priority shifted to the functioning of the respective programmes: PHARE (*Pologne et Hongrie Aide de la Reconstruction Économique*) on the European side, and SEED (Support for East European Democracy) on the US part. The third stage of EU–US endeavours in economic assistance has involved reorientation of both actors' programmes, with an emphasis on complementarity, and on rationalization of G-24 coordination.[9] PHARE continues to be highly active, but its efforts have switched from general reform in the CEEC to specific preparation for EU membership.[10] SEED's objectives are different, focusing on: (1) creating market economies through privatization, particularly of small-and medium-sized businesses, and economic restructuring based on new policy and legal environments; (2) embedding democratic institutions through public-sector reform, retrained public administration, vigorous decentralization, strengthened elected bodies, and through promotion of independent media and non-governmental organizations; and (3) enhancing 'quality of life' through health care, housing, labour and environmental reform.[11] It was specifically designed as a temporary programme, and has been phased out in the Czech Republic, Slovenia and Estonia. By the year 2000, it will have graduated Latvia, Hungary, Poland, Lithuania and Slovakia.

Divergences in the goals of PHARE and SEED point to a significant difference in approach. The United States looks for short-term, obvious programme results, in large part responding to domestic and congressional requirements for transparent progress. The EU displays a more long-term perspective that deems the steady process of preparation for EU membership just as important as the final result. US aid has been highly focused and bounded, whereas EU support has been more open-ended. With a longer-term orientation in much of its external activity, and without the same level of legislative oversight, the EU prefers a slower pace. As a result, the two actors have tended to have differing expectations regarding CEEC progress on reform, and, on occasion, diverging assessments of the outcome.

While both the United States and the European Union have agreed on the centrality of economic assistance for democratic transformation, the EU and its member-states have been the major donors. On the aid front, 53.5 per cent (ecu 46 billion) of all western aid between 1990 and 1995 was provided by the EU and its member states, and 11.3 per cent by the United States; international financial institutions accounted for 24.8 per cent of the total. The EU alone represented 15.6 per cent of the total.[12] The EU and the member-states also stand out in specific areas: 66 vs 22 per cent of grants, 52 vs 41 per cent of all food aid; 67 vs 26 per cent of emergency non-food aid; and 69 vs 27 per cent of technical assistance.

Similarly, while both have recognized the importance of trade liberalization, the EU has developed more instruments for its pursuit, particularly the Europe Agreements. Moreover, the EU trades more with the CEEC than any other actor does. For example, in 1994 it imported 15 times as much from the CEEC as the US did, and exported 20 times more. Moreover, except for the Europe Free Trade Area (EFTA) members, which negotiated similar agreements with the CEEC, no other country or organization has matched the Europe Agreements in their extensiveness.[13] The United States has done much to open up trade with the CEEC. It has extended most favoured nation (MFN) status or conditional MFN treatment to most of the CEEC, has trade agreements with a number of countries in the region, has granted Generalized System of Preferences benefits to many CEEC, and has promoted trade-related projects in the CEEC through the US Trade and Development Agency and the Export–Import Bank of the United States.

Both actors have highlighted investment, with the United States emphasizing from the beginning the role of the private sector as part of a classical market-economy approach in contradistinction to the EU's general social-market orientation. Accordingly, the US government has reinforced the American private sector's vigorous investment efforts through the activities of the Overseas Private Investment Corporation (OPIC) to provide loans, loan guarantees, investor services and insurance in most of the CEEC, and through bilateral investment treaties. Through 1996, OPIC's assistance amounted to $2.8 billion ($681 million in project-based financial packages, and $2.1 billion in political-risk insurance support). The seven Enterprise Funds the United States has created across ten CEE countries (with a capitalization of $576.5 million) typify the US strategy: they are non-profit corporations directed by boards from the private sector to stimulate, with great flexibility, the growth of private companies via equity investments, loans and grants.[14] Since March 1997, one of PHARE's chief priorities has been the financing of investment projects, to the tune of 70 per cent of the ecu 6.7 billion budget devoted to the applicant countries for the period 1995–99.[15] The European Bank for Reconstruction and Development (EBRD), in which the EU is the major shareholder, and the European Investment Bank (EIB) are also significant vehicles for EU investment, with the latter constituting the major source of external financing of infrastructure schemes in CEE (approximately ecu 1 billion per year, reaching ecu 1.7 billion in 1997).[16]

Washington and Brussels have trodden separate paths in the pursuit of the same goal – integrating Central and Eastern Europe – but collaboration can still occur. US–EU cooperation in Central and Eastern Europe does not require identity of views or of instruments, but it does presuppose mutual acceptance of roles, explicit recognition of policy philosophy and practice, and reasonableness of expectations. Such mutual tolerance was largely missing until the middle of 1995. After that point, the earlier acrimony over agenda-setting, priorities and responsibilities was significantly overcome, although each side on occasion still finds fault with the partner in specific areas. The mutual acceptance of roles is a natural consequence of cumulative experience, resources and the character of the two actors, and not the result of a formal assignment of tasks. The EU now appreciates that the United States has a special role to play in NATO and NATO enlargement. The United States recognizes the unique contribution EU enlargement can make to the stability of Central and Eastern Europe and to Europe as a whole, and broadly supports the EU's elaborate programme to prepare the countries for accession. As the US phases out the SEED programme and focuses on the future path of NATO enlargement, the EU's enlargement to the East assumes even greater significance. To understand the possibilities and limits of US–EU cooperation in Central and Eastern Europe, we must first appreciate the nature of the EU's enlargement process.

THE EUROPEAN UNION'S EASTERN ENLARGEMENT PROCESS

The Purposes and Significance of Enlargement

The EU's objectives in Eastern enlargement are varied – political, economic and psychological – but linked in the overriding purpose of creating and maintaining peace, security and stability in Central and Eastern Europe.[17] The EU's goal of embedding democratic polities and market economies in Central and Eastern Europe through enlargement is accompanied by a desire to create in the East a psychological environment of 'mutual trust', a 'feeling of belonging'.[18] Enlargement also provides a political–spiritual opportunity to 'undo the wrongs of half a century', and the economic advantage of low-cost production by a highly skilled workforce.[19] The CEEC share this triad of objectives in enlargement, for they are 'in search of a home', need 'an economic "modernization anchor"', and yearn for 'a political "security anchor"'.[20]

The goals of the EU and the CEEC have been clear, but the realization has involved a monumental task, comparable, in Leon Brittan's words, to 'that presented by the creation of the EC itself a generation ago at Messina'.[21] Expansion to the East represents a greater challenge than previous enlargements on four dimensions: number of applicants; magnitude of economic and social differences between applicants and current member-states (average GDP per person is approximately one-third of the EU-15 average); combined size of population (106 million, or 29 per cent of the EU total); and vastness of territory (1.1 million square km, or 33 per cent of the current EU area).

At least since the June 1993 Copenhagen summit, the EU has declared publicly the need to find a delicate balance between deepening (integrating further the current Community) and widening (admitting new members). Enlargement to the East provides, then, an acid-test for the EU's viability, institutionally, and conceptually. It provides an opportunity to show off the tools of the EU as a civilian power, yet simultaneously challenges the EU to demonstrate its capacity, or at least its intentions, regarding hard power – the use of military force.

Stages and Instruments of Enlargement

Despite some marked difference in member-state perspectives that has produced a gradual and cautious approach, the EU has managed to mount a comprehensive enlargement strategy, encompassing six stages since 1989:

1. A new relationship with the CEEC between 1989 and 1991 through trade and cooperation agreements and economic assistance.
2. The possibility of membership through the negotiation and conclusion of much more comprehensive Europe Agreements, mainly in the period 1992–93.

3. Commitment to the prospect of membership under specific conditions presented at the June 1993 Copenhagen European Council.
4. Detailed plans for adaptation to community norms and *acquis*, including the endorsement of a pre-accession strategy at the December 1994 Essen European Council; the presentation of specific papers at the June 1995 Cannes European Council and the December 1995 Madrid European Council; and elaborate country, budget and economic sector analyses that prepared the ground for the Commission's July 1997 Agenda 2000 opinions and its blueprint for enlargement.
5. The conclusions of the December 1997 Luxembourg European Council which endorsed the Commission's recommendation that five CEE countries should begin accession negotiations: Hungary, Poland, the Czech Republic, Estonia and Slovenia.
6. The implementation of the 'negotiation process' approach by convening two conferences in March 1998, a first one with all applicants to discuss transnational, regional and foreign policy issues, and subsequent opening negotiations with the first wave of candidates.

The EU's judgement about the readiness of applicants for membership is based on the political and economic criteria laid out at the 1993 Copenhagen European Council:

Membership requires that the candidate country has achieved stability of institutions guaranteeing democracy, the rule of law, human rights and respect for and protection of minorities, the existence of a functioning market economy as well as the capacity to cope with competitive pressure and market forces within the Union. Membership presupposes the candidate's ability to take on the obligations of membership including adherence to the aims of political, economic and monetary union.

The EU also has recognized that its structure and purpose must be able to digest enlargement:

The Union's capacity to absorb new members, while maintaining the momentum of European integration, is also an important consideration in the general interest of both the Union and the candidate countries.[22]

The main economic instruments the EU has devised to prepare applicants for candidacy and eventual membership, are: Europe Agreements, the Commission's White Paper on integrating the CEEC into the Internal Market, and aid. Political instruments include the 'structured dialogue' (also known as 'structured relations'), the Stability Pact, and regional cooperation.

The Europe Agreements with the ten CEEC cover cooperation in the political, scientific, technical, environmental and cultural arenas. Economic partnership aims to integrate the CEEC into the flow of trade and foster economic restructuring through the gradual creation of free trade in non-agricultural products. Special arrangements apply for tariff and quantitative restrictions in the areas of 'sensitive products', – that is, steel, textiles and clothing – and the Agreements contain safeguard, anti-dumping and shortage clauses.

The Commission's May 1995 White Paper on 'Preparation of the Associated Countries of Central and Eastern Europe for Integration into the Internal Market of the Union', whose drafting involved consultations with the CEEC, set out both the provisions of the Treaty and the key secondary legislation relating to the internal market; highlighted the purpose, organizational context and administrative structure of legislation; and suggested the order in which the approximations of laws could occur.[23] A comparable level of detail and prescription was evident in the Commission's subsequent Agricultural Strategy Paper for the Madrid European Council.

Aid, principally through the PHARE programme (subsequently applied to the rest of the region beyond Poland and Hungary), has been a focal point of the Community's efforts to support the process of economic and political reform in the CEEC. By the end of 1996, PHARE had committed ecu 6.6 billion in non-reimbursable grants; by 1997, 13 CEEC were eligible for participation. In general, PHARE has helped privatization, the development of a market economy, and economic restructuring in the CEEC through institution-building and through direct support to individual enterprises. By the mid-1990s, PHARE had evolved four different sets of programmes (national, cross-border, multi-country and horizontal), and extensive relations with other donors (both individual countries, and international financial institutions (IFIs)).[24]

The EU reconfirmed the centrality of PHARE at the Copenhagen European Council, refocused its attention specifically to accession at the Essen European Council, and renewed its financial commitment through 1999 at the Cannes European Council. To improve the membership chances of applicant countries, in March 1997 the Commission initiated a major reorientation of PHARE. The EU's evaluation of the aid programme identified PHARE's strengths – salience of support for transformation; magnitude of assistance; presence in relatively neglected areas such as democracy and civil society programmes; flexibility in response to frequent change in the CEEC; contribution to new thinking in recipient countries – but emphasized the need for major reform. By the mid-1990s, PHARE was suffering from a variety of problems: slowness in initial decisions and completion of projects; fragmentation, excessive complexity, and unfocused activities due to a demand-driven approach which came to elevate the priorities and agendas of recipient governments and contractors over the goals of the EU; and inefficiencies in organization, resulting in one-third of the funds remaining unused in the period 1990–96.

The new PHARE framework entails an accession-driven approach in which the EU specifies the priorities and is an active policy-maker rather than a passive policy-taker; simplified decision-making and streamlined management; more targeted relations with other donors; and regular evaluations of programmes. US policy-makers believe these management and stylistic changes reflect learning from the American approach to the administration of economic assistance. Substantively, the priorities lie in institution-building and administrative training (30 per cent of PHARE's budget), and investment accounts for the remainder. Functionally, the focus ranges across the environment, transportation, large infrastructural projects, modernization of industry, and regional cooperation.

The economic activity outlined above has been further reinforced by the EU's initiatives regarding the 'structured dialogue', the Stability Pact and regional cooperation, which have a distinctly political agenda, promoting security in both broad and narrow senses. The 'structured dialogue', has entailed participation of a consultative and advisory nature by CEEC ministers in a whole range of EU functional areas: economics, finance, agriculture, energy, environment, culture, education, research, telecommunications, transport, common foreign and security policy, justice and home affairs, as well as comprehensive meetings of heads of state or government and of foreign ministers. The structured relationship also has fostered coordination between the EU and the CEEC at the international level, both in international organizations (like the OSCE and the UN) and in third countries.

In seeking to develop habits of cooperation and intimate knowledge between the Community and the CEEC through the structured relationship, the EU is implicitly applying its own neo-functional and networking lessons. The notion of proffering a model for integration also informs its encouragement of regional cooperation within Central and Eastern Europe. As Commissioner van den Broek noted in January 1998:

> Another facet of the new Europe to which we attach considerable importance is regional cooperation. This is a valuable tool in bringing together countries which are linked with the European Union in different ways. The EU is actively involved in such initiatives from the Arctic to the Black Sea.[25]

The Pact on Stability in Europe, adopted in Paris in March 1995, incorporates the philosophy of peace and security through trade, functional and administrative cooperation, and good neighbourly relations, while also attending to the reality of ongoing disputes over borders and minorities. Launched as a French initiative and embroidered by the EU, the Stability Pact is now housed within the OSCE which monitors the bilateral agreements and arrangements. The Paris conference's final document included a list of 98 PHARE projects supporting the Pact's objectives.[26]

The effect of the EU's economic and political instruments on the CEEC candidacy for membership was gauged in the

July 1997 Agenda 2000 communication, in which the Commission explained its opinions on each membership application by applying the Copenhagen political and economic criteria.[27] In addition to specifying the grounds on which Hungary, Poland, the Czech Republic, Slovenia and Estonia were eligible for membership, the Commission proposed a two-pronged approach to reinforcing the pre-accession strategy: (1) creation of the Accession Partnerships, a single framework for all resources and types of assistance to prepare the CEEC for membership and to codify CEEC commitments in the areas of democracy, macroeconomic stabilization, nuclear safety, and adoption of the *acquis communautaire*; and (2) provision of additional assistance in agriculture (ecu 500 million per year) and in structural aid (approximately ecu 1 billion per year).

Implications of Enlargement for the EU

The Agenda 2000 report also listed the impact of enlargement on EU policies and future developments, elaborating on the Commission's December 1995 interim report. Eastern enlargement will have major internal and external implications for the EU, and the two are intertwined: a fractured, overextended, financially-strapped Union will have little impact in the international arena whereas a streamlined, purposeful, energized Union can exert influence.

Economically, enlargement could benefit the EU by expanding the Single Market, and by enhancing the EU's profile in global markets. At the same time, there will also be significant sectoral and regional adjustment challenges, particularly in the areas of labour-market competition, labour-intensive industries, and traditional sectors such as agriculture, coal and mining, and textiles. The task of adjusting to incipient or evolving EU policies and programmes – such as social policy, the environment, the transnational issues of Justice and Home Affairs, and EMU – is especially acute. The Commission predicts a reduction of 16 per cent in the average GDP per capita for the Community as a whole. The budgetary implications of enlargement are large, both in agriculture (between ecu 1.1 and 1.4 billion a year in market organization measures, plus eventually some ecu 2.5 billion in special modernization aid and other programmes), and in Structural Funds (ecu 45 billion of the total EU allocation of ecu 275 billion for the period 2000–2006).

As for institutional implications, enlargement does not cause new problems, but it magnifies the existing ones: weighting of votes; numbers of members of parliament; size of the Commission; and the nature of the Council presidency. The EU's failure to resolve these issues in the Amsterdam Treaty and its decision to revisit the problems before the next expansion complicate an already daunting enlargement agenda.

As in other areas, enlargement's consequences for security are at once clarifying and complicating. Given the depth of the EU and CEEC search for security in Europe, the potential for instability and conflict in the region and adjacent areas, and the fragility of the EU's CFSP, Eastern enlargement is bound to have a profound effect on the objectives, contours and instruments of the EU's foreign relations, as well as the Community's external image. Most generally, enlargement to the East will complete the process of undoing the Yalta system, render the EU a physically larger actor, modify its geopolitical milieu, and enhance the EU's capacity as a model for conflict-resolution.

The EU will be characterized by more heterogeneity, which can be a source of creativity and progress, but also can render more difficult (but by no means impossible) the setting of common goals in CFSP. CEEC accession will intensify the tangled mess of uneven participation of EU member-states in the WEU, and will cloud further the relationship between the EU and the WEU. However, the potential new members are also committed to CFSP, for with a self-image as small, vulnerable states, the CEEC ardently want to collectivize their security risks and burdens; membership will hinge on addressing extant bilateral disputes, and tensions over ethnic and national minorities. The long-term domestic economic requirements in the CEEC mean they will not be enhancing the soft power instruments of CFSP, nor will they add the most modern armies. But they will bring a peacekeeping expertise that can enrich the EU's preventive diplomacy goals; enlarged access to training facilities; and new fly-over possibilities.[28]

Russia and Ukraine will remain primary foci of EU security and foreign policy after enlargement. The EU's sensitivity to the danger of erecting new dividing lines in Europe can be detected in the priority it has assigned to the Partnership and Cooperation Agreements with Russia and Ukraine, the EU Action Plans for Russia and the Ukraine, and its promotion of regional cooperation schemes (Barents, Baltic and Black Sea areas). Historical and geographical ties of acceding countries, as well as enhanced market benefits of enlargement, also suggest the continued importance of relations with South-eastern Europe. Yet, the EU will have to avoid negative economic repercussions for South-eastern Europe, just as it will for the Mediterranean area.

In the end, beyond internal reform, Eastern enlargement may force the EU to make a choice it has avoided so far. It will have to confront the military dimension of power projection, and make a choice between remaining a civilian power, albeit with amplifications, or becoming a traditional power. Confidence in the former power role and uncertainty about the latter have featured prominently in relations with the United States over Central and Eastern Europe.

US–EUROPEAN COOPERATION IN CENTRAL AND EASTERN EUROPE

EU enlargement – and the process leading to accession – is the most prominent means by which the European Union has worked to integrate the CEEC more fully into Europe. It is part of a wider panoply of strategies which display varying degrees of cooperation with the United States. By the mid-1990s, three main types of cooperation had developed between the United States and the European Union in Central and Eastern Europe: coordination, division of labour and parallelism.[29] They are distinguished by the degree of jointness of enterprise, the level of dialogue, and the functional nature of the activity. There is direct reference or allusion to examples of all three in the December 1995 'The New Transatlantic Agenda: Joint US–European Union Action Plan' that resulted from a two-year effort to refashion the partnership for the post-communist world.[30] With respect to the CEEC, coordination has occurred mainly on economic assistance, but also on transnational issues and democratization. A form of division of labour has emerged on trade liberalization; and parallelism has characterized the respective approaches to military security issues.[31]

Coordination

The general attempt to coordinate in the region was consolidated by the establishment at the July 1994 US–EU Berlin summit of the *ad hoc* working group on Central and Eastern Europe. The effort has continued, more successfully because of its formal character, through the work of the Senior Level Group (SLG) (which has two representatives from the EU Council presidency, two from the Commission, and two from the United States) to monitor progress in the US–EU Action Plan. The SLG's first meeting in January 1996 included consideration of aid and environmental issues. The Senior Level Group meets several times a year, whereas the New Transatlantic Agenda Task Forces (which have representatives from the EU Council presidency, the Commission, and the State Department/USAID) maintain ongoing contact through meetings and video-conferences. The SLG's report to the EU–US Summit in June 1996 noted progress in general on the Joint US–EU Action Plan, but recognized also the need for greater persistence.[32] The December 1996 report listed the strengthening of civil society and the promotion of economic development in CEE as a priority; a year later the joint report included the development of free and independent media in the region as an additional focus.[33] An examination of specific efforts and outcomes between 1994 and 1998 regarding Central and Eastern Europe confirms the SLG's mixed assessment. However, compared to other areas of the New Transatlantic Agenda, officials on both sides deem US–EU cooperation in Central and Eastern Europe far-reaching.

In gauging the extent of coordination between the United States and the EU in economic assistance (the main area of cooperative activity), an important distinction exists between the coordination of policy and the coordination of programmes, between coordination across capitals (Washington and Brussels) and coordination *in situ*.

Policy Coordination

Given the similarity of overall goals in Central and Eastern Europe, coordination of policy has been 'natural' and 'organic' since fall 1989. It has occurred through meetings in Brussels and Washington and via the telephone between high-level officials (or their representatives) from a host of organizational units within the State Department, the US Agency for International Development, and the European Commission. In addition, US officials have made use of a standing EU invitation for them to stop off in Brussels when they visit Central and Eastern Europe. Finally, the network of traditional transatlantic consultations (summits, ministerials, cabinet meetings, sub-cabinet meetings, political director meetings and troika consultations) also cover Central and Eastern Europe.

After 1994, bilateral meetings focused less on general G-24 questions, as they did at the beginning, and more on specific countries. They involved information exchange (for example, the direction of the SEED and PHARE programmes), priority-setting and a broad commitment to passive programme coordination by seeking to avoid duplication. However, the meetings generally targeted neither specific, active coordination of separate programmes nor joint action. There is consensus among officials that this type of policy coordination has worked quite well by setting the right tone, but that it could have benefited from expansion, a more precise purpose, and a more direct relationship to the coordination of actual programmes.

Two structural innovations have reinforced the goal of US–EU policy coordination in economic assistance since 1996. The High-Level Assistance Consultations between USAID and the European Union, which began in September 1995 as a forum for exchanging information and ideas, evolved by October 1997 into an important venue for jointly diagnosing problems, reviewing activities, and targeting areas for further coordination. In addition to cataloguing US–EU cooperation, in other geographical regions, the 1997 consultations agreed to examine synergies in assistance programming for CEEC, including on the environment and civil society.[34] The increasing comfort level between USAID and the Commission reflected in the outcome of the October 1997 meeting has been aided by the presence, since 1996, of a full-time senior policy adviser for EU affairs in Washington and of a USAID official in the US Embassy to the European Union.

Programme Coordination
Programme coordination started much later than overall policy coordination, and for some officials on both sides it would have been preferable (for developments in the CEEC and in trans-atlantic relations) to commence active coordination with the onset of change in Central and Eastern Europe in 1989. Programme coordination has occurred, but officials on both sides have registered disappointment that there has not been more.

Given the rapid and often contradictory nature of transformation in the CEEC, it is not surprising that much of the actual coordination of EU and US programmes takes place on the ground in response to direct exposure to immediate or anticipated needs and problems. Because of its frequent lack of connection to the larger framework of policy coordination, and the inconsistency of local representatives' enthusiasm, on-the-ground US and EU cooperation in Central and Eastern Europe has been labeled 'coordination by coincidence' by some engaged in the process.

Coordination *in situ* has taken the form of ongoing informa-tion exchanges regarding separate US and EU programmes, synchronized activity within a particular sector of the economy or a particular project, and, more rarely, the evolution of joint programmes. Coordinating activity has often started infor-mally, for example in Hungary and Poland through lunch gatherings of major donors. It has been initiated by one side or the other and by the US and the EU together (and some-times by others, for example the Canadian aid representative in Hungary). Other donors, such as the British Know-How Fund, the World Bank or the EBRD, have also participated in coordination.

According to USAID documents, there are examples of US–EU programme coordination in development assistance for most of the CEEC.[35] Much of the coordination is on the looser side, but there are four oft-cited examples of focused, significant US–EU coordination: the project of making Ro-mania eligible for the World Bank's Financial Enterprise

Structural Adjustment Program; the restructuring of Hungary's banking system; reform of the Hungarian pension system; and the advice on energy policy in Poland.

There have been attempts to link the coordination of policy with the coordination of programmes in economic assistance, and fora have been established by the United States and the EU to mesh the two domains. One vehicle has been on-site meetings. Building on the work of the US–EU Ad Hoc Assistance Coordination Group in Brussels and Washington in 1994 and early 1995, the group convened in Warsaw with US and EU field representatives, as well as World Bank officials.[36] Besides linking policy and programme, and perspectives from headquarters and the field, the meeting sent a signal of western commitment and unity to the Polish government and provided a visible demonstration of progress in the New Transatlantic Agenda. Similar meetings were anticipated in Romania, Bulgaria and Lithuania.[37] According to American officials, an effort to convene all major donors locally was attempted in Bucharest in November 1997 by the USAID mission director, but failed due to the EU representative's unwillingness to participate on the grounds that the EU had the responsibility for coordination. From the EU perspective, there has been no repeat of the Warsaw meeting due to lack of initiative on the American side, and EU conviction that such a meeting (involving headquarters' input) would be superfluous given *in situ* coordination.

Despite such occasional differences over connecting policy and programme coordination, by 1998 a new joint effort emerged, which reflected the fruits of US and EU economic programmes in certain CEEC. Recognizing that Western activity can be seen as heavy-handed and threatening to some segments of the population, the United States and the EU have begun to promote the direct involvement of the successful Central and Eastern European countries in implementing US and EU economic-assistance agendas in the region. Poland, for example, can speak with conviction and historical connection to Slovakia (and Ukraine) about the benefits of the rule of law, a pluralistic and open political system, and an independent media.

Coordination of policy and of programmes clearly has occurred between the United States and the European

Union in Central and Eastern Europe, but less than one might expect in light of the monumental nature of the political and economic transformation challenge in the CEEC. We need to consider, then, both the logic for coordination and the obstacles to closer cooperation.

The Logic of Coordination
Coordination between the US and the EU is logical for financial, bureaucratic, programmatic and efficiency reasons. US aid budgets, which amount to less than one-half of 1 per cent of the American GNP, have been declining for the last decade and will not readily expand in the future.[38] In 1995, appropriated SEED funds declined to $359 million after having risen every year since 1991.[39] As a result, the United States is driven to work with foreign actors, among whom the EU stands out in terms of resources and commitment in the field of economic assistance in general, and Central and Eastern Europe in particular. USAID, in particular, is keen to publicize its collaboration with the EU as a demonstration to Congress of the efficiency, financial and multiplier benefits of pooling resources, and USAID documents are replete with references to coordination with the EU.[40]

With respect to bureaucratic and infrastructure resources, the picture is reversed. The presence of PHARE has been considerably thinner on the ground than USAID expertise, and it is a much newer organization. In addition, US embassies in CEEC capitals have more extensive facilities for meetings. The pooling of resources, whether financial or bureaucratic, permits the United States and the EU together to do what neither can do alone.

When combined, the different programmatic emphases of the United States and the EU have provided comprehensiveness and consistency for projects. Until the March 1997 reorganization of PHARE, EU activities were demand-driven, so undertakings resulted from host-country requests, and relationships were established with governments. The process was cumbersome, but also of longer duration. The United States could move much more quickly by seizing the initiative and readily using established, preselected contracting services; it could also disengage more abruptly. Budget cycles for the United States and the EU have been different, such that linkage of effort has ensured constancy of coverage. There is also a logic, formally recognized by officials, to gear USAID objectives more explicitly to CEEC integration into the EU and less to self-contained technical parameters traditionally employed in development assistance.[41] When PHARE was reconfigured to focus on accession, USAID officials took the initiative, with help from EU counterparts, to provide its field staff with copies of the EU's March 1997 blueprint.

By the end of the 1990s, therefore, a sufficient level of comfort and mutual learning has been reached between Washington and Brussels that differences in approach can be broached directly. The logic of coordination is understood well by US and EU officials, but the very differences between the two actors from which that logic of coordination derives can also militate against its realization. Obstacles in the areas of finances, bureaucracy, programmes and efficiency are both real and perceived.

Obstacles to Coordination

There has been hesitation on the part of some EU officials out of a concern that US enthusiasm for coordination reflects a desire to set the agenda and impose objectives without footing the bill, a tendency EU officials fear will grow as USAID leaves more countries. The European belief that CEEC integration is the acid-test of the EU's prowess as an international actor only heightens this urge to escape the role of junior partner, and to ensure that EU financial largesse receives proper credit. US officials perceive a decline in EU interest in cooperation coinciding with a shift from the phase of transition assistance for CEE to the phase of actual membership. EU officials acknowledge Central and Eastern Europe's special status as part of the 'family', whereas the United States views it as one (albeit highly important) recipient, among many, of American assistance.

This difference, in viewing CEEC as family members or aid recipients, has non-financial implications. The US initiative to include Central and Eastern Europe in the May 1997 Transatlantic Conference on 'Bridging the Atlantic: People to People Links' met with EU resistance for two reasons: the desire to preserve its special relationship with Central and Eastern Europe; and the fear of diluting and complicating the

transatlantic agenda. Central and Eastern European countries, therefore, participated only as observers. The United
States has continued its politics of inclusion by briefing Central and Eastern European countries at their embassies in
Washington after major transatlantic meetings, and on the
transatlantic dimensions of the Amsterdam Treaty and
the Commission's Agenda 2000 report; and by involving
the Europe Agreement countries in the next round of transatlantic people-to-people efforts, namely the NGO and civil
society dialogue.

Other bureaucratic impediments to coordination have
derived from interagency and intradepartment relationships
on both sides, and from differences in bureaucratic structure
between the United States and the EU. Melding regional
(Central and Eastern Europe) and functional (economic
assistance) tasks is never easy. Internal coordination appears
to have worked better, but by no means perfectly, on the
American side because of the interagency character of the
Office of the Coordinator for East European Assistance,
which is located in the State Department and draws on
USAID as lead agency.[42] The 1997 reorganization of
PHARE promises some improvement on the European side.
In addition, the inevitably differing objectives of the European
Commission's DG1 (transatlantic relations), DG1A (Central
and Eastern Europe), DG1B (North–South cooperation), and
DGXIII (development) can be profound. And, as environmen-
tal issues become woven into the fabric of USAID–EU cooperation in the CEEC, DGXI brings to deliberations an
additional perspective.

USAID and State Department officials are sensitive to turf
battles in the EU. They also note bureaucratic divergences in
the American policy-making community, which can colour the
relationship with the EU. The State Department's long-term
experience in dealing with the EU can add wisdom and
perspective, but also occasionally manifests itself as frustration
with USAID's enthusiasm and autonomous initiatives, while
USAID officials resent the 'imposition' of State's views. State's
traditional element of concern regarding EU interests in CEE
contrasts with the newer and less-experienced, but therefore
more open and less-critical, USAID attitude towards the EU.
Both the EU and USAID speak more eagerly the language of

soft power and preventive diplomacy than does the State Department.

Bureaucratic divergences have also been evident elsewhere in the United States. The Treasury Department has an active technical assistance programme in CEE that is built around US resident advisors operating in finance ministries. The tendency of resident advisors to have limited contact with US embassies, to avoid the appearance of promoting an American political agenda, precludes active coordination with the EU. With the National Security Council the problem is one of priorities, for the person responsible for dealing with the EU also handles many European and bilateral issues (including Northern Ireland), which have been high on the priority list of the White House.

Coordination has been hindered not only by internal difficulties among bureaucracies, but also by obstacles between the field and policy-makers. On both sides, aid representatives in the field inevitably concentrate on the details of their mission, without referring to the New Transatlantic Agenda, although the effort to communicate those goals is more easily and more frequently attempted by Washington than by Brussels. PHARE representatives have been overstretched as it is, so coordination with the United States is not necessarily a priority. In addition, the more circumscribed autonomy of PHARE representatives on the ground has at times hampered cooperation with the more independent USAID workers.

Regular and systematic reporting from the field on US–EU coordination is infrequent, despite the attempts of Washington and Brussels to gain an overview of the activity. USAID's Bureau for Europe and the New Independent States began to compile in a comprehensive report responses from the field on three issues: areas of continued collaboration with the EU; areas that the EU could take over as USAID missions are closed out; and new opportunities for collaboration.[43] Comparable efforts on the EU side apparently have not generated the same degree of responsiveness from the field.

US–EU coordination also has been hindered – not by the vast differences over goals, but by consensus over priorities. Both have made the Bosnian peace such a centerpiece of

their joint activity that other parts of Central and Eastern
Europe can be shortchanged. EU and US officials have
observed that cooperation in Central and Eastern Europe has
almost vanished from the New Transatlantic Agenda (as
demonstrated by the briefness of allusions in the most recent
SLG's reports), in part because a significant level of success has
been achieved, but also because crises that are ongoing (peace
in Bosnia) and potential (nuclear safety in the Ukraine) over-
shadow most other issues.

Finally, while efficiency arguments privilege coordination,
they also can mandate competition. Particularly on the American side, there is a view that arraying a set of alternative
programmes and models from which the CEEC can choose is
a healthy development, a natural part of democratic and market transformation. The latest incarnation of American promotion of alternatives is the Southeast Europe Cooperation
Initiative (SECI), housed in the State Department. Although
the SLG's December 1996 Report referred to SECI as a
complement to the EU's regional approach and the Royau-
mont process of Stability and Good Neighbourliness in Southeast Europe,[44] State Department officials see its origins in
American frustration with the EU's cross-border initiatives. In
turn, SECI has caused some disquiet among EU officials who
feel insufficiently informed about US activity 'in their back-
yard'.

Coordination in Other Areas

Coordinated activity has extended beyond the economic assistance arena to a variety of transnational issues. Both for
ecological and trade reasons, environmental issues have been
a primary common concern for the United States and the
European Union, exemplified in their Budapest Regional
Environmental Centre initiative. The Budapest initiative
spurred the agreement announced in June 1996, and
reiterated in the December 1997 SLG Report, to develop a
network of regional environmental centres in the NIS.[45] One
of the few results of the *ad hoc* EU–US working group on
organized crime and drug trafficking (mandated for a year at
the July 1994 Berlin US–EU summit) was cooperation to
establish the International Law Enforcement Academy in

Budapest. Trafficking in women has been a common concern also, leading to a joint US–EU information campaign in Poland (and Ukraine).[46]

Concerns about human rights and the development of political democracy have accompanied the economic assistance and transnational projects of the United States and the EU. The two actors have worked jointly to promote civic education, and have cooperated on local government issues. In May 1997, the United States and the EU announced a Democracy and Civil Society Awards Programme to promote local community, non-governmental and individual action on behalf of democracy.[47] Diverging US and EU programmatic conceptions have complicated the awards programme, but the process of joint US–EU nominations, and a joint US–EU working group to narrow the candidate list furthered practical cooperation and mutual learning.

Concerning democracy issues in Albania and Slovakia, the EU and United States first arrived independently at similar conclusions regarding the fragility of democracy, and increasingly are involved in joint assessments. The New Transatlantic Agenda has provided a useful framework to act on concerns in a coordinated manner. Consultation and coordination prevented Washington and Brussels from slipping into endorsement of the disputed Albanian elections in May 1996, and projected a united front to encourage new parliamentary elections (which took place in October 1996). A year later, when the collapse of several 'pyramid' savings schemes unleashed civil disorder, Washington and Brussels worked effectively together: assessing material needs and providing humanitarian relief, training for basic police-management and law enforcement to restore public order, auditing the pyramid schemes, and exploring the relative strengths of the World Bank, the IMF, the OSCE, the WEU and NATO for emergency programmes and contingency planning. In the Slovakia case, coordinated US and EU démarches since fall 1995 have defined unambiguously for the government the limits of Western tolerance of political illiberalism. By spring 1998, the United States and the EU began to explore ways to flag concerns jointly, particularly regarding defects in the election process and the absence of an independent media, and to identify new vehicles for influencing the Slovakian government. The United States and the EU also have pursued this political strategy – comparing notes and coordinating démarches – in the Baltics, for example on the question of border disputes with Russia.

Division of Labour

American efforts in privatization and democratization have simultaneously served US interests and the EU's objective of CEEC accession. As various American officials have stressed repeatedly, the United States firmly stands behind the EU's policy of enlargement and European integration in general.[48] It fully accepts the EU's unique role in anchoring the CEEC economically and politically just as the EU recognizes the special, though not exclusive, place the US occupies in NATO.[49] The United States can provide aid, investment and training, and devise programmes that explicitly and implicitly foster compliance with the EU's membership criteria. The United States can also remain a 'European power', to use Richard Holbrooke's term, yet knows that its capacity for economic and political integration of the CEEC is circumscribed. Since 1995, then, a division of labour has been forged.

Endorsement of this division of labour has not precluded occasional criticism, however. In the economic realm, the United States has found fault with the partial nature of the Europe Agreements, and the fact that agriculture and other sensitive products were excluded.[50] Proposals to formulate a common position regarding CEE on rules of origin, and to eliminate US and EU subsidies on agricultural exports to the CEEC foundered on domestic opposition in both parties.[51] While recognizing the complexity of the process, some officials, like Deputy Secretary of State Strobe Talbott, have chastised the EU for slowness, quoting Secretary of State Albright that European security should not be delayed until 'tomato farmers in central Europe start using the right kinds of pesticides'.[52] Others have criticized the EU for placing the burden of economic adjustment disproportionally on the CEEC.[53] Congressman Bereuter raised the idea of a US free trade area with the CEEC to nudge the EU's liberalization agenda.[54]

After actual enlargement, as with previous expansions, the United States and the EU will be engaged in negotiations over compensation, which could be arduous given the scale of this enlargement round. Washington has begun to construct its own dialogue with aspirant countries to air post-enlargement concerns on trade and economic issues. From the US perspective, the trade liberalization of enlargement could also be attended by trade deliberalization and diversion. One strand of the dialogue has been the promotion of a regional perspective, as displayed in the May 1997 speech of Stuart Eizenstat, then Undersecretary of Commerce for International Trade, to the first American conference on the Central European Free Trade Agreement.[55] Deputy Secretary of State Talbott has pleaded for 'openness of outlook and openness of access'.[56] Some of the trade problems the United States anticipated with actual enlargement had already emerged by spring 1998, due to the vigorous efforts of candidates and would-be candidates to apply strictly EU practice in advance of membership. The latter case revealed bureaucratic fissures on the American side, with the EU and the State Department working together while USTR threatened to hold up WTO accession for Latvia.

The accelerated pace of the enlargement process by spring 1998 has elicited four probable elements of a US post-enlargement strategy, for division of labour does not mean American economic retreat:

- The reorientation of development assistance to the south, although in some cases existing special programmes in northern CEEC – on the environment, nuclear safety and law enforcement – will remain, but with non-SEED funding from the State Department and the Department of Justice;
- the pursuit of trade relations with the new EU members on the model of established west–west relations;
- sustained facilitation of private American business interests in the region through the Commerce Department's Central and East Europe Business Information Center and the US and Foreign Commercial Service; and
- continuation of the hallmark of privatization in the US government's pre-enlargement activities through the promotion of existing players such as the Enterprise Funds and

various foundations (for example, the Eurasia Foundation), and of new initiatives such as those related to the Baltic Charter.

Collaboration with the EU in Central and Eastern Europe will continue to be important, as Under Secretary of State Stuart Eizenstat promised in September 1997:

> Looking ahead, I see the NTA playing an increasingly important role, especially as the EU extends its competence more deeply into new substantive areas and expands its borders to welcome Central European members.[57]

Politically, the United States has urged the EU to remain open, just as it has in the economic sphere. American officials such as Deputy Secretary of State Talbott used the occasion of actual enlargement negotiations in March 1998 to make the case for other CEE applicants beyond the first five, and, even more vigorously, for non-CEE countries such as Turkey.[58] Leon Brittan has downplayed the notion of a profound cleavage emanating from the division of labour, but has not ruled out differences from the EU's increased stature:

> We are already seeing that, in some respects, Europe has assumed the main leadership role, especially in our own continent. This is natural and should not be a cause of concern, as we exercise that role in directions which reflect our common interests. It is the EU that has led the effort to rebuild the economies of Central and Eastern Europe ... It is inevitable that we should now face the United States as an increasingly equal partner, sharing world leadership more and more as we develop still further our own capacity to act together in a united and effective way. That will not always be comfortable for the US. But the vision of the Marshall Plan foresaw, clearly and rightly, that the common interests of Europe and the US were so great that they tipped the balance overwhelmingly in favour of nurturing a strong Europe.[59]

Parallelism

NATO enlargement might be conceived of as the American side of the division of labour, but in fact the two enlargements are parallel processes, devoid of coordination and involving precious little dialogue. The Alliance's September 1995 'Study on NATO Enlargement' spelled out the relationship between the expansion processes in NATO and the EU: 'The enlargement of NATO is a parallel process with and will complement that of the European Union. Both enlargement processes will contribute significantly to extending security, stability, and prosperity'.[60] The Commission's Agenda 2000 Communication has referred to the two enlargements as 'autonomous processes'.[61]

Both the EU and the United States see clear advantages to keeping the two endeavours parallel and autonomous. In particular, there are perceived benefits of flexibility as the exercise unfolds and of fall-back possibilities if one process fails miserably, as long as membership in one organization does not provide an excuse for the other to refuse an applicant.[62] There is no desire to manipulate memberships, but American officials were pleased when Estonia appeared on the EU's list of the first five, given the inauspicious nature of its NATO candidacy. Although the two processes share the goal of stability, their dynamics and schedules are different. The active American leadership of NATO enlargement has not been matched by singular leadership in the EU case. The ultimate loss of sovereignty through accession and the intricate criteria for membership make the EU process more complex than NATO's, as recognized by US policy-makers.[63]

Despite the rationale for parallelism, there is also an obvious need for much more dialogue and synchronization to avoid the process of working at cross purposes, if not in outright competition with each other. The then US Ambassador to the EU, Stuart Eizenstat, described the situation bluntly in February 1996:

One part [of European security], which has received far too little attention given the crises of the day, is the need for cross-fertilization between NATO and the EU on two related issues: the future of the European Defense Identity and its relationship to the EU and NATO, and the roughly parallel enlargements of NATO and the EU . . . [We need] a careful effort to ensure that the . . . enlargements of NATO and the EU keep pace. NATO and the EU are both in Brussels, and we need to ensure that they do not act as if they were on different planets.[64]

The need for increased information exchange was also highlighted in the Senior Level Group's report to the June 1996 US–EU summit, and the Irish Council presidency placed the issue high on its agenda. High-level dialogue has occurred, in the framework of traditional US–EU consultations, on the relationship between the two enlargements. There has been increasing interaction among the various parties in Brussels (NATO Secretary General Javier Solana or his staff with European Commission President Jacques Santer or his staff; the US Mission to NATO with the US Mission to the EU), but less than the complexity and the stakes warrant.

Nonetheless, mutual sniping has still gone on. Compared to the highly public nature of the American NATO initiative, US officials believe the EU has squandered opportunities to be vocal and visible in its political commitment to EU enlargement, although they acknowledge improvement with the negotiation stage. They criticized the EU for being preoccupied with the conclusion of the Amsterdam Treaty and insufficiently focused on the East. American policy-makers, accordingly, have frequently employed the member-state route in their attempts to ensure and accelerate the agenda of EU enlargement.

EU officials have expressed concern about inadequate American sensitivity to the long-term nature of the two enlargement projects. Nevertheless, American policy-makers increasingly understand the benefits of the process itself, especially in preventing a search for other alternatives by those not at the head of the line. EU officials increasingly realize that the symbol of commitment is important, as is the publicizing of its work to prepare the CEEC for accession.

While slow and tentative, forward-thinking has evolved between the EU and the US about obvious difficulties in the two enlargement processes. Problems could arise regarding the complex of timing, candidates and security guarantees, as well as the conundrum of finding appropriate relationships with Russia. In terms of sequencing the entry, the EU and NATO will need to prevent squabbling within groups (the Visegrad 4, the six, the Baltic states and the special case of Slovenia) and between them. Given the reality that all full members of the WEU are also members of NATO, and the expanding connection between WEU and the EU, EU enlargement could imply the extension of NATO security guarantees. For this reason, the Alliance might 'give particular consideration to countries with a perspective of EU member-ship', so that membership between the WEU and NATO can remain congruent, a concern shared by the European Commission in its Agenda 2000 Communication.[65] In some cases, American officials cite the possibility of NATO enlargement being 'conducive to the enlargement of the EU', not just in 'setting an example', but also in broadening Europe's 'zone of security' that can facilitate the EU's eastward expansion.[66]

Despite the pockets of serious opposition among American elites to NATO enlargement, and the ambivalence of European publics towards EU enlargement, neither collectively nor separately have European and American policy-makers fashioned worst-case scenarios involving the failure of one or both enlargements. Yet, they have given considerable thought to avoiding Russia's isolation, and the attendant potential of malign nationalism, by establishing constructive relationships with Moscow. So far, Russia has not been perturbed by the prospect of EU enlargement in the way that it has by the thought of NATO enlargement. In fact, it has responded evenly, if at all, either because of the benefits of the extensive relationship it is offered through the Partnership and Co-operation Agreement with the EU, or because it does not fully recognize the degree of integration EU membership repre-sents. NATO and the EU have sought to prevent a situation where Russia attempts to play one organization off against the other.

As the process of EU enlargement has moved forward and reached the point of negotiation with the first five CEE candi-dates, the EU and the United States have cooperated to dif-ferent degrees, depending on the issue and the forum. The actual form accession assumes will have other, more long-term consequences for US–EU relations.

THE IMPLICATIONS OF CEEC ACCESSION FOR US–EU RELATIONS

Three scenarios for the EU as an international actor in the next century have been identified and they are operative for enlargement also.[67] If enlargement fails, it will be related to a general process of renationalization in the EU, resulting in a diffident Europe in the global arena. If enlargement occurs, but the process and the implementation are highly divisive, disruptive and piecemeal, then a multitier Europe could ensue (either single issue, *ad hoc* coalitions leading to variable geometry/differentiated integration; or consistent coalitions and adherence to deepening suggesting a core–periphery phenomenon). Such a Europe will still be assertive in the international system, but its purpose and coherence will be dented. If enlargement takes place in the context of overall reform of institutions and policies (inevitably a difficult, yet manageable undertaking), then the EU could emerge as a decisive actor internationally, possessing a sense of direction, streamlined instruments, and a reinvigorated agenda.

The first scenario – the failure of EU enlargement – could increase American involvement in Europe as a stabilizing factor, but, under congressional pressure, it also could push the United States to wash its hands politically and militarily. The failure of EU enlargement would expand NATO's burden and antagonize Russia by making NATO the premier organization. If NATO were the sole club, it could create divisions in Central and Eastern Europe among applicants, and in NATO (between new members from Central and Eastern Europe and those not yet in, between new CEEC members and long-standing West European members). In the final analysis, American officials consider the failure of EU enlargement 'disastrous', for it would invalidate the conception of security that combines the strengths of both NATO and the EU.

The second scenario – enlargement occurs, but in a diverse fashion – militates in favour of a continued partnership of relative equals between the United States and the European Union. The third scenario – enlargement coupled with effective institutional reform – would establish the EU in a position of dominance on the continent, with the United States playing a supporting role.

CONCLUSION

The preceding review of the political and economic integration of Central and Eastern Europe yields four principal conclusions: First, the EU's efforts to make the CEEC part of Europe are extensive and show progress, even if the results are not trumpeted. Second, the EU as a regional power and the United States as a global power approach integration in distinctive ways, but the common goal of stability has permitted cooperation in Central and Eastern Europe. Third, the consistency of programme coordination is relatively new, but it occurs predominantly on the ground, and mainly in the economic assistance arena. Fourth, intensified coordination is impeded by bureaucracy and institutional culture on both sides.

Prescriptively, there are four key lessons for the EU and the US as they enter post-enlargement territory: first, although neither side is interested in proliferating new institutions, US–EU cooperation towards countries that remain outside the first rounds of enlargement will require a regular, formal mechanism to improve vertical and horizontal communication by assembling headquarters and field perspectives, regional and functional expertise, and sensitivity to the importance of CEEC for transatlantic relations. Coordination cannot depend on personalities. If there is no further enlargement, or if it is significantly delayed, such a mechanism will be even more crucial. Second, to prepare for worst-case scenarios there should be increased sharing, in the framework of the NTA, of status reports on CEEC eligibility for membership in the EU and NATO. Information-exchange should go beyond bilateral connections between the United States and those countries who are members of both NATO and the EU.

Third, to reduce the possibility of politicians and public opinion in the United States, the European Union and Central and Eastern European countries obstructing accession at the last minute, both the successes in helping the CEEC to adapt to NATO and EU norms and the logic of enlargement and coordination should be publicized more. Finally, although geography and the opportunities for large-scale transformation render the CEEC a unique region for US–EU cooperation, it nonetheless behooves US and European Union officials to contemplate the lessons of their ten-year experience of cooperation, and their half-decade pursuit of collaboration in the NTA. If the B+ grade Undersecretary Eizenstat has given the New Transatlantic Agenda in general also applies to coordination on Central and Eastern Europe, then there are significant conclusions to be drawn for other regions in terms of agenda-setting, burden-sharing and structures.[68]

The task of continued cooperation and fresh evaluation are large and will require creative thinking and new patterns of behaviour, but the cost of failing to integrate Central and Eastern Europe and to learn from experience are gigantic for the European Union and the United States.

Notes

1. The designation 'Central and Eastern Europe' in this chapter embraces the following eleven countries: Albania, Bulgaria, the Czech Republic, Hungary, Poland, Romania, Slovakia and Slovenia; plus the three Baltic states of Estonia, Latvia and Lithuania. The EU refers to the CEEC (Central and Eastern European Countries) or CEC (Central European Countries); the US prefers CEE (Central and Eastern Europe) and Central Europe.

2. United States Department of State, *SEED Act Implementation Report*, fiscal year 1996 (Washington, DC: United States Department of State, Bureau of European and Canadian Affairs, February 1997), p. 1.

3. Sir Leon Brittan, 'The Next Enlargement: Challenges and Opportunities', speech to the Europolitischer Kongress of the CDU/CSU Group in the European Parliament, Berlin, 11 September 1995.

4. Hans van den Broek, 'The Challenge of Enlargement', speech to the East–West Institute, Brussels, 1 December 1995.

5. This chapter does not examine the attitude of individual member-states to enlargement, nor public attitudes in Western and Eastern Europe. For a disaggregation of the EU enlargement strategy, and of public opinion in the EU, see Lily Gardner Feldman, 'Reconciliation

and Legitimacy: Foreign Relations and Enlargement of the European Union', in Thomas Banchoff and Mitchell Smith (eds), *Legitimacy and the European Union: The Contested Polity* (New York: Routledge, 1999 forthcoming). For examples of Central and Eastern European leadership perspectives, see Vaclav Klaus, 'The Czech Republic, NATO and European Union Enlargement', speech at Georgetown University, Washington, DC, 10 November 1997; Joan Lofgren, 'A Different Kind of Union', *Transitions*, vol. 4, no. 6 (November 1997); Adrian Evtuhovici, 'Slovakia Courts the European Club', *Transitions*, vol. 4, no. 2, (July 1997). For Central and Eastern European public opinion, see European Commission, *Central and Eastern Eurobarometer. Public Opinion and the European Union* (19 Countries' Survey) (Brussels: European Commission, no. 6, March 1996).

6. See, for example, United States Department of State, *SEED Act Implementation Report*, fiscal year 1997 (Washington, DC: United States Department of State, Bureau of European and Canadian Affairs, February 1998); and US Agency for International Development, *The USAID FY 1998 Congressional Presentation* (visited 26 February 1998) at <http://www.info.usaid.gov/pubs/cp 1998/eni/countries/>.

7. Secretary Christopher, 'Charting a Transatlantic Agenda for the 21st Century', Address at Casa de America, Madrid, 2 June 1995, *US Department of State Dispatch*, vol. 6 (Washington DC: United States Department of State, Bureau of Public Affairs, Office of Public Communication), p. 2; Department of State, 'Statement by Secretary of State Madeleine Albright, Senate Foreign Relations Committee, 7 October 1997', pp. 2–3.

8. Jeremy Rosner, 'NATO Enlargement's American Hurdle: The Perils of Misjudging Our Political Will', *Foreign Affairs*, vol. 75, no. 4 (July/August 1996) p. 10. Office of the Secretary of Defense, 'Statement of The Honorable William S. Cohen, Secretary of Defense, before the Senate Committee on Appropriations, 21 October 1997 on the topic of NATO Enlargement', pp. 3–4.

9. On the reorientation of G-24 coordination, see the conclusions of the senior officials' meeting of the Group of Twenty-Four, European Commission, Spokesman's Service, Brussels, 10 March 1995.

10. For an evaluation of the PHARE changes, see European Commission, *The Phare Programme: An Interim Evaluation* (Brussels: Evaluation Unit, DGIA F5, June 1997).

11. For details of programmes and purpose, see United States Department of State, *SEED Act Implementation Report*, fiscal year 1995; fiscal year 1996; and fiscal year 1997, *op cit*. See also USAID/ENI, Bureau for Europe and the New Independent States, US Agency for International Development/Office of the Coordinator for East European Assistance, Department of State/Office of the Coordinator of US Assistance to the New Independent States, Department of State, 'Monitoring Country Progress in Central and Eastern Europe and the New Independent States', September 1997.

12.   For assistance figures, see European Commission, Directorate General IA, 'G-24 Scoreboard of Assistance Commitments to the Countries of Central and Eastern Europe, 1990–95', 4 June 1996.

13.   For details of trade, see European Commission, *Towards Greater Economic Integration. The European Union's Financial Assistance and Trade Policy for Central and Eastern Europe and the New Independent States* (Brussels: European Commission, 1995).

14.   US Department of State, *SEED Act*, fiscal year 1996, *op cit.*, pp. 180, 209.

15.   European Commission, *The Phare Programme Annual Report 1996* (Brussels: European Commission, 25 September 1997), final draft, p. 3.

16.   Wolfgang Roth, 'Eastern Enlargement of the European Union', speech to the American Institute for Contemporary German Studies/The Johns Hopkins University, Washington, DC, 30 March 1998, p. 10.

17.   For a general discussion of Eastern enlargement, see Werner Weidenfeld (ed.), *A New Ostpolitik – Strategies for a United Europe* (Bertelsmann Foundation Publishers: Gütersloh, 1997).

18.   See the Essen summit conclusions in *Bulletin of the European Union*, no. 12, vol. 27, December 1994, p. 12; and Commission of the European Communities, 'The Europe Agreements and Beyond: A Strategy to Prepare the Countries of Central and Eastern Europe for Accession', Communication from the Commission to the Council, COM(94) 320 final, Brussels, 13 July 1994, p. 4; Commission of the European Communities, 'Interim Report from the Commission to the European Council on the Effects on the Policies of the European Union of Enlargement to the Associated Countries of Central and Eastern Europe', CSE (95) 605, Brussels, 6 December 1995, p. 6; Hans van den Broek, 'The Council of Europe and the Enlargement of the European Union', speech to the Parliamentary Assembly of the Council of Europe, Strasbourg, 29 January 1998 (visited 13 February 1998) <http://www.europa.eu.int/rapid/cgi/rapcgi.ksh>, p. 1.

19.   Leon Brittan, *op. cit.*, p. 5.

20.   Vladimir Handl, 'The Czech Republic in Search of a Home', *WIRE*, Foreign Policy Research Institute, Philadelphia, vol. 3, no. 2, June 1995.

21.   Leon Brittan, *op. cit.*, p. 2.

22.   *Bulletin of the European Communities*, no. 6, vol. 26, 1993, p. 13.

23.   Commission of the European Communities, White Paper on 'The Preparation of the Associated Countries of Central and Eastern Europe for Integration into the Internal Market of the Union', COM(95) 163 final (Brussels: 3 May 1995).

24.   For details of PHARE's operations, see: European Commission, *Phare Programme Annual Report, op. cit.*; and *The Phare Programme: An Interim Evaluation, op. cit.*

25.   Van den Broek, speech to Council of Europe, *op. cit.*, p. 2.

26. See Conference sur la stabilité en Europe, Paris, 20–21 mars 1995, *The Pact on Stability in Europe*, annex 1-part (b). The document also includes a list of agreements and arrangements between the interested countries and the Member States of the European Union (pp. 5–7) and a list of agreements and arrangements concluded between the CEEC and between CEEC and others invited to the regional round-tables (pp. 8–12).

27. See European Commission, *Agenda 2000 – Volume 1 – Communication: For A Stronger and Wider Union* (visited 16 July 1997) <http://www.eurunion.org/legislat/agd2000/volume 1.html>; and *Agenda 2000 – Volume II – Communication: Reinforcing the Pre-Accession Strategy* (visited, July 16, 1997) <http://www.eurunion.org/legislat/agd2000/volume 2.html>.

28. For a discussion of the CFSP implications of Eastern enlargement, see Bertelsmann Stiftung, 'CFSP and the Future of the European Union', Interim Report of a Working Group (Bertelsmann Stiftung: Gutersloh, July 1995), pp. 5–9; Roy Ginsberg, 'The Impact of Enlargement on the Role of the European Union in the World', in John Redmond and Glenda Rosenthal (eds), *The Expanding European Union: Past, Present, and Future* (Boulder: Lynne Rienner, 1997).

29. For an assessment of EU–US cooperation in foreign policy in general, see Thomas Frellesen and Roy H. Ginsberg, *EU–US Foreign Policy Cooperation in the 1990s. Elements of Partnership* (Brussels: Centre for European Policy Studies, 1994), CEPS Paper no. 58. In discussing the range of EU–US interaction in the international arena, they distinguish between coordination and complementarity, and between action and declaration.

30. United States Department of State, Bureau of Public Affairs, 'The New Transatlantic Agenda: Joint US–European Union Action Plan', 3 December 1995.

31. Much of the information on US–EU cooperation was gathered from interviews with individuals at the following agencies: United States Department of State: 11 June, 12 June, 28 June, 5 July 1996; 28 January, 5 February 1998; USAID: 8 July 1996; 13 February, 22 February, 27 February 1998; National Security Council: 17 June 1996; European Union, Delegation of the European Commission to the United States, 7 June, 17 June, 25 June, 28 June 1996; 29 January 1998; World Bank, 28 June, 1 July 1996. The author is grateful for their observations. She also thanks Annette Hussong for research assistance.

32. 'New Transatlantic Agenda Report to the US–EU Summit, 12 June 1996' (visited 16 April 1997) <http://www.eurunion.org/partner/nta9606.html>, p. 1.

33. 'New Transatlantic Agenda, Senior Level Group Report to the US–EU Summit, 16 December 1996', (visited 16 April 1997) <http://www.eurunion.org/partner/nta9612.html>; and 'New Transatlantic Agenda: Senior Level Group Report to the US–EU Summit', 28 May 1997 (visited 3 February 1998) <http://www.state.gov/www/regions/eur/eu/970528slgrpt.html>; and Department of State, 'New

Transatlantic Agenda: Senior Level Group Report to the US–EU Summit, 5 December 1997.'

34.	US Agency for International Development, 'Third Annual High-Level US/EC Assistance Consultations, 23–24 October 1997' (Washington, DC: USAID, 1997).

35.	US Agency for International Development, 'USAID/EC Collaboration: Central and Eastern Europe', internal document (Washington, DC: USAID, 1997); US Agency for International Development, 'Mid-Course Review: USAID-EU Assistance Cooperation' internal document (Washington, DC: USAID, 1998) and US Agency for International Development, *The USAID FY 1998 Congressional Presentation*, *op. cit.*

36.	For different examples of US–EU activity and dialogue on Central and Eastern Europe in 1994–95, see European Commission, 'Progress Report on EU–US Relations' (Brussels: European Commission, December 1994); 'Progress Report on EU–US Relations' (Brussels: European Commission, July 1995).

37.	'New Transatlantic Agenda Report to the US–EU Summit, 12 June 1996', *op. cit.*, p. 3.

38.	On this point, see US Agency for International Development, *Agency Performance Report 1995* (Washington, DC: USAID, 1996), p. 5.

39.	See the introductory note from the Coordinator for East European Assistance in United States Department of State, *SEED Act Implementation Report*, fiscal year 1995, *op. cit.*

40.	See, for example, US Agency for International Development, *The USAID FY 1998 Congressional Presentation*, *op. cit.*, in which the detailed project descriptions for each country include references to collaboration with the EU (under 'Other Donors').

41.	US Agency for International Development, 'USAID/EC Collaboration: Central and Eastern Europe', *op. cit.*; and US Agency for International Development, *The USAID FY 1998 Congressional Presentation*, *op. cit.*

42.	According to State Department officials, the general success of US coordination on CEE has prompted a suggestion to replicate this structure for other regions of the world.

43.	US Agency for International Development, 'USAID/EC Collaboration: Central and Eastern Europe', *op. cit.* (a similar document was produced for the NIS); and U.S. Agency for International Development, 'Mid-Course Review', *op. cit.*

44.	'New Transatlantic Agenda, Senior Level Group Report to the US–EU Summit, 16 December 1996', *op. cit.* p. 2.

45.	'New Transatlantic Agenda: Senior Level Group Report to the US–EU Summit, 5 December 1997', *op. cit.* pp. 2, 5.

46.	*Ibid.*, p. 4.

47.	*Ibid.*, p. 6; and 'New Transatlantic Agenda: Senior Level Group Report to the US–EU Summit', 28 May 1997, *op. cit.*, p. 1.

48.	Stuart E. Eizenstat, 'Farewell Remarks to the EU Committee of the American Chamber of Commerce', Brussels, 8 February 1996, pp. 1, 9–10; Under Secretary Eizenstat, 'NATO Enlargement and US

Business Interests', speech at the Hungarian Embassy, Washington, DC, 13 January 1998, pp. 3–5; Stuart E. Eizenstat, Under Secretary for Economic, Business and Agricultural Affairs, 'Remarks at a meeting with the Presidents of the Baltic States, Washington, DC, January 15, 1998' (visited 21 April 1998) <http://www.state.gov/www/policy remarks/1998/980115 eizen baltics.html>, p. 1; and Deputy Secretary Strobe Talbott, 'Remarks to the US–EU Conference "Bridging the Atlantic: People-to-People Links", Washington, D.C., May 6, 1997' (visited 3 February 1998) <http:www.state.gov/www/regions/eur/eu/ 970506.html>, p. 4; Deputy Secretary of State Strobe Talbott, 'Address to the Conference, "A Wider Europe: EU Enlargement and U.S. Interests", Washington, DC, March 12, 1998' (Washington, DC: Department of State), p. 2; Delegation of the European Commission, 'Discuss New Transatlantic Agenda's First Year', Worldnet with Eizenstat, Brittan, Others, 4 December 1996 (Washington, DC: Delegation of the European Commission, 10 December 1996), pp. 7–8.

49. For the American perspective, see Eizenstat, 'NATO Enlargement and US Business Interests', *op. cit.*, p. 5. For the EU viewpoint, see Sir Leon Brittan, '"Creating a Partnership of Equals", speech given by [the] Vice-President of the European Commission at the Transatlantic Conference, Washington, 5th May 1997' (visited 3 February 1998) <http://www.europa.eu.int/en/comm/dg01/prconf.html>, pp. 5–6.

50. Stuart E. Eizenstat, 'Farewell Remarks', *op. cit.*, p. 17.

51. Anthony Laurence Gardner, *A New Era in US–EU Relations?: The Clinton Administration and the New Transatlantic Agenda* (Brookfield, Vermont: Ashgate Publishing Company, 1997), pp. 59–60.

52. Deputy Secretary Strobe Talbott, 'Remarks to the US–EU Conference "Bridging the Atlantic: People-to-People Links", Washington, DC, May 6, 1997', *op. cit.*, pp. 4–5.

53. See, for example, The Atlantic Council of the United States, 'The Marshall Plan: Lessons for US Assistance to Central and Eastern Europe and the Former Soviet Union', *Occasional Paper Series*, December 1995, p. xii.

54. Report of a European Institute conference, 12–13 September 1995, on the implications for transatlantic relations of CEEC accession to the EU, *Europe in Washington*, European Institute, vol. 6, no. 1, Spring 1996, p. 5.

55. United States Department of Commerce, 'Remarks of The Honorable Ambassador Stuart E. Eizenstat, Under Secretary for International Trade, US Department of Commerce, As Prepared for Delivery Before the CEFTA Conference, New York City, May 5, 1997' (US Department of Commerce, Washington, DC), p. 7.

56. Secretary of State Strobe Talbott, 'Address to the Conference, "A Wider Europe"', p. 2.

57. Stuart E. Eizenstat, Under Secretary for Economic, Business and Agricultural Affairs, 'Remarks before the American Chamber of Commerce, European Union Committee, Brussels, Belgium,

11 September 1997' (visited 21 April 1998) <http://www.state.gov/www/policy remarks/970911 eizen brussels.html>, p. 3.

58.   Deputy Secretary of State Strobe Talbott, 'Address to the Conference, "A Wider Europe"', pp. 3–4.

59.   Sir Leon Brittan, 'Creating a Partnership of Equals', *op. cit.*, pp. 1–2, 6–7.

60.   US Department of State, Office of Policy and Public Outreach, Bureau of European and Canadian Affairs, 'Messages on the Study on NATO Enlargement,' 20 September 1995, p. 3.

61.   European Commission, *Agenda 2000 – Volume II, op. cit.*, p. 19.

62.   Deputy Secretary Strobe Talbott, 'Remarks to the US–EU Conference', 6 May 1997, *op. cit.*, p. 5.

63.   Deputy Secretary of State Strobe Talbott, 'Address to the Conference', *op. cit.*, 12 March 1998, p. 3.

64.   Stuart E. Eizenstat, 'Farewell Remarks', *op. cit.*, Brussels, 8 February 1996, p. 14.

65.   U.S. Department of State, Office of Policy and Public Outreach, Bureau of European and Canadian Affairs, 'Study on NATO Enlargement', 20 September 1995, p. 8; European Commission, *Agenda 2000 – Volume II, op. cit.*, p. 19.

66.   Deputy Secretary of State Strobe Talbott, 'Address to the Conference', *op. cit.*, 12 March 1998, pp. 2–3.

67.   See Lily Gardner Feldman, 'The EC in the International Arena: A New Activism?' in *Europe and the United States: Competition and Cooperation in the 1990s,* Study Papers Submitted to the Subcommittee on International Economic Policy and Trade and the Subcommittee on Europe and the Middle East of the Committee on Foreign Affairs, US House of Representatives, June 1992.

68.   Stuart E. Eizenstat, 'Remarks before the American Chamber of Commerce', 11 September 1997, *op. cit.*, p. 5.

4 Russia in Europe's New Equation

Renée de Nevers

The end of the Cold War and the disintegration of the Soviet Union in late 1991 created a new international political and security climate. The new states generated by the upheavals in Eastern Europe and the Soviet Union have faced substantial obstacles in their efforts to construct – or reconstruct – working market economies, democratic political systems, and the basic elements of civil society that undergird them.

These changes have also created new dilemmas for those states that had opposed the Soviet Union and its allies during the Cold War. The most important challenge confronting the established Western democracies in this new environment has been the task of shaping new ties with Russia. How can they help Russia move in directions that are perceived to be beneficial, both to Russia and to its former opponents in Europe and North America?

That Russia continues to matter to Western security is clear. Russia is the most important country among the new states in Eurasia. It inherited the lion's share of the USSR's territory and material resources, and is the sole nuclear successor state to the Soviet Union. The task of restructuring has been particularly difficult for Russia both because of its great size and because it experienced a greater sense of loss from the collapse of Soviet power. One would expect, then, that the West would pay special attention to the development and implementation of policies intended to promote democracy and prevent conflict in Russia. Such policies must be designed to address Russia's singular circumstances and history if they are to be effective.

Nonetheless, the Western response to the end of the Cold War and the collapse of the Soviet Union has been inconsistent. The major Western powers and institutions have not fully used this opportunity to ensure a more stable and less-threatening environment for Europe and the United States, and they have been slow to incorporate Russia into new or existing Western institutions. Moreover, by failing to follow through on early promises of substantial support to Russia, the West damaged relations with Moscow in the short run, and may have complicated longer-term relations with the Russian Federation.

Cooperation among the Western powers to formulate policies toward Russia has been limited. This is understandable, since the West has faced significant problems of its own following the Soviet Union's collapse. The United States and its major allies in Europe and Japan have been struggling to adapt their own relationship in light of the changed international system. Yet, as a consequence of their competing concerns and their subsequent inattention to Russia, Western policies towards Russia have sometimes worked at cross-purposes. Simultaneously with efforts to encourage democratization and steps towards a market economy in Russia, the West has also been searching for new ways to ensure stability and security in Europe and the broader international system. These two goals have not always been compatible. Most conspicuously, NATO's decision to enlarge undermines Western efforts to integrate Russia into the Western community and has exacerbated fears in Russian political circles about Western intentions towards Russia.

To be sure, efforts to establish new relations with Russia in the post-Soviet period had to deal with Russia's need for assistance, training and support in establishing a market economy and democratic institutions, while at the same time trying not to offend Russian sensitivities about their weakened circumstances. And whether by plan or by accident, different Western multilateral organizations have focused on different tasks in establishing new relations with Russia. Among the more important fora have been the Group of Seven (G-7) and the International Monetary Fund (IMF), which have supported financial aspects of Russia's transition, while the North Atlantic Treaty Organization (NATO) has worked to formulate new security ties with Russia.

This chapter will assess the efficacy of policies undertaken by the United States and Europe towards Russia. I will first outline how internal conditions in Russia affect its relations with the West. Next, I will briefly examine external financial assistance to Russia by international financial institutions, as well as the efforts of the United States and the European Union (EU) both independently and together to promote cooperation with Russia. I will then examine NATO's policy towards Russia since the early 1990s, and review efforts to ensure nuclear safety in Russia. Finally, I will make some recommendations for improving policies in the future.

RUSSIA'S INTERNAL CONDITIONS AND THE INTERNATIONAL ENVIRONMENT

Developments in Russia will help determine the climate within which US–European relations will evolve. Russia's economic success or failure may not have a significant impact on Europe or the United States; like the USSR before it, Russia is not a major international economic player. The socialist economic system was in large part separate from the global economy, and Russia today is of relatively low economic importance to the major industrialized countries as a trade partner, and this is not likely to change soon under even the best of circumstances. Should Russia's economic conditions worsen, it will simply fall further behind the West in economic development.

Although, a faltering Russian economy will have few economic consequences for the West, the political and social instability that is likely to accompany such problems could create difficulties for the West. Western institutions and governments face a quandary in deciding how much aid and advice is appropriate for Russia, as well as how to support Russian economic and political reforms without causing a negative domestic backlash in Russia. This reinforces the importance of determining how effective Western cooperation has been, and whether it can better address Russia's economic and political needs.

Internal Conditions in Russia

Western efforts to improve relations with Russia have been impeded both by the turmoil in Russia since the Soviet Union collapsed and by Russian perspectives on its changed circumstances. First, Russians are suspicious about what the West is doing and what it has done. The 'loss' of the Cold War and then subsequently of Russia's former empire left a legacy of resentment and humiliation at Russia's diminished status.[1] Some politicians have encouraged this resentment by arguing that Russia, like Germany in 1918, was betrayed or deceived by its former leaders or the West. This led to attempts to bolster 'Russian' traditions to prevent further encroachment by the West. Arguments that Russia is somehow different and separate from the West have gained greater prominence, accompanied by a corresponding sense that Western ideas, both political and economic, are 'inappropriate' for Russia.[2] This stands in sharp contrast not only to the early euphoria with which Russians greeted 'democratization', but also to the attitude of most Central and East European countries, which have embraced Western ideas and policies as their own.

Russia has faced the challenge of simultaneously establishing a market-based economy and a democratic system of government. While it is not alone in confronting this dual challenge, Russia's history makes this task more difficult. Seventy years of communist rule distorted the Russian system both intellectually and physically. Intellectually, by emphasising egalitarianism and punishing initiative or dissent, communist rule damaged the conception of initiative or entrepreneurship among a broad spectrum of the Russian populace. Moreover, particularly during Stalin's tenure, the communist system destroyed the fabric of civil society in Russia (most notably during the purges), and created instead an atomized society in which scant sense of community or popular participation remained. Added to this, Russia had little experience with democracy prior to communist rule; it was isolated from the West throughout much of its history, in spite of conspicuous efforts by rulers from the time of Peter the Great to modernize and 'westernize' the empire. This has hindered the state's efforts to introduce market mechanisms, and to revitalize the political structure. Finally, communist rule made the Russian people extremely suspicious of political parties and of involvement in the political system, which has complicated efforts both to establish a political party system on the Western model, and to encourage full and active popular participation in day-to-day politics.

In spite of this, Russia has made significant progress in introducing a democratic system. It not only weathered the disbanding of the parliament and the shelling of the parliamentary of building – known as the White House – in 1993, but it has gone through a succession of elections since then: two parliamentary elections in December 1993 and December 1995; presidential elections in the summer of 1996; and gubernatorial elections in 1997. Though hardly perfect, these elections were perceived to be generally free and fair, and relatively free of violence. Thus, though slightly tarnished and occasionally waylaid, Russia's progress towards a more democratic system persists.

Russia's presidential structure remains imperfect, however. The Constitution of the Russian Federation, approved by referendum in December 1993, gives substantial authority to the President and his government. The Duma has little ability to legislate or to influence government policies, with its most significant power the right to vote on presidential legislation like the budget. But it has used this limited power to maximum effect. Dominated since 1993 by opponents of Yeltsin's government, the Duma has complicated efforts to pass legislation designed to speed Russia's move towards a stable market-based economy. Notably, Russia has been unable to establish a tax code that is perceived to be equitable and enforceable, and poor tax collection has been a serious obstacle to government efforts to pay budget arrears and steady the economy.[3]

Russia also made tortuous, but notable, progress towards establishing a market economy. Yeltsin's victory in the 1996 presidential elections enabled him to push further economic reforms. Efforts to privatize the economy made progress, though not without problems, and in 1997 Russia's GDP showed positive growth for the first time since the collapse of the Soviet Union.[4] Until August of 1998, stabilization appeared to be more or less secure, and the Russian economy looked likely to recover from the negative growth it experienced in the 1990s.

This positive progress has been marred by two factors: the criminalization of Russia's economy and its apparent domination by a handful of entrepreneurs who benefit from their ties to high-level government officials. Yeltsin himself has warned that criminal groups could threaten Russia's ability to sustain control over the state.[5] The danger to Russia's economic growth from its new business class lies in the latter's unwillingness to accept free and fair competition as the basis for economic transactions; this was borne out during the currency crisis in the fall of 1998.[6] The Russian state suffered when these insiders gained control of its resources at bargain prices, while doing little to restructure the assets they control or to invest in Russia.

Finally, perennial questions about Yeltsin's health make Russia's future uncertain. Though often more tacit than expressed, one of the main goals of Western policy from the collapse of the Soviet Union until well into 1996 was to ensure the continuation of Boris Yeltsin's rule as president in the newly-independent Russia. Partly as a result of this, aid to Russia faced a chicken-and-egg problem. Sustaining Yeltsin's rule was perceived in the West as critical to the continuation of democratization and market reforms in Russia, and to ensure an enduring climate favourable to Western investment. At the same time, Western aid and support are perceived to be critical to preserving Yeltsin's rule – with the caveat, of course, that Yeltsin cannot risk appearing to be too close to the West, since this might work against him in domestic politics. While Western leaders have stressed in recent years that they support the Russian state and its elected officials, rather than Yeltsin *per se*, there is no obvious successor with both the ability to win a presidential election and with proven credentials as a reformer. Given Yeltsin's ill-health, Western policy needs some longer-term strategies with regard to Russia. It is against this fragile domestic background that international efforts to assist Russia in its transition to a stable market democracy must be seen.

FINANCIAL ASSISTANCE TO RUSSIA

International Community Efforts

Western financial aid to Russia has suffered from several problems. First, the early promises of substantial aid, in particular from the G-7, were not fulfilled. In 1992 and 1993, the G-7

countries promised first $2.5 billion, and then $24 billion
in aid and loans to Russia, little of which actually found
its way to Russia. The over-inflated rhetoric that accompanied
Western promises of substantial aid to Russia in these early
years created heightened expectations in Moscow both
about the amplitude of assistance that the West would provide, and about the degree and pace with which Russia in
particular would be welcomed into Western institutions. Not
surprisingly, when these expectations failed to be realized,
they led to heightened disappointment as well. US assistance
programmes came in for particular attack, since the most
visible of them appeared to be a means to subsidize high-
priced Western consultants to do studies in Russia, with little
clear benefit for Russians.[7] This hurt Western relations
with Russia by causing resentment both towards the West,
and towards the reformers who advocated closer ties with the
West. This in turn damaged efforts to promote reform
in Russia, notably following the parliamentary elections of
1993 and 1995.

It should also be noted that the overall amount of money
expended has been inadequate in light of the problems Russia
faces. This is particularly evident when aid for Russian reform is
compared to the amounts spent annually during the Cold War to
maintain the military defenses of the West.[8]

Second, while the G-7 stated its intention to aid Russia in
1992 and emphasised this at its Tokyo meeting in 1993, the
task of providing economic support over the next few years
was shifted from individual countries to international financial
institutions.[9] Moreover, the IMF, one of the major financial
actors dealing with Russia, tended to adopt a strategy similar
to that it relied on in other parts of the globe. The IMF's
policy was designed to establish and sustain a free market, on
the assumption that once countries have achieved macroeconomic stability, liberalized trade, freed prices and established
property rights, the market itself would be capable of promoting reform. The IMF's focus on stability in Russia and
Central and Eastern Europe has been criticized as ineffective
for the problems facing states in this region.[10] Nonetheless, it
has more or less stuck with policies that fall within the
bounds set by its mandate. And while its stress on monetary
stability was viewed by some as narrow, the amount of

funds involved rose by the mid-1990s – in March 1995, the IMF agreed to provide Russia a credit of about $6.5 billion over the period from April 1995 to February 1996; and in early 1996, it agreed to grant Russia a three-year loan of around $10 billion.[11] In July 1998, the IMF approved a loan of $11.2 billion to Russia as the government tried, with little success, to stabilize the ruble. While the crisis was exacerbated by speculation by Russian bankers and Western investment banks, IMF involvement, and its focus on monetary rather than social criteria, led many Russians to place the blame for the crisis with the West.

Third, immediately after the collapse of the Soviet Union, Western governments appeared to be most concerned with ensuring that the former Soviet Union's debt would be serviced. This left the IMF to stabilize the situation in Russia on its own, and engendered a sense that the West was more concerned with its own future than with Russia's.

In spite of these difficulties, there were several positive developments in 1997. First, Yeltsin attended the annual meeting of the G-7 leaders, carefully renamed the 'Summit of the Eight', as almost a full participant. While Russia's status as a regular member in this group is not fully established, other leaders stressed the importance of Yeltsin's participation as a sign of its significant political and economic progress.[12] Russia also joined the Paris Club of creditor nations in September 1997. This was significant both because of the prestige of this group, and also because membership as a creditor would improve Russia's ability to obtain debt-repayments from many of the states to which the USSR loaned money.[13] Finally, Russia reached agreement with the London Club of commercial creditors to restructure the enormous Soviet-era debt to commercial banks. This step was expected to help Russia improve its international credit-rating, which would encourage more foreign investment in Russia. Moreover, then First Deputy Prime Minister Chubais noted that this might enhance Russia's ability to join other international financial institutions.[14]

These positive developments were an indication that Western leaders recognized both the importance of ensuring Russia's continued economic progress and that Russia has made some significant gains. It also indicates their awareness of the need to mollify Russia's leaders, if they want to quell resentment towards the West.

Bilateral and EU Aid

US and other Western aid programmes to help Russia and other states in the region were initiated in haste shortly after the fall of communist regimes in this region, in order to protect those recent gains and to shore up what were perceived to be struggling attempts to establish democracy. Yet, little time appears to have been spent on ensuring that these efforts would be effective or appropriate to the countries in which they were implemented. Rather than considering what forms and institutions might have the best chance of success in the societies and circumstances of the recipient countries, programmes have often aimed to duplicate the institutional structure that exists in the donor country. Furthermore, Western donors tended to use the existence of programmes similar to their own state structures as an indication that 'democracy' was succeeding.

Of the major Western states, Germany and the United States have been the largest individual donors to Russia. Between 1990 and 1993, Germany committed over DM 100 billion to the Commonwealth of Independent States (CIS). It also extended a $650 million loan to Russia in May 1996 during the run-up to the presidential election. German Chancellor Helmut Kohl also worked hard to promote stable relations between Germany and Russia, particularly during Yeltsin's election campaign.

The US began a bilateral aid policy towards Russia at the end of 1991, couched within a broader programme of aid to the former Soviet republics. But because Russia was more advanced than other republics when the Soviet Union collapsed, and because Washington has sought to acknowledge Russia's political standing as the successor to the USSR, US policy has aimed at moving rapidly towards establishing a 'normal' economic relationship with Russia.[15] As a consequence of this, new US funding for technical assistance was scheduled to end in 1998. It is assumed that Russia will have absorbed what the West has to offer in this regard, and that it will then be ready for 'normal' trade and investment

relations with the West. In part, this assumption is based on
the fact that US assistance through the Freedom Support Act
was 'front-loaded', significantly higher amounts were committed through 1994 on programmes that are now under
way. Few new programmes have been initiated since 1994
on the assumption that the main programmes that were
needed already exist.[16] By 1994, US strategy also began to
shift more resources to other former Soviet republics, both
because it was perceived that programmes in Russia had
been established by then, and to offset the heavy emphasis
on Russia in the first few years of this programme.[17] The
greater emphasis on support for trade and investment in
Russia also reflected constraints on US aid due to congressional oversight, and the ongoing effort to get private US
corporations involved in aiding Russia's transformation.

Between 1992 and the end of 1994, the US committed
almost $2.3 billion in economic assistance to the Russian Fed-
eration. The stated goal in early 1995, reiterated in 1996, was
to continue the strategy to promote systemic change in two
ways: by working with Russian reformers to build and
strengthen the laws and institutions necessary for the functioning of democracy and a market economy; and by developing
and demonstrating models of successful solutions to particular
problems. US policy had, by 1996, shifted to an emphasis on
technical assistance, as well as support for trade and investment. Trade between the United States and Russia reached
about $5.8 billion in 1994.[18]

Individual European countries have offered assistance to
Russia at varying levels, and the European Union also developed programmes designed to assist both the states of Eastern
Europe and Russia after the Cold War ended. The EU
established the Technical Assistance to the CIS (TACIS) as
a programme in 1991, and Russia has been a major recipient
of funds under this programme – from 1991–94, the EU
made available $846 million to Russia to launch projects
designed to promote the reform process. TACIS focused during this period on helping Russia to stabilize its economy,
promote administrative reform, privatize agriculture, improve
infrastructure in both communications and transportation, and
enhance nuclear reactor safety.[19] The focal sectors for 1993–
95 were the restructuring of state enterprises, human

resources development, and reforming public administration at all levels throughout the Russian state.[20]

The TACIS programme has been sharply criticized for the way it has operated in Russia and the other states of the former Soviet Union. Critics argue that the EU headquarters demand strict adherence to plans drawn up by bureaucrats in Brussels, with little regard for their appropriateness to the situation in a given country. The EU relies heavily on short-term contracts and employs too many Western consultants, while giving scant consideration to the need for experience working in the region, or in the particular economic sector that a project is designed to help.[21] Moreover, TACIS efforts have been hampered by the bureaucratic considerations within the EU, such as the need to award contracts based on the EU country of origin, at the expense of favouring prior experience working in Russia or continuity on the ground in running projects.[22]

When the United States and the EU announced the New Transatlantic Agenda in December 1995, cooperation with regard to Russia was clearly included. What is striking, however, is how little attention Russia received in the formulation of cooperation between the United States and the EU. Russia fell third in the list of stated priorities in working for a stable Europe – after former Yugoslavia and the Central and East European states. Moreover, Russia was grouped with Ukraine and other Newly Independent States, with the emphasis given to consolidating democracy and the transition to market economies in these states, through their integration into the global economy and the provisions of technical assistance. This suggests that Russia remains low on the list of priorities in US–EU discussions, and could easily be submerged in importance as more immediate crises, or the complexities of EU expansion and trade ties with the United States, take precedence.

NATO and Russia

NATO's relationship with Russia remains complex for a variety of reasons. Moscow still sees NATO as an instrument of the Cold War, and, accordingly, an opponent of the USSR and hence Russia. From Russia's perspective, there has been little obvious change in NATO's structure or mission in response to recent changes in the international system.[23] Moreover, NATO's decision to expand to the east is perceived as threatening by Moscow.

NATO's members consider that the Alliance has worked hard to adjust to the political changes in Europe. Though some would argue that it was slow to respond to Gorbachev's initiation of *perestroika* in the Soviet Union in the 1980s, NATO began to change its policies towards the USSR with issuance of the London Declaration in July 1990.[24]

The upheavals in Europe following the USSR's collapse, and the dramatic shifts in Russian foreign policy behaviour that ensued in 1992 and 1993, led many states in Eastern Europe to feel that their security needs were not sufficiently met by membership in the North Atlantic Cooperation Council, which the Alliance had extended to them in 1991. The NACC was a discussion forum, and it involved neither active cooperation between NATO and the former East bloc countries nor any security guarantees. In an effort to assuage their fears without simultaneously exciting new ones in Russia, NATO invited the members of NACC to join a 'Partnership for Peace' (PfP) programme in January 1994.[25] The unstated goal when it was created was that PfP should be a holding operation, to put off any decision about NATO enlargement until after the next round of presidential elections in both Russia and the United States.

The Partnership for Peace and Russia

The Partnership for Peace has been one of the central pillars of NATO's hopes for a better relationship with Russia. Its stated aim was to expand and intensify political and military cooperation with non-NATO states on a bilateral basis, so as to enhance European stability. Twenty-six states within NACC joined the PfP, as well as Austria, Finland, Malta, Sweden and Slovenia.[26]

Russia originally praised this programme, and it signed the initial framework document declaring its intention to join PfP in June 1994.[27] Yet in December 1994, Foreign Minister Andrei Kozyrev refused to sign the final cooperation agreements to formalize Russia's participation. The main reason was that, in the interim, the discussion of NATO enlargement had significantly shifted. In June and July 1994 President Clinton publicly stated that expansion was 'no longer a question of if, but when';[28] and by December 1994, NATO announced its decision to study the implications of enlargement. Since 1994, NATO's efforts to improve relations with Russia through PfP have had mixed success. Russia has shown interest in working with NATO in some areas, such as NATO's Science Programme and in Civil Emergency Planning.[29] Yet building cooperation with Russia's military organization has been less successful.

NATO intended to use two main channels for improving links with Russia: its participation in the PfP programme, and a separate 'strategic partnership' between NATO and Russia. The latter was designed after Russia's objections to NATO enlargement became obvious, and was meant as a way to recognize Russia's special status in Europe without giving it veto power over enlargement. NATO's aim was to have the two processes of enlargement and its strategic relationship with Russia proceed in parallel, but not simultaneously, since aiming for simultaneity might provide Russia with a means to obstruct the process of enlargement. However, until mid-1997, Russia was unwilling to formalize the idea of a strategic partnership, because it did not want to do anything that would make it look like Russia was willing to accept NATO expansion.

Russia has been generally unwilling to participate actively in the military aspects of PfP. Moscow has made clear that, as far as Russia is concerned, the PfP is absurd since it treats Russia, a great power, and tiny states like Albania as equal participants. Moreover, some Russians argue that the PfP is merely a way for the imperialist West to move east, at the expense of Russia's security.[30]

Russia remains resistant to many aspects of the PfP menu from which states can design their cooperation, for some understandable reasons. First, since it does not expect to be invited to join NATO, why should it try to improve interoperability with the Alliance? There are few benefits to Russia or its defense industry in this. Second, both the Russian military and most Russian politicians have shown little interest in learning about how civil–military relations work in democracies. NATO has run seminars for parliamentarians to discuss the ways in which parliaments can ensure oversight of the military. While this has been quite successful in Central and Eastern Europe, the Russians have been less keen to participate. Nonetheless, the Russian military has made clear that it does not think it needs to learn about civil–military relations from the West. Instead Russians argue that the USSR, and hence Russia, has long had civil control of the military through Communist Party oversight.

Third, the Russian Army has resisted participation in joint training exercises and exchanges under the PfP. This is due to three reasons: first, the Russian military and Defense Ministry are suspicious of the West and the United States in particular regarding joint training and other cooperative activities. Both have been unwilling to expose the Russian Army to Western, and particularly US, influences. Instead, the Defense Ministry has earmarked two divisions for peace-keeping activities in cooperation with Western armies; and the divisions are, in effect, isolated from the Russian Army proper.[31] Second, the Defense Ministry may not want to expose the Russian military to scrutiny by Western armies, so as to hide its miserable condition. The Army has become increasingly demoralized, both because of the lack of financial support and its sense of a diminished position within society. Its pitiful performance in Chechnya was both an indication of the Army's declining circumstances, and an additional source of demoralization. Third, the Russians seem unwilling to *regularize* contacts with militaries. The Russians have not been willing to accept contacts as a 'normal' part of their relationship with other Western militaries. Similarly, at least initially, the Russian military seemed suspicious of those members of its own forces who did get involved in joint activities with NATO.

At the same time, Russia has been willing to regularize military-to-military contacts with the United States,[32] which highlights an additional factor: Russia perceives itself as the equal of the United States, but does not want to be treated as one among many. The consequence has been that Russia does not want to participate in multilateral exercises. From its perspective, if the United States and Russia, the major players, have a joint exercise and a few smaller countries are allowed to join in, this is acceptable, but Russia is unwilling to be only one of many countries in a NATO exercise.[33]

Russian participation in the Bosnia operation is the clearest example of this. The United States and its NATO allies felt that Russian participation in any peace-keeping force in Bosnia–Herzegovina would be critical not just to the success of this mission, but also to improving and stabilizing relations between Russia and the West at a time when the discussion of NATO expansion was causing friction between NATO and Russia. As with the Dayton Accords in general, the United States was instrumental in obtaining Russia's agreement to participate in the Implementation Force (IFOR) and in succession, the Stabilization Force (SFOR).[34] Yet the final agreement on Russian participation left Russia officially *outside* the NATO chain of command. The Russian military agreed to accept orders from General Joulwan in his capacity as commander of US forces in Europe, not as the allied commander of NATO, and they have insisted on a command chain which was separate from Joulwan's command over NATO troops.[35]

The fact that the United States was willing to accept a circumvention of NATO's chain of command may have disturbed other Alliance members. To all intents and purposes, this separation is a fiction; IFOR and SFOR are NATO operations, and Russia is *de facto* participating under NATO via US command. NATO member-states undoubtedly agree on the importance of Russian participation to ensure that IFOR/SFOR proves a success, and this could clearly be a valuable step towards expanding Russian trust of NATO and improving its overall relationship with the Alliance. Nonetheless, this separateness did concede to Russia a status different to that of other states, and it was established virtually without European participation in the decision.

In spite of IFOR/SFOR's success at promoting cooperation with Russia, NATO has been frustrated in its efforts to establish stronger military ties with Russia. The PfP cannot be seen as a success without this element of cooperation, and IFOR/SFOR is the only small sign of progress in this direction. Even with the difficulties involved in reaching an agreement for Russian participation, this still gives at least those Russians involved in IFOR a glimpse of how NATO works, and how civil–military relations work in Western armies.

The NATO–Russia Founding Act

In spite of Russia's earlier cool reception to the idea of a strategic partnership, NATO proposed a founding charter between NATO and Russia to ease the sting of NATO enlargement. President Yeltsin and the leaders of NATO's 16 nations signed the NATO–Russia Founding Act on 27 May 1997, shortly before the Alliance invited Poland, Hungary and the Czech Republic to begin the process of joining NATO. In addition to defining areas of cooperation between Russia and the Alliance, the Founding Act provided for the establishment of the NATO–Russian Permanent Joint Council, which will be 'a mechanism for consultations, co-ordination, and...where appropriate, for joint decisions and joint action with respect to security issues of common concern'.[36]

Despite the Founding Act, the level of Russian hostility to NATO expansion has not waned, though Russia appears to have chosen to live with current expansion for now. Notably, Yeltsin described the Founding Act as 'enshrining NATO's pledge not to deploy nuclear weapons on the territories of its new members countries...not [to] build up its armed forces near our borders...nor carry out relevant infrastructure preparations'[37] – an interpretation which NATO representatives and the Act's text rejected. A further indication that Russia was not totally resigned to NATO expansion was evident in the response of Russian Defense Minister Igor Sergeyev during a visit to Germany in January 1998, in which he noted that the prospect of a joint German–Danish–Polish force based in Szczecin, Poland, meant that NATO was 'advancing towards the Russian border with weapons in its hands'.[38]

The long-term impact of NATO expansion on relations with Russia remains to be seen. The fact that Russia did not break ties with the West, and that its democratic government does not seem to have been weakened significantly, are positive signs. Yet NATO's decision to expand may make the ratification of the START II Treaty by the Russian Duma more difficult, if not impossible to achieve. This would postpone further nuclear reductions between the US and Russia.

WESTERN EFFORTS TO ENSURE NUCLEAR SECURITY IN RUSSIA

While the collapse of the Soviet Union significantly lessened the threat to the West from nuclear war, the USSR's breakup could create new dangers for the US and its allies. US efforts to address this danger have concentrated primarily on the Cooperative Threat Reduction (CTR) programme.

Cooperative Threat Reduction

The logic of CTR is geopolitical: US security would be threatened if current nuclear safeguards in the former Soviet Union fail, or if fissile materials, either weapons-grade or otherwise, fall into the wrong hands. With this consideration the Nunn–Lugar programme was initiated in November 1991. Its goal is to provide funds to help the former Soviet republics in which nuclear weapons remained to dismantle and destroy these weapons, to keep the 'chain of custody' of nuclear warheads secure, and to help demilitarize the industrial and scientific infrastructure that supported the USSR's military power.

The importance of this issue notwithstanding, the CTR programme got off to a slow start in 1992. When funds were initially allocated in late 1991, no one knew what needed to be done to aid the former Soviet Union, much less how to do it; this was not something the Department of Defense or anyone else had experience with. Moreover, 1992 was an election year in the United States, and the normal resistance within different branches of the government and the Pentagon itself to changing priorities and reallocating money undoubtedly slowed progress on the programme.

The CTR programme became a central focus in US relations with Russia and the former Soviet Union once the Clinton administration took office. The programme has had some notable successes, such as the trilateral agreement reached between Ukraine, Russia and the United States in January 1994. Under this agreement, Ukraine renounced its nuclear status and agreed to return all nuclear warheads in its territory to Russia in return for Russia's agreement to compensate Ukraine by providing nuclear reactor fuel, and the

US provision of security assurances to Ukraine and economic aid through CTR assistance. The CTR programme is expected to continue in operation until 2001. During fiscal years 1996 and 1997, over $600 million was allocated in the CTR budget for assistance to Russia to cover projects ranging from the elimination of strategic nuclear arms to provisions of fissile material containers.[39] Management of the programme was also streamlined; the Pentagon now works specifically on defense-related issues, while the Department of Energy and the State Department have taken direct responsibility for some programmes that had earlier been included under the CTR framework.

In spite of its successes, a variety of problems have impeded efforts to promote denuclearization programmes in Russia. First, early implementation of the CTR programme was frustrated by the form in which its authorization was written by Congress. Because funds for this programme did not initially come from a specific 'line' in the defense budget, they had to be allocated from other sources within the Pentagon's budget. This created a continual struggle for funds.[40] Moreover, and critically, the amount of funds allocated to denuclearization has been far too low, given the scope of the problem. This illustrates the second major problem confronting CTR; the problem of nuclear leakage from Russia and the former Soviet Union may be far more serious than many in Washington have recognized, or are willing to acknowledge.[41]

Third, the design of US funding for the CTR programme has hindered its implementation. The CTR legislation stipulates that US contractors should be used whenever possible. This does not help cooperation with Russia, because those responsible for maintaining nuclear security and secrets in Russia are not anxious to have Americans, either from the Pentagon or its contractors, snooping around in very sensitive facilities within Russia.[42] Further, Russians question why the US will not give them contracts to carry out CTR provisions if it wants to aid in the restructuring of Russia's economy.

Fourth, the Defense Department has faced a difficult task in trying to sustain congressional support for this programme. That Congress does not appear to recognize the seriousness of this issue is apparent in congressional efforts to continue limiting funding for the CTR programme and other efforts to promote nuclear safeguards.

Critics have also argued that the danger of nuclear leakage is so grave that it ought to be the Clinton administration's top foreign policy priority. The rash of smuggling incidents in recent years that involved fissile materials is an indication of the potential seriousness of the problem.[43] Yet to date, they argue, the administration simply has not devoted enough attention to this issue, either in terms of shaping its policies towards Russia, or in trying to focus congressional attention on the gravity of this issue in order to achieve greater bipartisan support for CTR and related programmes. One consequence of this inattention is that the administration has pursued policies in other areas of its foreign policy that make cooperation in this critical area more difficult – notably NATO expansion.

Nuclear Safety and Science Programmes

While its programmes to secure Russia's nuclear materials have thus had mixed success, the US is nonetheless the country most actively working to contain this threat. In addition to the CTR programme, the Energy Department conducts a substantial programme of laboratory-to-laboratory exchanges designed to enhance the security of the entire chain of nuclear materials in Russia. This is part of the Material Protection, Control and Accounting effort.[44] The Gore–Chernomyrdin Commission has also addressed some issues relating to nuclear security in Russia, most recently overseeing the conclusion of a series of agreements on the conversion of two nuclear reactors so that they will no longer produce plutonium.[45] Finally, the State Department oversees efforts to work with Russia to prevent proliferation.[46]

Fissile materials present a danger to all the major Western powers. Yet few are working either with the United States or on their own to limit the danger of nuclear leakage. When it began the CTR programme, the Clinton administration tried to gain allied support for it but soon gave up because of a lack of positive response. Britain has contributed some trucks and containers to help transport nuclear warheads within the former Soviet Union, and it is working to help improve security at one nuclear fuel reprocessing plant in Russia. The only other efforts by European powers to ensure nuclear security in Russia and the former Soviet Union fall under the EU's TACIS programme. These activities focus on funding efforts to improve the security of Russia's nuclear power plants and other civilian nuclear fuel and waste facilities. From 1991–94, approximately one-fourth of TACIS funding to Russia was earmarked for nuclear safety. In 1995, TACIS was funding 17 nuclear safety-related projects in Russia, ranging from electricity upgrades at nuclear power plants, re-engineering emergency power systems, and improving the physical security of various facilities.[47]

One of the few clear areas of cooperation between the US, the EU and also Japan, has been in organizing support for an International Science and Technology Centre (ISTC), which was formed in cooperation with the Russian Federation and is funded by the US, Japan and the EU's TACIS programme. The ISTC was established in March 1994 and is based in Moscow. Its aim is to provide funding for scientists and engineers in Russia who were involved in the Soviet Union's nuclear and missile complex, to redirect their research in new, more peaceful directions.[48] NATO has a similar project supporting scientific exchanges between the West and Partnership for Peace countries, including Russia.[49]

CONCLUSIONS

Given the complexities of the post-Cold War period, and the challenges this has presented to both the US and the EU, it may be unreasonable to expect that these countries would have succeeded in coordinating and expanding their policies towards Russia. And, in fact, US–EU cooperation has been limited since the end of the Cold War. Yet all sides, both the Western actors and Russia, would be better served by greater coordination among Western donors, as well as with Russia. This is true both with regard to aid for Russia, and in examining ways to integrate Russia into Western and international institutions.

Insofar as Russia continues to need Western assistance, the nature of its needs have changed since the Soviet Union's collapse. All parties would benefit from a clearer understanding both of areas where Russia still wants technical or financial assistance, and by recognizing what assistance is available, and under what constraints. Moreover, the US and the EU should discuss ways to ensure that their assistance efforts do not work at cross-purposes. A serious assessment is needed, first, of whether current aid strategies have achieved their stated goals in Russia, and how existing projects should be adjusted to take into account the findings of such studies.[50] Second, the US and the EU need to determine whether coordination of aid strategies would improve their efficacy. They should also strive to share successful policies, and to incorporate strategies that have worked for others into their own programmes. This goes against the standard tactics of many of the organizations in the field that are competing for funding from governmental and EU sources. Yet the outcome in Russia is sufficiently important that strategies to ensure success should take precedence. There is also no reason to waste money on duplicate efforts or inefficient projects.

Russia's expanded participation in international institutions may be a positive trend, and to the degree that its inclusion in financial institutions meant that Russia's economy was improving, international involvement would bolster this trend. Since Russia's entry depends on its meeting certain standards of economic practice and trade, this could also help regularize business practices in Russia; moreover, this could encourage more investments. This is true, however, only so long as Russia abides by the rules of existing international organizations, rather than demanding inclusion under special conditions. The severe fiscal crisis it faced in 1998, however, is likely to slow Russia's further integration in international institutions.

On a related note, one area in which the West should provide assistance and urge Russia to continue reforms is in the establishment of legitimate and open business practices. Russia's revival has been seriously impeded by corrupt business practices and the Russian people's faith that capitalism and democracy can bring them a better future has been severely damaged. To a large extent, Russia must solve this problem on its own. The West, however, can continue to offer advice on legal structures and business ethics, and continue its cooperation with Russian law-enforcement agencies.

In addition, debate over NATO expansion is not over. Rejection of the decision to include new members might be more detrimental to the Alliance than enlargement will be. Yet the United States and Europe face conflicts over possible future enlargement, as well as over the Alliance's mission. In combination with differences about appropriate policies towards countries like Iraq, these tensions may provide Russia an opportunity to try to undermine Alliance cohesion.

The West should strive to ensure that Russia's interests and concerns are not ignored in the process of determining NATO's future. The NATO–Russia Council may prove helpful, but more important will be to ensure that cooperation with the Russian military expands. Active interaction may be the most effective proof that NATO's missions and expectations have changed, which would help to convince Russia that Western intentions are benign. At a minimum, the United States and the EU should determine some shared priorities with regard to Russia. As noted earlier, Yeltsin's success was one such guiding principle; new ones are necessary now. Cooperation in areas like nuclear safety which is, if anything, more critical to European security than to that of the United States, would be a good place to start.

Notes

1.   This is a very brief summary of a series of very complex issues. For a more detailed examination, see Sir Rodric Braithwaite, 'The Changing Political Landscape of Russia', *Survival*, vol. 36, no. 3 (Autumn 1994); and Alexei Arbatov, 'Russia's Foreign Policy Alternatives', *International Security*, vol. 18, no. 2 (Fall 1993).

2.   Yuriy Antonivich Borko, 'Russia and the European Union are Trying to Overcome Old Fears – The Prospects for Partnership with the EU are Still Obscure', *Segodnya*, 19 August 1995, p. 6.

3.   This has caused problems with the IMF as well. Ron Synovitz, 'Russia: IMF's Fischer Endorses Proposed Tax Changes', *RFE/RL Research Report*, 12 November 1997.

4. GDP apparently fell 38.5 per cent between 1992 and 1996. US Department of State Background Notes: Russia, June 1997, p. 8 (http://www.state.gov/www/background_notes/russia-0697_bgn.html).

5. Interior Minister Anatoly Kulikov claimed in June 1997 that over 9000 crime groups were operating in Russia. *RFE/RL Research Report*, 13 June 1997; *RFE/RL Research Report*, 26 September 1997.

6. This became painfully apparent during the summer and fall of 1997 as the 'banker's scandal' unfolded. See David Hoffman, 'Russia's Clans Go to War: Phone Giant's Sale Splits Tycoon's Tight Ranks', *Washington Post*, 26 October 1997; and Floriana Fossato '1997 in Review: Russian Reforms Suffer a Setback as Year Ends', *RFE/RL Research Report*, 26 December 1997.

7. See Renée de Nevers, *Russia's Strategic Renovation: Russian Security Strategies and Foreign Policy in the Post-Imperial Era*, Adelphi Paper no. 289 (London: International Institute for Strategic Studies, 1994), p. 12.

8. By one calculation, the West spent over $10 trillion to defend itself from the Soviet Union during the Cold War. See Martin Wolf, 'How the West Failed Russia', *Financial Times*, 7 May 1996, p. 12.

9. Hans-Hermann Hochmann and Christian Meier, 'The Halifax G7 Summit and Western Assistance for Russia and the Ukraine', *Aussenpolitik*, vol. 47, no. 1 (1996), pp. 53–60.

10. Michael Dauderstädt, 'A Comparison of the Assistance Strategies of the Western Donors', unpublished manuscript, Friedrich Ebert Stiftung, Bonn, January 1996.

11. Indeed, in the run-up to Russia's elections in 1996, there were some questions about whether the IMF was easing its policy guidelines in an effort to ensure Yeltsin's victory. See 'Mr. Yeltsin's Flexible Friend', *The Economist*, 13 July 1996, pp. 71–2.

12. Stephanie Baker, 'Russia: Deal on Paris Club Entry seen as Political Victory', *RFE/RL Research Report*, 26 June 1997; and 'Russia: Paris Club Welcomes New Creditor Nation', *RFE/RL Research Report*, 17 September 1997.

13. Russia assumed the USSR's debt in 1992, with the breakup of that state.

14. Stephanie Baker, 'Landmark Debt Restructuring Deal Signed', *RFE/RL*, 7 October 1997.

15. 'United States Assistance and Economic Cooperation Strategy for Russia', update by the Coordinator of US Assistance to the New Independent States, 3 February 1995; see also *US Assistance and Related Programs for the New Independent States of the Former Soviet Union: 1994 Annual Report*, pp. 20–23.

16. For FY 1990–93, 19 US government agencies committed $10.1 billion for bilateral grants, donations and credit programmes to the FSU. $6.7 billion took the form of direct loans, grants and insurance (for investment). $1 billion was obligated, and $434 million spent of $1.8 billion which was originally authorized for grants. $1.6 billion was obligated, and $1.22 billion spent, of the allocations for donations in the form of food assistance, among other things. See 'Former

Soviet Union: US Bilateral Program Lacks Effective Coordination', US Government Accounting Office, GAO/NSIAD-95-10, February 1995, p. 2.

17. *US Assistance and Related Programs for the New Independent States of the Former Soviet Union: 1994 Annual Report*, pp. 20–3.

18. Fact Sheet: US–Russian Economic Relations and Military Issues, US Department of State, 2 January 1996.

19. See *TACIS Russia: The European Union's TACIS Programme* (Brussels: European Commission, 1995).

20. *TACIS: Summary of Indicative Programmes, 1993–1995* (Brussels: European Commission, 1995), pp. 31–4.

21. Joel Blocker, 'Europe: EU Promises Most, Delivers Least to the East', *RFE/RL*, 11 November 1997.

22. Alexander Kennaway, 'What is Wrong with Western Aid to the FSU and Central and Eastern Europe and how to Improve It', draft discussion paper, Conflict Studies Research Centre, RMA Sandhurst, May 1995.

23. This is not to suggest that NATO has not changed, but that Russia does not recognize its changes as substantial. See Andrew J. Pierre and Dmitri Trenin, 'NATO's New Tasks: Developing NATO–Russian Relations', *Survival*, vol. 39, no. 1 (Spring 1997), p. 9.

24. See Michael Brown's chapter in this volume.

25. 'Partnership for Peace Invitation', issued by the heads of state and governments participating in the meeting of the North Atlantic Council held at NATO headquarters, Brussels, 10–11 January 1994.

26. Given that not all PfP partners are likely at any point to be invited to joint NATO, it is quite useful to have several states participating in the PfP programme who clearly have no interest in joining the Alliance, in particular Sweden and Finland. For a good assessment of the aims of PfP, see Nick Williams, 'Partnership for Peace: Permanent Fixture or Declining Asset?', *Survival*, vol. 38, no. 1 (Spring 1996), pp. 98–110.

27. See for example Alexei Pushkov, 'Russia and the West: An Endangered Relationship?', *NATO Review*, vol. 42, no. 1 (February 1994), pp. 5–7.

28. 'Clinton Hints NATO Would Defend East From Attack', *International Herald Tribune*, 13 January 1994; and The White House, *A National Security Strategy of Engagement and Enlargement* (Washington, DC: US Government Printing Office, July 1994), p. 22.

29. One area of clear success in relations between NATO and Russia has been in the area of Civilian Emergency Planning (CEP). CEP accounts for 12 per cent of the efforts made with all partner countries in the PfP, though it receives at most 1 per cent of the PfP budget. Based on interviews at NATO headquarters, Brussels, March 1996. On NATO's cooperation with EMERCOM, see also 'Memorandum of Understanding on Civil Emergency Planning and Disaster Preparedness Between Ministry of Russian Federation for Civil Defense, Emergencies and Elimination of Consequences of Natural Disasters (EMERCOM of Russia) and the North Atlantic Treaty Organization',

signed on 20 March 1996; and 'NATO Secretary General Signs Memorandum of Understanding on Civil Emergency Planning and Disaster Preparedness with Russia', NATO press release (96)44, 20 March 1996.

30. Marina Sergeyeva, 'Moscow has few Trump Cards, But not all Cards have been Dealt', *Kommersant-Daily*, 8 June 1996, p. 4; Vasiliy Safronchuck, 'Seven and a Half or Chernomyrdin goes Cap in Hand in Lyon', *Sovetskaya Rossiya*, 1 July 1996, p. 3.

31. An airborne battalion has also been assigned to peace-keeping. Yeltsin also announced that the MOD was forming a 'special military contingent to participate in maintaining and restoring international peace and security'. See Kevin O'Prey, 'Keeping Peace in the Borderlands of Russia', Henry L. Stimson Center Occasional Paper 23, July 1995, p. 6.; and Doug Clarke, *OMRI Daily Digest*, no. 88, part 1, 6 May 1996.

32. US military officers are frustrated with their ties with the Russians, however; there are many exchanges, but the Russians have been less interested in joint training exercises. For analysis of US–Russian military contacts, see Kimberly Marten Zisk, 'Contact Lenses: The Realist Neglect of Transparency and US–Russian Military Ties', *Program on New Approaches to Russian Security Working Papers Series*, no. 2 (September, 1997), pp. 4–10; Michael J. McCarthy, 'Comrades in Arms: Russian–American Military-to-Military Contacts since 1992', *Journal of Slavic Military Studies* vol. 9, no. 4 (December 1996), pp. 743–78.

33. Based on interviews in Bonn and Brussels, March 1996.

34. Defense Secretary William Perry's close relationship with then Minister of Defense Pavel Grachev was critical to Russia's final agreement on participation. Based on author's interviews in Brussels and Bonn, March 1996.

35. Zisk, 'Contact Lenses', *op. cit.*, p. 9.

36. As quoted in Jack Mendelsohn, 'The NATO–Russian Founding Act', *Arms Control Today*, vol. 27, no. 4 (May 1997), p. 19.

37. As quoted in Mendelsohn, 'The NATO–Russian Founding Act', *op. cit.*, p. 20.

38. Douglas Busvine, 'Russia Defense Chief Unimpressed by New Corps', *Reuters*, 29 January 1998.

39. Overall allocations by Congress were $2.5 billion between 1992–96. Jason Ellis, 'Nunn-Lugar's Mid-Life Crisis', *Survival*, vol. 39, no. 1 (Spring 1997), p. 84; US Department of State Background Notes: Russia, June 1997, p. 12.

40. 'Former Soviet Union: US Bilateral Program Lacks Effective Coordination', *op. cit.*, p. 46.

41. See William C. Potter, 'Before the Deluge? Assessing the Threat of Nuclear Leakage from the Post-Soviet States', *Arms Control Today*, vol. 25, no. 9 (October 1995), pp. 9–16; and James Blaker, 'Coping with the New "Clear and Present Danger" from Russia', *Arms Control Today*, vol. 25, No. 3 (April 1995), pp. 13–16.

42. This is not unique to Russia; the US Navy, for example, has been recalcitrant about allowing reciprocal inspections that might help promote cooperation with the Russians. Potter, 'Before the Deluge?', *op. cit.*, p. 15.

43. Oleg Bukharin and William Potter, 'Potatoes were Guarded Better', *The Bulletin of the Atomic Scientists* (May/June 1995), pp. 46–50; Potter, 'Before the Deluge?'

44. Ellis, 'Nunn-Lugar's Mid-Life Crisis', *op. cit.*, pp. 88–9.

45. 'Agreement between USG and Russia Concerning Cooperation Regarding Plutonium Reactors', 23 September 1997, Gore–Chernomyrdin Web page, http://www.usia. gov/regional/bnc/usrussia/gcc9/pluto/usruagre.htm

46. Ellis, 'Nunn-Lugar's Mid-Life Crisis', *op. cit.*, p. 89.

47. TACIS 'Contract Information Update July 1996', Nuclear Safety 1995, European Commission; see also *Russia: The European Union's Tacis Programme* (Brussels: DG IA, European Commission, 1995).

48. *Guide to TACIS Framework Programmes: What they Are and How to Apply* (Brussels: DG IA, European Commission, 1995), pp. 32–3.

49. 'NATO Science Programme: Priority Area on Disarmament Technologies' (Brussels: Scientific Affairs Division, NATO, 1996); see also *Avoiding Nuclear Anarchy: Containing the Threat of Loose Russian Nuclear Weapons and Fissile Material* (Cambridge: The MIT Press for CSIA, 1996), pp. 142–3.

50. A few studies of this sort have appeared in recent years, such as those by Nancy Lubin, 'Aid to the Former Soviet Union: When Less is More', Draft Preliminary Report, 9 December 1995; Thomas Carothers, *Assessing Democracy Assistance: The Case of Romania* (Washington, DC: Carnegie Endowment for International Peace, 1996); Alexander Kennaway, 'What is Wrong with Western Aid to the FSU and Central and Eastern Europe and How to Improve It', draft discussion paper, Conflict Studies Research Centre, RMA Sandhurst, May 1995.

5 'Rogue States' and Transatlantic Relations*
Philip H. Gordon

Differences over how to deal with the international system's malcontents – the regimes that challenge the international status quo and global leadership of the United States – has perhaps been the greatest area of divergence between the United States and its European (and North American) allies in the post-Cold War world. Whereas other transatlantic disagreements (such as those over trade policy, the Middle East peace process, Africa, and even Bosnia) worsened or improved according to a wide range of factors, the 'rogue states' dispute has been a constant, and steadily growing, irritant to the transatlantic partnership in the 1990s. Because the dispute is based on deep-seated perspectives that derive from history, political culture and economic interests, it seems unlikely to disappear – unless and until the rogue regimes themselves change or disappear.

The source of the transatlantic disagreement about rogue states was the intensification, beginning in 1993, of US efforts to contain, punish, influence or even oust a small group of regimes that Washington claimed were responsible for a range of threats to international peace and US interests. According to then US National Security Adviser Anthony Lake, who first publicly set out the strategy in March 1994, Cuba, Libya, Iran, Iraq and North Korea were international 'outlaws' that merited not only the disdain but also the sanction and containment of the international community.[1] As Congress and some leading press commentators pressured the Clinton administration to do more to contain these hostile regimes (particularly after certain terrorist and other incidents drew greater attention to the issue and as the 1996 elections approached), the US rogue state policy intensified.

* Part of this chapter draws on the author's *The Transatlantic Allies and the Changing Middle East*, Adelphi Paper no. 322 (London: International Institute for Strategic Studies, 1998).

In 1996 it erupted into a full-blown effort not only to contain or even topple rogue regimes, but to punish other states – even close allies – who deal with them. By the time Clinton's second term began, the punishment and containment of rogue states became one of the central elements in US foreign policy. It was the 'stick' in a global 'carrot and stick' approach to spreading democracy and freedom around the world.[2]

It is not yet clear what effect US policy has had on the rogue states; not even its proponents claimed that it would bring quick results. What is clear, however, is that Europeans (as well as Canadians, Japanese and Mexicans) have strongly opposed US policy and have been vociferous in denouncing it. The allies vehemently rejected the logic of cutting off disagreeable regimes and argued that openness and dialogue was a wiser strategy. Even more important, they resented US legislation passed in 1996 that sought to punish their companies that did business with the so-called rogues. By the end of that year, Europeans were retaliating in their own legal systems against the US laws, refusing to curtail their diplomatic or business dealings with the targeted states, and asserting their right to pursue different foreign policies from those of the leader of the Western alliance.

The current transatlantic dispute about rogue states is in some ways just another episode in a long series of transatlantic disagreements about NATO's 'out-of-area' policy going back to the 1956 Suez crisis, the Algerian and Vietnam wars in the 1950s and 1960s, and the US bombing of Libya in 1986. But the current dispute is in one way even more problematic than those in the earlier period because it threatens the cohesion of the Atlantic Alliance when that cohesion is no longer ensured by a common threat. Quarrels over out-of-area issues never really threatened NATO during the Cold War, because the common need to stand together was always far more important than any extra-European disputes. Today, as NATO becomes more an alliance of common values and interests than a mere defense pact, and when it occupies itself with issues that are no longer 'existential', external differences will matter more than in the past. If Americans come to see Europeans as free-riding appeasers of states that threaten global US interests, and Europeans come to see Americans as simplistic crusaders who seek to assert their authority unilaterally over their own allies, the result cannot help but threaten the unity of the Alliance and the willingness of Americans and Europeans to stand by each other in times of need.[3]

Even short of its effect on transatlantic cohesion, the rogue states dispute is problematic because transatlantic policy differences undermine the effectiveness of either US or European strategy. Sanctions and containment are less likely to influence or bring down a regime when applied by the United States in isolation, but trade and dialogue are equally unlikely to foster change when the world's largest economy and political player is not involved. A divided Western strategy towards rogue states, in other words, leads neither to the defeat of the unwanted regimes nor to their integration into civilized international behaviour, but rather to tensions within the Atlantic Alliance and the chance for rogue states to play the allies off against each other. Although it might be argued that this unintended 'division of labour' – US pressure and European engagement – serves the useful purpose of allowing outsiders to wield both pressure and influence (the United States applies sanctions on Iran while German diplomats negotiate with it, for example), the more likely result is that the targeted states see it as a sign of Western weakness and division, which they exploit. The result is that the Western allies end up with worse relations with each other, but that their relations with the rogue states do not change.

ALLIED POLICIES AND ROGUE STATES

Western policies towards each rogue state are different, but in each case the pattern is similar: the United States urges containment and punishment, while the Europeans seek change through dialogue and trade.

North Korea

The divergence in US and European policy towards rogue states is probably smallest concerning North Korea, not only because Europeans are not leading actors in East Asia but also because it is the one case where US policy has been moving towards increased dialogue and trade rather than towards sanction. Although US military containment of North Korea continues, Washington has been tentatively moving towards engagement ever since Pyongyang agreed in October 1994 to freeze its suspected nuclear weapons programme in exchange for food and energy aid and trade with the West. The US opening to North Korea is still highly tentative and uncertain, and it is perhaps not a healthy sign that the opening came about in this case not because Pyongyang's behaviour was improving, but because of the opposite: North Korea had apparently developed its illicit nuclear programme to the point of becoming a truly dangerous menace. The message from this experience to Iran and other rogue states – 'we will talk to you only once you have nuclear weapons' – was perhaps not what the United States had in mind, but it was sent nonetheless. Since Europeans had no better ideas, and few stakes in the country, they went along.

Iraq

US and European policies towards Iraq have also not yet led to serious and open disputes that could damage the Alliance, but only because the post-Gulf War set of sanctions on Iraq allows the United States to impose its policies of containment and isolation on sometimes unenthusiastic allies. Contrary to the perception of some Americans, it is not that anyone in Europe is arguing for dialogue and openness with Saddam Hussein, or claims that Iraq does not pose a potential regional threat. It is the case, however, that many in Europe accuse the United States of continuing the confrontation with Saddam Hussein for domestic political purposes, and of 'moving the goalposts' where the lifting of UN sanctions is concerned. France, a traditional ally of Iraq and the first Western country to break with the post-Gulf War policy of ostracizing the Iraqi leadership (when it welcomed Foreign Minister Tariq Aziz in January 1995), has been openly critical of US policy there, and Paris seems poised to promote and take advantage of an opening towards Iraq as soon as that becomes possible.

When in September 1996, US air forces attacked Iraqi targets in response to an Iraqi incursion in the Kurdish fighting in northern Iraq, many Europeans distanced themselves from the action; only Britain offered full support, and France made its objections publicly known. And from November 1997–March 1998, when Iraq created a crisis by expelling US members of the UN weapons-inspection teams and then denying inspectors access to so-called 'presidential sites', again only Britain gave its full backing to US preparations to respond militarily if necessary. Most Europeans eventually came around to lend at least political support to the US–UK threat of military action, but France again insisted on the need for a diplomatic solution and called for Iraq to be given more hope that sanctions might one day be removed. A number of French and Italian construction and oil companies have already made visits to Iraq to position themselves for the eventual contracts that will be signed after the lifting of sanctions. And almost all European countries disassociate themselves from American suggestions that sanctions on Iraq could be lifted only when Saddam Hussein leaves the scene. Saddam Hussein's continued mistreatment of his own citizens and reluctance to cooperate completely with UN resolutions have prevented Europeans from fully making the case for engagement, but there is little doubt that they are more prepared to do so than the United States.

Cuba

Far more openly contentious than Iraq is the issue of Cuba, the first of the rogue state problems to explode into a legislative dispute between the United States and the European Union (EU). Long an area of policy disagreement between the EU, which is Cuba's largest single trading partner, and the United States, which has maintained an embargo on trade with and travel to Cuba since Fidel Castro's 1959 revolution, Cuba policy became a high-profile issue with the passage on 12 March 1996 of the 'Cuban Liberty and Democratic Solidarity Act', known as Helms–Burton after its congressional sponsors. Helms–Burton seeks to support the claims of US and naturalized Cuban-American citizens whose property was expropriated after the 1959 revolution. Title IV of the Act, which took effect immediately, gives the US government the right to deny entry into the United States to anyone who 'traffics' in such property. Even the family members of shareholders in a firm that uses Cuban sugar made in an expropriated plant, for example, could be barred from the United States. The first company to be affected by the law was a Canadian mining firm, Sheritt International, whose directors, including former Bank of England Deputy Governor Rupert Pennant-Rea, were banned from the United States.

An even more controversial aspect of the Helms–Burton Act is Title III, which allows US companies to sue foreign firms and affiliates that have profited from the use of seized property. On 16 July 1996, President Clinton announced that he was suspending implementation of Title III for six months in order to give foreign firms more time to comply with the spirit of the law. Nevertheless, the Europeans and Canadians were still outraged, and condemned the law as both unwise and illegal. The Canadian government immediately took measures to allow its companies to continue to trade with Cuba, and the Europeans threatened both to disregard the US threats and to take the United States to the World Trade Organisation (WTO). In October, the European Commission approved legislation to make it illegal for EU companies to comply with the Act and which gave them the right to counter-sue in European courts.[4] European officials denied that Cuba posed any threat whatsoever to international security, and argued that rather than tightening the US embargo by threatening allies, the embargo should be dropped altogether.

On 3 January 1997, citing progress in getting Europeans to pressure Cuba, President Clinton delayed the implementation of Title III for another six months, and promised to continue to delay implementation so long as European policy towards Cuba got tougher. In April, the EU agreed to let its WTO case expire while both sides sought a solution to the problem. But Brussels continued to strongly resist the legislation and the principle of extraterritoriality, pressuring EU companies not to comply, and maintaining its threat to renew the WTO case if a solution is not found.[5]

Iran

Among all of the rogue state disputes, the greatest, and most consequential, concerns Iran. Ever since the 1979 Islamic revolution in Tehran and the holding of American hostages there for 444 days, Iran has been a particularly determined adversary of the United States – 'the Great Satan' to the adherents of the Islamic regime. (The US negotiator with Iran during the hostage crises was Warren Christopher, who showed no signs of having forgiven his former antagonists when Secretary of State 15 years later.[6]) The United States cut off diplomatic relations with Tehran in 1980, and Iran is consistently placed on the State Department's annual list of state supporters of terrorism. US leaders have accused Iran of threatening its neighbours, seeking to sabotage the Middle East peace process through its backing of anti-Israel groups like *Hizbollah* and *Hamas*, pursuing an illicit nuclear weapons programme, and murdering Iranian dissidents abroad.[7] Whereas Europe – which does not deny all the Iranian regime's wrongdoings – has sought to influence Iran through a process of 'critical dialogue' and continued trade, the United States has been resolute in its determination to isolate and punish Tehran.

Whereas the United States has long been an adversary of the regime in Iran, it was only from 1995 that the Clinton administration began its more active campaign to contain and penalize the Islamic regime.[8] In January of that year, Tehran signed a $1 billion contract with Russia to build two nuclear reactors in Iran, and in March, Iranian leaders seemed to approve of Palestinian terrorist attacks on Israeli civilians. Washington decided to take tougher action.[9] The first step was to put an end to the inconsistency that condemned other countries for trading with Iran but allowed US companies to do so. As late as 1994, US companies were the largest purchasers of Iranian oil, and US exports to Iran were more than $1 billion and increasing. The import of Iranian goods into the United States has been banned since 1987, but 'indirect' trade, whereby US companies bought and sold Iranian goods elsewhere, was allowed. On 30 April 1995, President Clinton ended the apparent hypocrisy by announcing a ban on all US trade with and investment in Iran, and he forced an American company, Conoco, to drop the oil exploration deal it had signed the previous month.[10] Going even further, in July 1996 the US House of Representatives passed the Iran–Libya Sanctions Act (ILSA), which had already been approved by the Senate. Like Helms–Burton, ILSA would punish even foreign companies that did business with Iran. The act, sponsored by New York Republican Senator Alfonse D'Amato, obliges the President to implement at least two of six possible sanctions, ranging from an import ban to lesser penalties, on all companies that invest more than $40 million in either the Iranian or the Libyan oil and gas sectors. President Clinton signed ILSA into law on 5 August 1996.

The European reaction to ILSA was even more vehement than to Helms–Burton, given the much higher levels of trade and investment at stake.[11] European leaders argued that it was wrong to try to change Iran by crippling its oil sector, and that such measures would actually be counterproductive by giving the Islamic regime an excuse for its poor economic performance, and by making the West seem hostile to Islam. More specifically, the Europeans and Canadians protested against the principle of 'extraterritorial' legislation, the idea that Washington could impose its own laws on foreign companies and countries, that was common to Helms–Burton and D'Amato. EU trade commissioner Leon Brittan called the US acts 'objectionable in principle, contrary to international trade law, and damaging to the interests of the European Union', and the EU began to apply similar countermeasures to those it took against Helms–Burton.[12] The problem came to a head when, in September 1997, the French oil company Total announced that together with Russia's Gazprom and the Malaysian company Petronas it had signed a $2 billion gas development deal with Tehran, a move that seemed likely to trigger US sanctions and a European reaction to them.

If the Iran case is brought before a WTO dispute panel, the outcome would be of enormous significance. The United States would almost certainly appeal to provisions that allow countries to suspend international trade rules to protect 'essential security interests', and the Europeans would counter that national security was not at stake. If the WTO found in favour of the United States, the precedent of appealing to national security could undermine the whole system; if it found against the United States, American support for the WTO could be undermined.

Libya

The transatlantic debate about Libya in many ways mirrors that about Iran. Like Iran, Libya is seen in the United States as one of the world's foremost supporters of state-sponsored terrorism, and Libya's leader, Moammar Gadaffi, is as reviled in the United States as any of Iran's leaders. Europeans are not exactly supportive of Gadaffi's regime, but they oppose trade sanctions on it, just as most of them (the exception being the UK) opposed the punitive air strikes on Tripoli taken by the United States in April 1986 in response to what Washington claimed was evidence of Libyan-supported terrorism. Libya, unlike Iran, is the object of sanctions that were imposed by the UN after Gadaffi's unwillingness to turn over two Libyans accused of bombing Pan Am flight 103 in 1988, but the UN sanctions only cover air travel to and from Libya, and not trade or oil development, and sanctions on these would be opposed by Europeans. Frustrated with the European unwillingness to support harsher sanctions on Libya, the US Congress included Libya in the D'Amato Act, which had originally been designed to apply only to Iran.

THE SOURCES OF TRANSATLANTIC DIVISIONS

Why do Americans and Europeans (and Canadians) have such different views about rogue states, and why are their policies so different? At the heart of the dispute is a genuine difference in policy analysis between Americans and Europeans about how best to deal with, and eventually change, objectionable regimes.[13] Europeans argue that dialogue and trade are the best tools of leverage, and that prosperity and human contact are ultimately better means of spreading democracy and cooperation than anything else. Trade, in this view, fosters common interests and greater harmony among nations, and stimulates business activity and political change. Europeans are convinced, in any case, that US policies of punishment and containment simply do not work, and that policies of containment and the demonization of elites in rogue states will only promote their determination to resist

Western hegemony and give them a public excuse for their poor economic and social performance.

The Americans respond that the European view is either cynical or naive. The leaders of rogue states are probably unreformable, and even if it were possible to change them over time, they would do so much damage in the meantime that the risk of trying is too great. Trade and dialogue with rogue states, thus, does not foster openness and political change, but simply gives the hostile regimes more resources with which to carry out their destructive programmes, and takes away any incentive they might have to amend their ways. The US objective is thus to keep the pressure on so that they are forced to change, and keep them from doing much damage in the meantime. It would be misleading to conclude, however, that the transatlantic dispute over rogue states is simply a difference in analysis, and that the positions on the issue could just as easily have been the other way around. In fact, of course, the US and European positions on the issue have as much to do with the domestic politics, economic interests, military roles and political cultures of the two protagonists as they do with a genuine policy dispute.

It is hard to deny that domestic politics have played a critical role in both US and European policies toward Cuba, Iran, Iraq and Libya over the past several years and even decades. Cuban-Americans have long been influential in US domestic politics, and it is certainly no coincidence that it was in an election year that the Helms–Burton Act was signed into law by a President known to be uncomfortable with it. The states of Florida and New Jersey, where many Cuban-Americans live, have between them 40 electoral votes (nearly 15 per cent of the 270 needed to win a presidential election), and it is in any case hard to argue that Cuba, especially after the end of the Cold War and death of communism, poses a strategic threat to American interests. The 'strategists' of Helms–Burton would have a hard time explaining why Fidel Castro and his regime in Cuba are a greater threat to human rights or US interests than many regimes around the world with which the United States maintains close relations.

Iran does pose potential threats to US interests, and certainly mistreats its own citizens, but there also seems little doubt that those threats are often exaggerated in the United

States. The D'Amato Act faced an uncertain fate in the Congress until the bombing of a US military base at Dhahran in Saudi Arabia on 25 June 1996, and the explosion of TWA flight 800 a month later made it seem imperative to get tough on Iran even though there was no solid evidence that Tehran had anything to do with either incident. Taking tough action against Iraq and Libya – whose abominable leaders are seen by many Americans as responsible for acts of international terrorism in the past – is also popular in the United States, which has little to lose by doing so as it has few economic interests in either country.[14] Economic sanctions are thus a favoured tool of leaders who want to be seen as 'taking action' but who are unprepared to run the risks involved with the use of military force.[15]

Europeans, of course, do a lot of business with all of these states, and that is one of the main reasons why their domestic politics lead them in a different direction from the United States. Whereas the United States has not traded with Cuba for more than 35 years, the EU and Canada are the source of more than 70 per cent of Cuba's imports, at a value of over $1.3 billion per year.[16] European trade with Iran and Libya is even greater. The EU does more than $20 billion in annual trade with Iran and Libya, which together account for more than 20 per cent of EU oil imports.[17] Some large European companies (such as France's Total and Elf, and Italy's Agip) have investments of hundreds of millions of dollars in both countries. Iran also has debts with Germany of $8.6 billion, meaning that even though its exports to Iran are falling, the German interest in Iranian economic situation remains great.[18] Europeans would surely be more willing to sanction Iran if they did not have such significant economic interests at stake.

A third reason why the United States takes a harder line on rogue states is that Americans see themselves as, and in fact are, more responsible for containing threats to international order than Europeans. If a rogue state challenges regional or global security, it is the United States and not Europe that must deal with the problem, and the United States has often come into conflict with those states that have challenged the international status quo. It is thus not a coincidence, or even solely due to geography, that Europeans trade more with

Iran, Iraq, Libya and Cuba than does the United States. These states have all directly challenged Washington's global leadership – sometimes through propaganda, sometimes through terrorism, and sometimes through war – and thereby provoked far more American hostility than European. It was the United States that was targeted by Soviet nuclear weapons in Cuba during the 1962 missile crisis, the United States whose diplomats and other citizens were seized by Iranian 'students' for over a year during the Iranian revolution, and the United States that led the international coalition against Saddam Hussein. The situation today is not altogether different from during the Cold War, when the United States was the self-appointed (and widely accepted) leader in the fight against communism, leading to what the Europeans often considered excesses in Central America, Asia, and even in Europe itself. Today just as then, some Americans believe they are responsible for coping with challenges to regional or international order, and that Europeans are able, and all too willing, to 'free ride' behind them.[19]

A final explanation for the greater American hostility is the difference in the political cultures of the United States and Europe. Americans, with their idealistic (some Europeans would say naive) vision of their own place and role in the world, have always been more ready to divide states and causes between good and evil. American wars have thus been fought for causes as grand as 'making the world safe for democracy', 'defeating fascism', and 'creating a new world order', rather than for such crass goals as national interests. Europeans, on the other hand, perhaps because of their much longer and more complicated histories in which all states have at various times been 'good', 'bad' or both at the same time, seem more willing (in some American eyes all too willing) to take moderate views of the behaviour of other states. US political culture thus seems far more susceptible to 'demonization' and differentiation between 'friends' and 'enemies' than European political culture. All of this leads Americans to view rogue states as not merely a little bit more problematic than others, but as adversaries who must be reformed. Europeans are more ready to live with what they believe they cannot change.

FUTURE PROSPECTS

The deep-seated European–US differences in domestic politics, economic interests and political culture make the rogue state dispute far more difficult to resolve than it would be were it simply a matter of policy analysis. Since there is little sign that the rogue state problem is going to disappear anytime soon, the chances that these differences will continue to be an irritant to transatlantic relations – or perhaps even worse – are therefore very great indeed.

Which side is right in the dispute? It must be said that neither strategy for influencing hostile regimes has an impressive track record, and neither 'quintuple containment' nor 'critical dialogue' is without flaws. Americans would have to admit, for example, that neither 38 years of sanctions against Castro's Cuba nor 17 years of confrontation with Iran has undermined either regime's hold on power (the opposite might be true, since US hostility is a convenient scapegoat for the regimes' failings), and the historical record for bringing about regime-change through economic sanctions is exceedingly weak.[20] Whereas the United States might make the case that the sanctions would have worked better had they been applied universally rather than just by the United States, the record from Iraq – where universal sanctions do hold – is also not good: the country is destroyed and the population suffering, but the regime survives. The international track record of changing authoritarian regimes through engagement and economic development seems better (look, for example, at South Korea and Taiwan), as the United States itself has implicitly admitted in its own, selective pursuit of contact with many unappealing leaders.[21] There is thus apparent inconsistency in the US approach – it seeks change in China, Saudi Arabia and even North Korea through trade, dialogue and engagement, but denounces those methods when applied to Cuba, Libya and Iran.

Where the United States clearly has a point, however, is in the argument that change through engagement takes a long time, and that the rogue regimes have potential to do enormous damage to regional and international security, as well as to their own people, in the meantime. Perhaps

Iran or Libya would, if left to trade and interact in the community of nations, one day develop into status quo, or even liberal powers. But what should the world do in the meantime if they are murdering their own citizens at home and abroad, developing weapons of mass destruction, seeking to sabotage Arab–Israeli peace, and issuing death edicts against Western authors? Money is fungible, and every dollar earned by rogue regimes can be put to use by those regimes to maintain their grip on power and pursue their interests abroad. Europe's critical dialogue might appease European consciences and sound good in theory, but it must be admitted that there is little evidence of it influencing rogue states in what the West would consider to be a positive direction.

Because the issue of how best to deal with rogue states is therefore inconclusive in the abstract, policies will doubtless continue to be made based on national interests, perceptions and politics, and will therefore continue to differ across the Atlantic. There might, however, be something to be gained in efforts to develop a common strategy, whereby senior US and European officials would seek to identify areas of 'unacceptable' policy, and agree what should trigger sanctions to which both sides would agree.[22] These areas might be proof of state-sponsored terrorism and the pursuit of weapons of mass destruction.[23] If taken seriously on both sides, such an effort could also give political leaders protection against domestic criticism if the United States and EU together decided on policies one of their publics, business communities or legislatures did not like. The Clinton administration could refuse Helms–Burton-like legislation, for example (which it was known privately to oppose anyway), on the grounds of the need for Alliance cohesion, arguing that unilateral policies would not work anyway. This was not altogether different from the administration's stance during 1995 on the issue of lifting the arms embargo on the Bosnian Muslims – the administration opposed Congress with the argument that the Europeans would have to be on board for it to work. European leaders could also cite the need for transatlantic consensus in applying sanctions on a rogue state that their business communities might oppose. Such efforts would not ensure transatlantic harmony or convergence of views (or interests), but it could foster at least a better understanding of the arguments of the other side and provide a measure of political cover for leaders whose views are not as extremist as those of some of their legislators.

Ultimately, of course, there is no simple institutional solution for the problem of rogue states and transatlantic relations. But if the Atlantic allies cannot find a way to agree on policy, they must at least understand the negative consequences of their failure to do so. By failing to appreciate the importance to Americans of constraining states that threaten US interests around the globe, Europeans may be undermining US support for Europe at a time when such support is no longer guaranted. And by seeking unilaterally to impose their will on dissenting allies, the United States might well be provoking the very sort of independent European foreign policies that they are seeking to avoid. None of this is very healthy for a transatlantic security alliance whose truly common threat has disappeared.

Notes

1. See Anthony Lake, 'Confronting Backlash States', *Foreign Affairs*, vol. 73, no. 2 (March/April 1994), pp. 45–55. Lake was building on, and broadening, the policy of 'dual containment' of Iran and Iraq articulated more than a year earlier by National Security Council official Martin Indyk in a speech to the Washington Institute for Near East Policy. See Indyk's 'Keynote Address: The Clinton Administration's Approach to the Middle East', 18 May 1993.

2. On spreading democracy as a centrepiece of the Clinton foreign policy, see President William Jefferson Clinton, *A National Security Strategy of Engagement and Enlargement* (Washington, DC: Government Printing Office, 1994); and Deputy Secretary of State Strobe Talbott, 'Democracy and the National Interest', *Foreign Affairs*, vol. 75, no. 6 (November/December 1996), pp. 47–63.

3. For the case that a European failure to support US global strategy will undermine the Atlantic Alliance, see Ronald D. Asmus, Robert Blackwill and F. Stephen Larrabee, 'Can NATO Survive?' *The Washington Quarterly*, vol. 19, no. 3 (Spring 1996), pp. 79–101; and the various chapters in David C. Gompert and F. Stephen Larrabee, *America and Europe: A Partnership for a New Era* (Cambridge: Cambridge University Press, 1997). For one (of many) European

arguments that the post- Cold War United States is trying to 'rule the world', see the editorial 'L'inadmissible prétension américaine', *Le Monde*, 13 July 1996.

4. The EU legislation was initially held up by Denmark, which supported the EU retaliation but had reservations about the use of the catch-all article 235 of the Treaty of Rome to do so. EU foreign ministers reached a compromise on 28 October that allowed the European counter-measures to go ahead. See Lionel Barber, 'Brussels Finesses Danish Threat to Cuba Law Riposte', *Financial Times*, 29 October 1996.

5. On Clinton's July 1996 and January 1997 decisions to delay implementation of Title III, see John F. Harris, 'Clinton Postpones Disputed Provision of Anti-Cuba Law', *International Herald Tribune*, 17 July 1996; and Thomas W. Lippman, 'US Extends Delay On Anti-Cuba Law', *International Herald Tribune*, 4–5 January 1997. On the continued European opposition, see Neil Buckley, 'EU Seeks Help for Helms–Burton Case', *Financial Times*, 27 February 1997.

6. See Thomas W. Lippman, 'For Christopher, Iran Is Public Enemy No. 1', *Washington Post*, 5 August 1995.

7. See, for example, Warren Christopher's description of Iran as 'the foremost sponsor of terrorism in the world...one of the greatest if not the greatest threats to peace and stability in the region', in 'Statement by Secretary of State Warren Christopher Regarding US Sanctions Against Iran', State Department Briefing, *Federal News Service*, 1 May 1995; and the similar statements made by President Clinton in 'Remarks by President Clinton at a Dinner of the World Jewish Congress', *Federal News Service*, 30 April 1995, p. 4.

8. Already in late 1994, under pressure from Republicans in Congress (in particular Speaker of the House Newt Gingrich), President Clinton authorized a secret Central Intelligence Agency operation designed to change the nature of the government of Iran. Gingrich had apparently conceived of a plan that would seek to oust the Iranian government, but the administration insisted on the more modest goal of changing Iran's behaviour before agreeing to the plan. See Tim Weiner, 'US Plan to Change Iran Leaders is an Open Secret Before it Begins', *New York Times*, 26 January 1996.

9. On the Russian reactor deal and the Iranian comments on terrorism in Israel, see Fawas Gerges, 'Washington's Misguided Iran Policy', *Survival* (Winter 1996–97), p. 7. The tougher US policy was also prompted by press and intelligence reports in early 1995 that suggested Iran was closer to being able to build a nuclear weapon than previously thought. See Chris Hedges, 'Iran Almost Has A-Bomb, US and Israel Conclude', *New York Times*, 5 January 1995; and Thomas W. Lippman, 'Stepped-Up Nuclear Effort Renews Alarm about Iran', *Washington Post*, 17 April 1995.

10. Conoco was to develop Iran's Sirri oil fields, located in the northern Gulf. A few months later the Sirri deal was given to a French firm, Total, making the transatlantic divergence all the more distinct – and bitter. See 'L'Europe refuse que Washington sanctionne des firmes

étrangères', *Le Monde*, 7 August 1996. According to Fawas Gerges, Iranian President Hashemi Rafsanjani claims to have offered the deal to an American firm as a 'message' to the United States, 'which was not correctly understood'. See Gerges, 'Washington's Misguided Iran Policy', *op. cit.*, p. 11.

11. For examples of criticism from France, Britain, Germany, Spain and Italy, see 'L'Europe refuse que Washington sanctionne des firmes étrangères', *Le Monde*, 7 August 1996, p. 2. Also see the (unsuccessful) attempt by UK Foreign Secretary Malcolm Rifkind to influence the debate in Washington as the Iran legislation was being considered, in Malcolm Rifkind, 'Secondary Boycotts are Not a Good Way to Fight Terrorism', *Washington Post*, 30 May 1996.

12. See Tom Buerkle, 'EU Steps up Campaign Against US Sanctions; In Rebuff to Clinton, Bloc Taking Dispute to World Trade Body', *International Herald Tribune*, 2 October 1996.

13. For a useful recent discussion of the debate over how best to change undesirable regimes, see Franklin L. Lavin, 'Asphyxiation or Oxygen? The Sanctions Dilemma', *Foreign Policy*, no. 104 (Fall 1996), pp. 139–53.

14. No less than 63 per cent of Americans polled in June 1996 supported not only punishing Cuba, Iran and Libya, but also 'punishing foreign companies that do business with Cuba, Iran, and Libya by preventing them from selling products in the US.' Only 25 per cent of those polled were opposed. See the *Wall Street Journal*/NBC poll cited in Peter Rudolf, *Konflikt Oder Koordination? Die USA, Iran und die Deutsch–Amerikanischen Beziehungen* (Ebenhausen: Stiftung Wissenschaft und Politik, October 1996), p. 18.

15. The domestic political explanation for sanctions is an old one. Already in 1935, David Lloyd George quipped that the League of Nations sanctions against Italy 'came too late to save Abyssinia, but, they are just in the nick of time to save the Government'. Cited in Gary Clyde Hufbauer, Jeffrey J. Schott and Kimberly Ann Elliot, *Economic Sanctions Reconsidered: History and Current Policy* (Washington, DC: Institute for International Economics, 1990), p. 3.

16. Canada is Cuba's largest trading partner and alone accounts for $500 million per year in trade, helped by the 100,000 Canadian tourists who visit Cuba each year. See 'L'Europe se mobilise contre la politique d'embargo des Etats-Unis', *Le Monde*, 17 July 1996; and also the figures in International Institute for Strategic Studies, 'US–EU Trade Wars', *Strategic Comments*, vol. 2, no. 7 (August 1996).

17. Germany alone accounts for 15 per cent of Iran's imports, with France accounting for 7 per cent, Italy 6 per cent and the United States just 3 per cent. See the table 'Parts de Marché des Principaux Fournisseurs', in *Le Monde*, 7 August 1996. Also see IISS, 'US–EU Trade Wars', *op. cit.* Detailed data on trade with Cuba, Iran and Libya can be found in International Monetary Fund, *Directions of Trade Statistics Yearbook, 1996* (Washington, DC: IMF, 1996), pp. 171–72, 253–54 and 288–89.

18. Germany's exports to Iran have fallen from $5.2 billion in 1992 to $1.6 billion in 1995. See Rick Atkinson, 'Washington and Bonn

Collide on How Best to Deal With Iran', *Washington Post*, 28 June 1996.

19.   See David C. Gompert and Richard Kugler, 'Free-Rider Redux', *Foreign Affairs*, vol. 74, no. 1 (January–February 1995), pp. 7–12.

20.   Most of the academic work on sanctions suggests that they can often be effective if widely applied and targeted at modest and very specific goals, but that they can rarely achieve maximalist aims such as bringing down a government or changing a regime. One of the most influential studies is Hufbauer, Schott and Elliot, *Economic Sanctions Reconsidered, op. cit.* Also see the discussion in Lavin, 'Asphyxiation or Oxygen?', pp. 143–7; and an updated version of the Hufbauer, Schott and Elliot study: Kimberly Ann Elliot and Gary Clyde Hufbauer, '"New" Approaches to Economic Sanctions', in Arnold Kanter and Linton F. Brooks, *US Intervention Policy for the Post-Cold War World: New Challenges and New Responses* (New York: W. W. Norton & Co., 1994), pp. 133–58.

21.   Whether or not economic development leads to democratization is one of the most widely debated and studied questions in comparative politics, but most scholars accept that there is a positive link between the two. For the case that socioeconomic modernization and economic development promotes democracy, and some hypotheses as to why this might be the case, see Robert A. Scalapino, 'Democratizing Dragons: South Korea and Taiwan', *Journal of Democracy*, vol. 4, no. 3 (July 1993), pp. 70–83. For a recent study that argues that rising income has a 'statistically significant democratizing effects', see John B. Londregan and Keith T. Poole, 'Does High Income Promote Democracy?', *World Politics*, vol. 48, no. 4 (October 1996), pp. 1–30. Other recent studies suggest that economic development is not particularly helpful in bringing about democracy, but that it helps sustain democratic systems once they come about. See Adam Przeworski and Fernando Limongi, 'Modernization: Theories and Facts', *World Politics*, vol. 49, no. 2 (January 1997), pp. 155–83.

22.   See the calls for such efforts in Shahram Chubin, 'US Policy Towards Iran Should Change – But It Probably Won't', *Survival*, vol. 58, no. 4 (Winter 1996–97), pp. 16–18; and Rudolf, *Konflikt Oder Koordination? op. cit.*, pp. 26–9.

23.   The issue of providing 'hard intelligence' for US claims of misbehaviour by the rogue regimes is a difficult one. As former CIA director James Woolsey has argued, calls 'to see yet more "hard evidence" of Iranian government sponsorship than has already been made public hits an obvious problem: some of the convincing detail (hard evidence indeed) must remain in governments' hands in order to protect intelligence sources and methods. Unfortunately, if governments were to inform...the public about some details, they would also perforce inform...the Iranian Minister for Intelligence and Security, who would promptly see to it that outsiders did not learn any more about how the Iranian terror apparatus operates'. See R. James Woolsey, 'Appeasement Will Only Encourage Iran', *Survival*, vol. 38, no. 4 (Winter 1996–97), p. 19. In fact, the issue between the

US and European intelligence services is less the willingness to share information (though that sometimes also takes place), but differences over just what constitutes 'proof'. As one US intelligence official told me, 'When Iranian leaders want something done, they rarely issue signed orders on paper with letterhead'.

6 Managing Proliferation: A View from the United States

Brad Roberts[1]

'Managing proliferation' sounds deceptively simple: organize to address the problem, throw some resources as it, periodically underscore the urgency of success, and hope for the best. In fact, responding with effective policy to the challenges posed by proliferation is a task of considerable complexity. The challenges, after all, are multidimensional. Proliferation is in part a military problem, posing force-planning and defense-preparedness requirements unlike those known to NATO allies during the Cold War. Proliferation is in part an economic problem, associated with an evolving global economy marked increasingly by the flow of technologies, materials and expertise with both civilian and military applications. Proliferation is also a political problem, reflecting the competition for influence, status and turf in the international system. Proliferation management entails the use of myriad instruments of policy to dampen the incentives of states to acquire nuclear, biological or chemical (NBC) weapons and their means of delivery; to cap or roll back proliferation where that is possible and desirable; and to take the steps necessary to ensure that such acquisitions do not change the world in ways we would not like. Effective proliferation management entails keeping these myriad tools both up-to-date and in balance.

Proliferation management has proceeded at the global level for decades. Throughout the Cold War, the transatlantic community played a strong role in support of these global processes, although sometimes with sharp disagreements about specific problems or policies. In the years since the end of the Cold War, global instruments have undergone significant evolution. The role of the transatlantic community has also evolved. The increasing prominence of disputes among the allies about the global proliferation agenda has raised a question about whether and for how long the community can continue to play a constructive role. Looking to the future, should we anticipate a divergence of interests and a weakened transatlantic role in supporting global processes? Or, alternatively, is the prospect brighter? Are there lessons to be drawn from the experience of managing proliferation that are relevant for the larger questions posed in this volume?

In a search for answers to these questions, this chapter proceeds as follows. It begins with a description of the principal proliferation management mechanisms pursued in the global arena, and reviews the transatlantic role in support of each. This analysis moves seriatium through the political, economic and military agendas. The chapter then speculates about the implications of this analysis for the larger study, and concludes with a general discussion of the nature of the interests that will shape future cooperation.

MANAGING PROLIFERATION BY POLITICAL MEANS

The first aspiration of policy is to prevent proliferation by addressing the incentives that give rise to NBC weapons-acquisition programmes. At the global level, a number of political processes are in place aimed at dealing with those incentives. In a general sense, the global effort to preserve stable relations among states, to construct an open trading system, to promote shared values, and to foster peaceful development is part and parcel of ensuring that states are not motivated to acquire massively destructive weaponry to provide for their well-being. In a more specific sense, mechanisms have been created to deal with proliferation incentives among states. Some of these are *ad hoc*, whereas others are formal and legalistic.

Ad hoc cooperation occurs in response to specific proliferation problems. The break-up of the Soviet Union, for example, posed significant proliferation risks both globally and within Europe. In order to address concerns that post-Soviet successor states other than Russia might retain or acquire NBC capabilities, the United States cooperated with partners in Europe and elsewhere to provide the political, economic and military incentives sufficient to induce states such as Ukraine, for example, not to do so. In order to address concerns about the loose control of weapons, weapons technologies and materials, and weapons-related expertise, the United States has enlisted European partners in helping Russia to implement relevant controls more effectively. The successes enjoyed by these efforts are substantial, although it is clear that risks remain and are likely to exist for an extended period into the future.

But this *ad hoc* cooperation has not proceeded according to everyone's highest expectations. Washington remains disappointed with the extent of European commitment to the so-called Nunn–Lugar process, the funding mechanism established by the US Congress to address the so-called 'loose nukes' problem. Among others, Senator Richard Lugar believes that the level of European commitment to this effort, both fiscal and political, is not commensurate with Europe's stake. Europeans, on the other hand, are typically of the view that the United States is better positioned than they to engage the Russian leadership on this question. They also note the very different capacities of the transatlantic economies to generate the funds necessary to assist Russia in this regard at this time.

The primary global processes aimed at the proliferation problem are formal, not *ad hoc*. An arms-control regime has been created over the last few decades aimed at imposing legal restraints on NBC proliferation. This regime includes the nuclear Non-proliferation Treaty (NPT), the Biological and Toxin Weapons Convention (BWC), and the Chemical Weapons Convention (CWC). How are these useful as political tools? They codify agreed rules of behaviour concerning the use of militarily sensitive technologies and materials of particular international concern, given their potential for mass destruction and their unsettling effect on interstate relations when employed for purposes of aggression. They create mechanisms for monitoring compliance with those rules, and they create the political basis for forming coalitions against non-compliant states. In a more general sense they represent an agreed allocation of rights and responsibilities in the international system, tying states of all different orientations, ideologies and capacities to the common task of preventing particularly damaging types of proliferation.[2]

A cursory glance at this global treaty regime in the mid-1990s suggests that it is in good shape. The NPT has been extended for an indefinite period (and by consensus). The BWC is the subject of a broad-based international effort to tighten its terms and strengthen compliance. The CWC entered into force in spring 1997.

But appearances may be deceptive. The manner in which NPT extension was achieved has alienated many developing countries that wanted to see the treaty survive but not to lose their leverage over the nuclear weapon states (by granting indefinite and unconditional extension of the treaty, rather than making its extension conditional on more progress by the nuclear weapons states in implementing their commitment to eliminate their nuclear stockpiles). The process of strengthening the BWC may yet falter on the basis of disinterest in arms control generally among leading Western nations, or because of their failure to agree on how to strengthen it. CWC implementation may also go awry, if significant numbers of possessors of chemical weapons choose to remain outside the regime or fail to meet their destruction obligations within the agreed timeframe. Failure to carry forward the momentum towards a strengthened global treaty regime could have significant consequences, casting sharp doubt on the institutions that remain in place and eroding the foundations of consensus and principle that have brought the international community together to criminalize certain types of state behaviour.

The transatlantic community has a particular role to play in this process of sustaining momentum. In the past, it has cooperated as the so-called Western group in negotiating and implementing the treaty regimes, and its ability to focus analytical and political resources on key problems has been instrumental in overcoming obstacles. In the endgame of the CWC negotiation, for example, Western group consensus proved the core of the final treaty bargain. Today, no other group of countries – and indeed no single country – has the capacity to carry forward the multilateral effort. (To be sure, many single countries or groups have the capability to spoil the process.) But the Western group identity has weakened as its erstwhile negotiating partners – the non-aligned and Eastern groups – have lost and/or remade their identities. It is no longer quite as clear as it once was what particular interests set the transatlantic community apart from the rest in these global processes. Identities are inchoate, even if the will to cooperate in these venues remains.

In looking to the future of this global arms control regime, the transatlantic community will face a common challenge in responding to the growing prominence of developing countries in the multilateral arms control process. It must be attentive to the necessity of supporting the aspirations of other countries to play more prominent roles in overseeing and implementing these treaties. It must also be attentive to their view that such treaties are useful not least for helping to adjudicate changing relations of power and authority in the international system. At a time when the developing world is developing (at least, significant parts of it), the developed world must respond to the new stature and impact of countries outside the transatlantic community and should more firmly attach international institutions to the aspirations of those countries.

In the future, the transatlantic partners will also face the specific challenge of responding to changes in their own relative power positions. One of the central roles of the Europeans is to keep the United States engaged in and focused on these various tasks. As a country more attuned to its status as 'the world's only superpower' than to the requirements of multilateralism, the United States needs good friends to ensure a sufficient element of constancy in its work on the treaty regime – especially those who have worked with it in its most strikingly successful multilateral enterprise, namely NATO. The United States can also play an essential role for Europe, by encouraging it to speak with a unanimity sufficient to the task of consensus within the various arms-control regimes.

The Compliance Conundrum

The most basic emerging challenge to the global treaty regime is posed by the compliance agenda, which is a political issue par excellence. Political emphasis is clearly shifting,

from the negotiation of treaty elements to treaty implementation. Implementation entails enforcement. Here global processes are not so well advanced, and transatlantic friction is
already pronounced.

Ensuring compliance with existing treaty obligations is
bedeviled by the fact that it is up to the states parties
themselves – and not to some supranational treaty organization – to determine for themselves whether others are in
compliance (although they may draw upon the findings of
the International Atomic Energy Agency or the Organization
for the Prohibition of Chemical Weapons for that purpose).
To deal with particular instances of suspected non-compliance
entails building international political coalitions among key
interested states. Part of the utility of arms control today is
that it helps to assemble such coalitions, by elaborating common values, interests and undertakings. At the same time, one
of the shortcomings of these arms-control mechanisms is that
they ultimately must turn to the UN Security Council to
ensure compliance where differences of opinion on whether
or how to secure compliance are manifest. Such differences
have been evident in the debate about how to restore North
Korea's compliance with its NPT obligation. A transatlantic
rift has been especially visible in the debate over how to
secure Iraqi compliance with its international treaty obligations and with the duties imposed upon Baghdad by the UN
Security Council to abandon and destroy its weapons of mass
destruction.

The history of the transatlantic relationship on the treaty
compliance question is a troubled one, with sharp debates in
the 1970s and 1980s about the scale and importance of Soviet
non-compliance with its treaty obligations and sharp debates
today about Iraq and Iran. Hints remain of Cold War vintage
ways of thinking about such compliance, in the form of
Americans too willing to rely on privately-held information
to charge non-compliance, and Europeans too automatically
skeptical of US charges. If Europeans and Americans are to
speak with one voice on compliance issues, and are to build
broader coalitions within the multilateral regime on problems
of non-compliance, it seems necessary to depoliticize somewhat that aspect of their relationship concerned with the hard
end of arms control, the enforcement end. Depoliticization

might be well-served by some greater sharing within the community of proliferation-related intelligence.

One further facet of this compliance debate relates to Article VI of the NPT – the article committing the nuclear weapons states to move toward nuclear disarmament in the context of general and complete disarmament. Among European arms controllers, pressures are mounting on the United States to get on with the task of implementing this commitment. (The pressures on Britain and France are less, given their substantially smaller nuclear weapons inventories.) But among European security specialists, the US nuclear guarantee remains an article of faith. Until now, it has been possible to ignore these sharply different perspectives, but with the Cold War gone the two seem headed towards a clash. Either Article VI implementation will come to be broadly accepted as a long-term and relatively remote possibility, or the Alliance – and its three nuclear-armed states – will abandon its nuclear element. Making this choice, and building consensus around it, appears a daunting task.

MANAGING PROLIFERATION BY ECONOMIC MEANS

Economic tools are also employed to dampen proliferation incentives. These tools include both sanctions and export controls.

Sanctions

Sanctions are employed to isolate states and to punish them for behaviours deemed unacceptable by others in the international community. Sanctions have often been brought into being by the UN Security Council and applied with broad international support, such as those directed against Iraq after its invasion of Kuwait. Sanctions have sometimes been employed on an *ad hoc* basis by groups of states focused on a particular problem, such as those adopted by the Group of Seven and targeted on state sponsors of terrorism. Sanctions are sometimes employed unilaterally, frequently by the United States, with the hope that others will follow suit. At times these unilateral sanctions have some long-term impact, as in

Cuba; at other times they are the source of immediate international friction, as in the case of Iran. Unilateral sanctions typically offer little leverage in a global economy in which sources of supply and exchange are numerous and increasing, although they can have some utility when they can be targeted against firms that wish to participate in major markets abroad and/or against states without large reserves of natural resources, such as oil.

The history of transatlantic cooperation on proliferation-related sanctions is particularly complex. Europeans and Americans have often agreed on countries of particular concern and on the sanctions likely to have most effect – as for example against countries known to sponsor terrorism. Sometimes they have agreed that specific countries pose proliferation risks, but not on the means to induce future behaviours desirable from the non-proliferation perspective. This is true for example of Iran.

The transatlantic community shares concerns about the future direction of Iranian NBC weapons programmes and desires to shape Iranian strategic choices so that it chooses cooperation over confrontation with the international community. But very different ideas exist – and not just between but within states of the transatlantic community – on how best to secure this outcome, and on the utility of sanctions towards that end. Many Europeans believe that the United States is motivated more by animosities related to the fall of the Shah and the hostage crisis than by a sound reading of Iran's nuclear weapons programme; they especially criticize US efforts to extend the extraterritorial reach of US law to firms located in Europe and doing business with Iran. Many Americans believe that Europeans are simply looking the other way while setting an unreasonably high standard of proof for the nuclear allegations, simply to curry political favour with Iran, advance economic interests, and demonstrate a bit of independence from Washington. This dispute is reminiscent of earlier ones over oil pipelines from the Soviet Union and policy towards Pakistan.

Transatlantic frictions on sanctions-based non-proliferation strategies have been amplified by efforts from Washington to coerce a greater degree of cooperation from its European partners. Under the aegis of legislation encompassed in the

Helms–Burton and D'Amato Acts, the Clinton administration has been compelled to attempt to exploit US economic leverage over the Europeans in order to induce them to curtail commercial relationships between firms in their nations and countries suspected in Washington of not complying with US non-proliferation expectations. These acts have eroded European and Canadian willingness to cooperate with Washington to deal with proliferation risks. To some Europeans, they smack of a time now past when they had to bend to US preferences because of its leading role in confronting the Soviet threat. To some Americans, European umbrage at these acts belies a resistance to American leadership and a wavering commitment to non-proliferation principles. So far at least, the corrosive effect of these matters has been limited. But it could well grow if greater transatlantic agreement is not built on the desirability and utility of such sanctions.

Export Controls

If sanctions are one type of economic tool, the other is export controls. The utility of such controls in combating proliferation is not well-understood. Such controls do not hinder trade so much as they direct it in certain desirable directions, make it more transparent, and bring it into alignment with international agreements and norms. They are also useful for helping to dampen the competitive commercial pressures among states of the kind that Saddam Hussein exploited to assemble Iraq's NBC weapons programmes. Export controls are in fact export licensing systems. Because of the diversity of supply internationally, such licensing systems can only be effective in achieving these purposes if they are pursued in concert with other suppliers, so that the licensing decisions can be informed by common knowledge.[3]

This points to the necessity of coordinating mechanisms in each of the areas of sensitive trade. Over the decades, such mechanisms have been elaborated by interested states. This began in the nuclear domain early in the Cold War with creation of the Nuclear Suppliers Group, and expanded in the 1970s with the Zangger Committee. It continued in the 1980s with creation of the Australia Group, aimed at enhancing cooperation among suppliers of materials and technologies sensitive from the point of view of chemical warfare, whose members extended their interest to biological matters in the early 1990s. The Missile Technology Control Regime (MTCR) was created in the mid-1980s with a similar purpose.

The transatlantic community has cooperated extensively and effectively in bringing these mechanisms into being and promoting their good use. By and large, transatlantic partners have shared intelligence, opted not to pursue narrow commercial advantage, and enforced licensing provisions. They have also supported expanded participation in each of these mechanisms over the last decade, in response to the emergence of new suppliers or newly-willing partners (such as Russia). An important friction has existed, however, between those who see such controls as interim measures, to be pursued on a short-term basis until formal negotiated disarmament measures can be implemented, and those who see such controls as the primary tool of policy for the foreseeable future. This is sometimes expressed as a conflict between Europeans and Americans, but the debate appears to be split along different lines and to reflect differences of opinion within many governments about the optimal balance of economic, political and military instruments.

This *ad hoc* form of cooperation in the economic domain to secure non-proliferation goals is most troubled in its newest phase. This is also where the deepest transatlantic divisions currently exist. That phase has to do with the effort to create a post-Cold War framework for cooperative export licensing in the generic dual-use domain (that is, on those materials and technologies with both civilian and military applications). During the Cold War, the Soviet Union was the target of a large Western effort to prevent it from acquiring such materials and technologies. Under the aegis of the Coordinating Committee on Export Controls (COCOM), the Western allies coordinated sensitive exports under a system largely dictated by Washington.

In autumn 1994, COCOM ceased to exist. In late 1996, its successor, the so-called Wassenaar Arrangement, came into being. Its goal is improved international coordination of the transfer or sale of militarily-sensitive materials not otherwise controlled by previously existing mechanisms. From the perspective of formal, legalistic control, it is a disappointment. It

represents the lowest common denominator among the participating states (including states from what used to be called
West, East and the Third World). Its function is strictly consultative and its work is based on limited information-sharing;
controls are nationally implemented and not subject to veto by
others. To prevent or interrupt sales or transfers deemed unacceptable requires a great deal of cajoling and arm-twisting.
Especially on sales of major conventional weapon systems,
lack of agreement seems certain given the sharply differing
commercial interests among major participants and different
perceptions of various regions. From the start it has been
bedeviled by the unwillingness of its participants to offend
any country or countries by singling them out by name as
countries of proliferation concern. Europeans wish not to be
tarred as merely doing Washington's bidding in its ideological
wars with those it deems rogues. Washington sees European
reluctance as feckless.

On the other hand, the Wassenaar Arrangement, like the
Australia Group and MTCR before it, may gain in size and
impact with time. Membership has already expanded beyond
the original 28 states, and more seem likely to join in future
years. The list of controlled items may well expand over time.
Consensus about which transfers and sales are stabilizing and
which destabilizing may prove easier to achieve than past
experience suggests, given the passing of the bipolar Cold
War order. The pattern of dialogue and cooperation that it
establishes may prove essential if, at some later time, a crisis
tied to an ill-considered transfer or sale leads to heightened
political interest in controlling such trade.

Prospects

This effort to coordinate economic tools of policy seems likely
to face a number of additional pressures in the future.

One arises from the US domestic political scene. Some in
America are attempting to mobilize a political constituency
around the view that the Clinton administration has been soft
on proliferation issues and has failed to exploit full US economic leverage to gain achievable non-proliferation goals.
They look with nostalgia upon COCOM and call for its re-
creation, without explaining how it might be possible to

recreate the constellation of international forces that gave rise to COCOM in the first place.[4] Some on the Right also attack export controls as contrary to the nation's economic interests or as dangerously naïve in preventing weaponization by willful adversaries. Of course, others on the Left attack sanctions as contrary to the spirit of international cooperation. This is a view that resonates greatly in the developing world, where the most vocal members of the Non-Aligned Movement attack such controls as tools of the rich and secure aimed at keeping the rest weak and insecure. This points to an important European role in working to sustain common international views of the necessary and appropriate role of export controls.

A second pressure arises from the changing nature of dual-use technologies and materials. During the Cold War, there was a relatively small set of technologies and materials generated in military research and development (R&D) programmes and spun off into the commercial sector. Today, the technology flows in reverse, with an ever-larger set of commercial items lending themselves to military applications – including electronics, biotechnology and advanced manufacturing techniques, for example. This seems likely to require an increasing emphasis on transparency and self-policing in balancing the right to reap economic benefits with the need to prevent misuse for war-making purposes.[5]

A third pressure arises from the task, discussed elsewhere in this volume, of managing the emerging global economy. The effort to institutionalize a global free trade system has proceeded largely independently of the effort to ensure the necessary measure of export licensing coordination in the dual-use areas. If major problems erupt in either area, the other is likely to pay a price. A breakdown of the effort to channel dual-use trade towards commercial and not military purposes could induce a political backlash against expanding international trade, if the public comes to believe that individual firms are exploiting war and war-making tyrants in the pursuit of profits. A breakdown of the effort to build a global economy based on liberal principles, with the result that trade-blocs emerge and trade relations become more competitive and less cooperative, would have a more ambiguous effect on export controls. It could be counted on to increase interest among like-minded states to cooperate on an *ad hoc* basis to constrain dual-use trade, at precisely the same time that their leverage in the global economy would be slipping.

MANAGING PROLIFERATION BY MILITARY MEANS

Military means are also a tool of proliferation management. In a general sense, the existence of military alliances can help to dampen proliferation incentives, much as US security guarantees to Germany and Japan in the early Cold War years helped to allay concerns about their future weapons prowess. At the global level, the UN Security Council also operates on the security perceptions of key proliferators, whether as a final guarantor of the major arms-control treaties or as a body of states specially charged with preserving international peace and stability. In 1992, the permanent members of the Security Council, meeting for the first time at the head-of-state or head-of-government level, stated their view that proliferation constitutes a threat to the peace and thus potentially legitimizes Security Council military action.[6]

Military tools of policy are potentially useful for a number of purposes. From the perspective of the proliferator, effective military counters to NBC threats can help to establish that any attempt to use NBC weapons for aggressive purposes, whether for coercion or battlefield success, will prove unsuccessful. If such weapons are acquired only with international opprobrium and at some risk and, moreover, promise no likelihood of success, then the incentives to acquire them in the first place should decline. Military preparations by security guarantors are also useful for reassuring the potential victims of NBC attack that such attacks can be deterred and, if not deterred, that their effects can be minimized if not neutralized.

Looking to the past, Europeans and Americans have found it possible to cooperate on many elements of this agenda. As permanent members of the Security Council, Britain, France and the United States have made common cause to support the statement cited above. NATO defense preparations have also helped to reassure a number of European states that NBC acquisition would be unnecessary.

In recent years, NATO planners have come to a new understanding of potential proliferation challenges. As NATO undertakes out-of-area operations in the Balkans, it must contend with the possibility that chemical and biological weapons left over from the Yugoslav arsenal (or newly-manufactured) may be used against its forces. As it contemplates other out-of-area operations in zones of conflict, it must contend with the vulnerability of its forces to NBC attacks and with the availability on the international arms market of many high-leverage weapon systems. As it rethinks the challenge of protecting member nations from direct attack, it must cope with the realities created by the diffusion of NBC weapons mounted on long-range delivery systems. Looking to the future, NATO defense planners recognize that the means to produce and stockpile chemical and biological weapons, long-range delivery systems, and many advanced conventional munitions will have diffused broadly around its perimeter.

To think through the challenges of mounting successful military operations in this type of evolving security environment, NATO in 1993 composed a Defense Group on Proliferation (DGP). Its work has proceeded in phases, under joint cochairmanship by the United States and a rotating European partner. It has proceeded 'at 16', meaning that France has been a full participant in the process. Much of its agenda has been driven by the US counter-proliferation initiative.

In phase one, the group undertook to better understand the military risks posed by the proliferation of NBC weapons. This work helped to break down ways of thinking about the problems of nuclear, biological, and chemical warfare that developed during the Cold War. Among DGP participants, chemical and biological warfare are now subjects to be taken seriously and, analytically speaking, nuclear warfare has been stripped of its mutual-assured-destruction context. One of the striking features of this work was the willingness of group members other than the United States to begin to contemplate the ways in which military capabilities beyond the European theatre might influence NATO interests.

In phase two, the group undertook to assess the gaps between the military requirements created by NBC proliferation and the existing capabilities of NATO forces, as broadly defined to include not just deployed combat systems but operational art and effectiveness. This work helped to bring into focus specific ways in which proliferation translates into military advantages for aggressors *vis-à-vis* NATO forces.

In phase three, the group undertook to identify the steps necessary to close the gaps between threats and capabilities. The result was an agreed agenda of hardware procurement, doctrine reform, training activities and operational steps that can be acted upon by broader NATO leadership and member nations. This agenda was endorsed at NATO ministerial meetings in June 1996. Subsequently, NATO members sought to fund and implement the agreed agenda.

This transatlantic dialogue on proliferation has gone farther than many expected when it began.[7] Europeans were reluctant to engage in a discussion of the US counter-proliferation agenda, not least because they perceived counter-proliferation to be a cover for an aggressive campaign of preemptive attack by the United States on the NBC weapons programme of states it deems rogues.[8] The United States seemed in contrast to have done a good deal of thinking about proliferation as a challenge to US global interests and roles, but relatively little thinking about what issues might be of distinctly transatlantic interest – and about how to translate its concerns about proliferation into a suitable military posture. Europeans seem to have satisfied themselves that counter-proliferation is not about preemption, except perhaps in circumstances analogous to the campaign of strategic bombing that preceding the ground attack in Desert Storm. And Americans seem to have determined that NATO has something important to contribute to the task of meeting proliferation challenges.

Nevertheless, four challenges appear on the horizon. The first of these is translating the DGP's agenda into a programme of action that is politically and economically sustainable within key NATO countries. This will be a difficult task at a time of shrinking defense budgets. Towards this end, carrying forward the educative function of the DGP is necessary. Both up the decision-making ladder to more senior policy-makers, as well as down the ladder to officers responsible for operations, old ways of thinking about the NBC problem remain deeply engrained. The United States will have a particularly important role to play in sustaining the commitment to improved counter-proliferation capabilities; but its leverage will be diminished if it fails to sustain its own commitment to improved NBC defenses. Indeed, the contrast between statements by senior Clinton administration policy-makers supportive of improved chemical and biological war-fare defenses, and the chronic weakness of those defenses as exacerbated by ongoing defense cuts and base closures, is already a subject of discussion among Europeans who count on US leadership to carry forward the DGP agenda.

This will be tied to the second, more general, challenge of building consensus about the desirability of NATO out-of-area operations. NATO members remain divided about the Alliance's role in promoting security in other regions of the world. They are uncertain of the risks posed by such insecurity and thus of their stake in dealing with it. Calculations of risk and stake are likely to be significantly reshaped if regional conflicts come to be seen as NBC conflicts. Their perceived risks are likely to increase, but so too the perceived stake in finding a solution that reaffirms existing non-proliferation norms and mechanisms.

The third challenge is achieving consensus on missile defenses – whatever the final point of consensus might be, whether no deployment in Europe, limited deployment or deployment of a robust system. The threat posed to Europe by ballistic missiles, and increasingly by cruise missiles, seems certain to grow in the years and decades ahead. Some Europeans have become interested in a European missile defense, while others see the American urgency about such defenses as nothing more than an effort to get Europeans to buy some expensive American goods. Moreover, the United States appears headed towards at least some limited form of strategic defense in the next decade or two, and more definitely and immediately towards improved theatre missile defenses.[9] These trends will put onto the NATO agenda an issue that it seems to find quite difficult – whether, when and how to deploy missile defenses.

The fourth challenge relates to the future of nuclear weapons in NATO. Despite the long-familiar nuclear order in NATO, the transatlantic relationship has been characterized by a variety of approaches to a string of nuclear items. In both the 1950s and 1990s, the United States has found itself at odds with its European partners on the control of fissile materials, as manifest most recently in the dispute over extension of the agreement between EURATOM and the United States. The sharp international criticism of the French nuclear testing programme of 1995 is a strong reminder of the historical tensions between the three nuclear-armed members of the NATO Alliance on items like testing, test bans, force modernization, force structures and nuclear arms control.

Looking to the future, nuclear matters seem likely to continue to fester in transatlantic relations. NATO nuclear doctrine has firm foundations in the strategic realities of transatlantic cooperation and the transatlantic balance of power, and it is virtually inconceivable that the US nuclear guarantee will be withdrawn from Europe at any time in the foreseeable future. But issues of NATO nuclear strategy will inevitably emerge as its nuclear-armed members make plans for the future disposition of their arsenals. Decisions about nuclear modernization and nuclear arms control seem likely to be driven by debates about how such forces can be used to deal with strategic problems of the twenty-first century, and thus not least with the weapons programmes of proliferation concern. Issues of nuclear strategy also seem likely to be forced onto the NATO agenda as its members begin to think through the challenges of meeting a regional aggressor armed with NBC weapons, especially if that aggressor were to conclude that it might be possible to split the transatlantic alliance by exploiting differences in the nuclear policies and interests of NATO members. An open review of NATO nuclear strategy at this time would raise many questions about the utility of nuclear weapons and their role in Alliance strategy, questions that many would find difficult, not least because they would challenge so much of the accumulated sentiment within interested publics about such questions. The DGP process evidently concluded that such a review is not necessary at this time.

PROSPECTS

This survey reveals a high level of transatlantic cooperation in meeting the global proliferation problem. The existence of focused and effective strategies backed by institutionalized mechanisms and a track record of common effort leads logically to an assessment that, despite the challenges enumerated above, the future will see continued cooperation and success. How valid is this assessment?

Clearly, the history cited above is punctuated by a good deal of conflict within the transatlantic community, some of it heated. On the political agenda, the crisis over Iraqi compliance with its international obligations has brought to the fore fundamentally different notions about how to cope with states whose leaders reject the norms and institutions of international community. The appearance of deep fissures among the permanent members of the Security Council on questions as fundamental as non-proliferation and arms-control enforcement could embolden future aggressors to target and exploit those fissures. This could well have the effect of accelerating the passing of an era in which the major powers have seen the world in more-or-less similar terms.

On the economic agenda, disputes over sanctions and states like Libya and Iran are a reminder of the sharply competitive economic interests that coexist with transatlantic cooperation. In the future, there is certain to be a continuing need to balance competitive economic interests with shared security ones. The end of the Cold War took away the monolithic military threat that had compelled Western countries to a significant degree of cooperation, even when separate national economic interests were hurt. As argued above, proliferation does not so readily translate into a monolithic threat and thus competitive pressures seem likely to be intense in the years ahead, especially as disappointing economic performance in many countries induces many politicians to put heightened emphasis on job-creation.

On the security agenda, disputes ring loudest on preemption. NATO members have very different perceptions about the value and propriety of preemptive military strikes. Although counter-proliferation is not a preemptive strategy, the United States does consider the possibility of such strikes to eliminate weapons stockpiles seen to pose particularly urgent and immediate military threats, as, for example, in the context of the air campaign that preceded the Gulf War. The willingness of NATO allies to prepare themselves to participate in defensive coalitions to reverse NBC-backed aggression will not readily translate, if at all, into a willingness to back Washington in punitive strikes on NBC arsenals and production plants.

But the existence of disputes past, present and future does not spell the end of transatlantic cooperation on proliferation. It is a reminder of how much cooperation has achieved and how much work there is yet to be done. The key issue is whether interests overlap sufficiently to counterbalance the frictions noted here.

Seen in long-term perspective, the shared transatlantic interest in preventing the proliferation of weapons of mass destruction and of other forms of high-leverage military capability seems clear. Proliferation cuts across every facet of the transatlantic community's interests. Failure to generate the necessary political resolve to deal with proliferation issues is likely to greatly impair the transatlantic community's ability to cooperate on the cross-cutting issues with which proliferation intersects. Failure to coordinate sufficiently in the economic domain will have negative consequences for future economic growth. As argued throughout this volume, the transatlantic community has a general interest in deepening patterns of cooperation in the international system and broadening the stability upon which such cooperation is built; this interest would be threatened by the prospect of a more anarchic system that might result if proliferation emboldens predatory states or generates arms race instabilities. Singling out the proliferation issue as somehow separate and distinct from the larger post-Cold War security agenda is likely to be as useless as Cold War vintage attempts to separate arms control from the political realities of East–West confrontation.

Another way to illustrate the shared long-term interest in non-proliferation is to speculate about the consequences of a breakdown in transatlantic cooperation on proliferation. In meeting future regional contingencies, especially along Europe's periphery, NATO members might find themselves blackmailed into inaction and otherwise coping with the ambitions of a challenger warmed to aggression by NATO's appeasement. In meeting the stresses of a competitive economy, Europeans and Americans could find themselves drawn into a competition for sales to NBC weapons programmes in the developing world, which seems certain to produce a public backlash, a clampdown on the trade of sensitive industries, and the related economic burden. If Europeans and Americans fall out over the arms-control agenda, they may find that the existing global treaty regime slips rapidly into history. Given the rapid ongoing diffusion of the technologies and materials to make weapons of mass destruction, the transatlantic community could find itself coping with sudden shifts in the global balance of power and with the emergence of new challengers to Western interests and to global norms.

So long as interests overlap, some form of cooperation seems likely. The essential question then is whether those interests will be seen to overlap sufficiently to permit effective cooperation, as opposed to cooperation at the lowest-common-denominator level. This is a matter of perceptions. Differences of perception sometimes get magnified in the transatlantic debate. For example, despite the friction over Iran, there is broad agreement that Iran is a nation ambitious for enhanced political and military standing and a sponsor of terror whose aspirations to a regional and global role could be unsettling within and beyond the region. Differences are over tactics in dealing with the Iran of the moment, not the overall goal of working to prevent its emergence as an aggressive and over-armed state. The history of debate on questions of military strategy, nuclear policy, arms control and non-proliferation suggests that the sharp words that sometimes fly across the Atlantic have tended to work over time to resolve differences of perception and to lead to common approaches on effective strategies – in other words, to get beyond perceptions to common interests.

Whether the transatlantic community can resist the lowest-common-denominator in the years ahead is of course uncertain. In the area of economic responses to proliferation, the lowest-common-denominator prevails for the moment, at least, in the Wassenaar Arrangement. But the other economic mechanisms discussed above strongly suggest that effective cooperation on economic matters and nonproliferation will continue. The transatlantic community has done much better on the military dimension, and the agenda sketched out by the NATO DGP process promises to carry forward Alliance debate and actions.

The community's future success on the political agenda seems the most uncertain. Europe remains half-born, its capacity to form and implement a common policy held hostage to the troubled process of building a united Europe. The United States remains a reluctant superpower, engaged but tempted by isolationism, still learning what it means to be first-among-equals. Europeans, Canadians and Americans could find common cause in a comprehensive global regime that shapes the way nations acquire, use and control weapons of mass destruction. Or they may allow this regime to fall prey to competing interests and perceptions and short-term national interests.

IMPLICATIONS

What does this look at the proliferation problem suggest about the larger questions posed in this volume? What does it indicate about the future direction of the transatlantic relationship and its capacity to act as a positive force in the global arena? Elsewhere in this volume, three propositions have been offered about the transatlantic relationship. One is that the United States takes a more global view, and Europe generally takes a more regional one. The second is that the United States prefers unilateral over multilateral approaches, unlike the Europeans, who prefer the opposite. The third is that the United States prefers military solutions to political ones, again unlike the Europeans, who prefer the opposite. This focused look at the proliferation problem provides an opportunity to test these hypotheses.

Global vs Regional

The disputes recorded in the history of transatlantic efforts to manage proliferation are a reminder of the different orientations of states on each side of the Atlantic. The United States tends to look at the world in global terms, given its far-flung Alliance commitments and role as a security guarantor. For example, it perceives the military challenges of proliferation largely in global terms. Europeans, on the other hand, tend to look a little closer to home. They are concerned primarily about the proliferation of NBC weapons along NATO's periphery, whether in Central and Eastern Europe where NATO has peace-keeping missions, or along NATO's southern flank. Members of NATO's southern flank are especially concerned about weapons proliferation to anti-Western states or groups across the Mediterranean.

But the image of America as a global power and Europe as a regional one is a bit too tidy. America enlists partners at every turn, and sometimes seems incapable of acting without them. Historically, it has shown a clear preference for employing its military forces in coalitions of nations. In dealing with future NBC-armed aggressors, Washington is again likely to find such coalitions indispensable. Because its capacity to act as the world's policeman is greatly inhibited by sociocultural norms against the hegemonic influence of power, it needs partners, especially European ones, to help legitimize in its own eyes the use of force abroad. Moreover, Europeans are not limited to regional perspectives alone. NATO is coming to terms with its post-Cold War role as a force for stability within and beyond its immediate vicinity. Furthermore, Britain and France have both power projection capabilities and historical reasons to look at the challenges of proliferation in transregional terms.

Unilateral vs Multilateral

The American effort to employ sanctions against countries it deems rogues, and its willingness to lean hard on its allies and their firms to adhere to Washington's expectations, certainly conforms to the view of the United States as a nation willing to go it alone. This is accentuated by the common criticism of the United States as not particularly effective at multilateral arms control, as it tends to pay, at best, episodic interest to multilateral processes and to play to its advantages of size and power in ways that sometimes grate on others in those processes. Moreover, many in Washington tend to see multilateralism more generally as inconsistent with the freedom of maneuver that they expect for America in its 'unipolar moment'.

But, these matters aside, it is clear that the United States is involved in all of the multilateral processes relevant to the proliferation problem, often in a leading role, but sometimes also in a role aimed at encouraging others to offer some leadership. Even in the military domain, the effort to enhance the capacity to act against NBC-armed adversaries embodied in the counter-proliferation initiative is matched by a high-level effort to assist US allies to make the same preparations. Counter-proliferation is often dismissed by critics as an exercise in punitive unilateralism by the United States, when in fact the transatlantic counter-proliferation agenda is aimed at ensuring that the European allies will have the capacity to act along with the United States when the first regional NBC-armed challenger appears. It is about promoting Europe as a global partner.

Military vs Political

On the counter-proliferation agenda, it is certainly true that the United States has been the primary driver of the NATO dialogue and that it has actively sought to improve the Alliance's capacity for military response to proliferation. It also possesses some unique military assets, including both a capacity to conduct precision attacks on well-protected facilities and to project military power over long distance on a theater-wide basis. Thus it is going to consider military options when others cannot.

But a strategic perspective of the overall US effort to manage proliferation reveals a full press on arms control, export controls, intelligence, and political and diplomatic strategies as a complement to the military dimension. The balance among them does not suit everyone's tastes – especially not in Washington – but it certainly calls into question the common criticism of the United States as single-mindedly pursuing military counters to proliferation. Moreover, there is an important question about just how viable the remainder of the agenda might be without a credible counter to aggressors armed with NBC weapons. If arms-control agreements depend ultimately for their credibility and viability on the ability of states parties to ensure compliance by particularly willful and aggressive states, then they will lose both if NBC attacks can be threatened by renegade states to dissuade others from taking the necessary steps to ensure compliance.

Moreover, if NBC weapons actually come to be seen as useful because they have been used successfully to commit acts of aggression, to secure acts of conventional aggression, or to defeat a coalition of major powers, then the world would likely change in quite fundamental ways. Thus, there is a necessary and appropriate place for military replies to proliferation, with special responsibilities falling on the United States in preparing for them, and in encouraging its allies to prepare as well. Military capabilities are essential, but so too are the other pieces of the puzzle.

The proliferation problem sheds some useful light on each of these three hypotheses. It shows them each to be simplifications of a reality that is a good deal more complex. It illuminates the changing nature of the transatlantic relationship, as well as the changing context within which it operates.

CONCLUSIONS

In summing up, it is useful to recall what this volume is *not* about: it is not about transatlantic relations *per se*. Rather, it is about how the transatlantic community operates on the global scene. This chapter has focused on one element of that global agenda: proliferation. The central conclusion will surprise many who have grown accustomed to decades of transatlantic dispute on pieces of the proliferation puzzle: managing proliferation is a task for which transatlantic cooperation is well-suited. On myriad military, economic and political agendas, past patterns and habits of cooperation translate today into new initiatives. Proliferation as such should not be mistaken as being the entire security agenda of the transatlantic community, but it does cut across a surprisingly broad set of shared interests. Its management appears truly a joint task, because no aspect of the problem is amenable to solution by one nation or even one group of nations.

In surveying future challenges, it seems likely, however, that proliferation will put new stresses on the transatlantic partnership. Translating a notional counter-proliferation agenda into sustainable military forces against NBC proliferation threats seems to require the articulation of new strategic concepts and new forms of political consensus, even as old ones prove long-lived. Sustaining cooperation on dual-use items in a changing global economy seems to require a willingness to set shared interests above national ones at a time when economic trends make this difficult. Ensuring the functioning of the arms control regime as a political instrument seems to require adjustments to the expectations and roles of many countries, at a time when some prominent ones may bristle at the necessity of accepting burdens commensurate with capabilities.

But these challenges appear surmountable. Managing proliferation involves doing things the transatlantic community is pretty good at – tending joint mechanisms, defining and enforcing rules of appropriate and inappropriate behaviour, sharing burdens, and talking both diplomatically and bluntly so that shared national interests are not swamped by competing perceptions and acrimonious rhetoric. As a community with foundations that transcend the Cold War epoch, the transatlantic community brings most of what it needs to this work. The one critical ingredient that remains in doubt is sustained political will. Happily, the process of diagnosing the proliferation problem may help to build this will, by identifying new interests, elaborating new strategic concepts, and deepening the habit of cooperation.

Notes

1. The author is grateful to Ellen Frost, Piet de Klerk, Steven Miller and Mitchel Wallerstein for their comments on earlier drafts of this essay. He alone is responsible for the arguments and conclusions presented here.
2. For more on this line of argument about the international political role of arms control in the post-Cold War era, see Brad Roberts, 'Arms Control in the Emerging Strategic Environment', *Contemporary Security Policy*, vol. 18, no. 1 (April 1997).
3. For more on export controls and dual-use materials, see US Congress, Office of Technology Assessment, *Export Controls and Nonproliferation Policy*, OTA-ISS-596 (Washington, DC: GPO, May 1994) and *Global Arms Trade: Commerce in Advanced Military Technology and Weapons*, OTA-ISC-460 (Washington, DC: GPO, June 1991). For more on the role of export controls as trade enablers, see Brad Roberts,

'Export Controls and Biological Weapons: New Roles, New Challenges', in *Critical Reviews in Microbiology*, vol. 24, no. 3 (1998), pp. 235–254.

4. See for example *The Proliferation Primer*, a Majority Report of the Sub-committee on International Security, Proliferation and Federal Services, Committee on Governmental Affairs, US Senate, January 1998.

5. Michael Moodie, 'Beyond Proliferation: The Challenge of Technology Diffusion – A Research Survey', in Brad Roberts, (ed.), *Weapons Proliferation in the 1990s* (Cambridge, Mass.: MIT Press, 1995), pp. 71–90.

6. See UN Security Council Resolution on proliferation: Note by the President of the Security Council, UN document S/23500 (31 January 1992).

7. For a history and summary of the NATO dialogue on proliferation and counter-proliferation, see Robert Joseph, 'Proliferation, Counter-Proliferation, and NATO', *Survival*, vol. 38, no. 1 (Spring 1996), pp. 111–30.

8. For a discussion of early European reactions to counter-proliferation, see Harald Müller and Mitchell Reiss, 'Counterproliferation: Putting New Wine in Old Bottles', *The Washington Quarterly*, vol. 18, no. 2 (Spring 1995), pp. 143–54.

9. See *Proliferation: Threat and Response*, 2nd edn (Washington, DC: Office of the Secretary of Defense, November 1997).

7 Managing Proliferation: A European Perspective

Harald Müller

The United States and Europe share a fundamental interest in maintaining and promoting global security, which includes stemming the proliferation of weapons of mass destruction. This common interest provides the underlying basis for future US – European collaboration on non-proliferation issues. Notwithstanding this fundamental commonality of interest, however, stark differences exist in approaching non-proliferation questions, and these pose a significant hurdle for strengthening common efforts in the future. The most notable differences between US and European approaches on this question are:

- a US preference for unilateral action against a conceptual and habitual appreciation of the Europeans for multilateralism;
- a US tendency to apply this unilateralism even after the establishment of commonly agreed rules, but before these rules have had occasion to prove their value; as against a European inclination to stick to such rules even after they have outlived their utility;
- a US inclination to deal with the Europeans one-on-one, rather than recognizing the specific institutional set-up that is characteristic of the European Union;
- differences of opinion about fuel-cycle policies that are exacerbated by a very determined US Congress that has little understanding of the intricacies of the European institutions, and tends to view the European countries as different units, not as an entity; and
- different interests and assessments concerning regional situations and concomitant appropriate strategies that could lead to acute crisis in transatlantic relations if actions are taken that violate the perceived vital interests of one of the partners.

These differences have made an impact in the various fields that have recently dominated non-proliferation policy, including: dealing with the inheritance of the former Soviet Union; handling the back-end of the nuclear fuel cycle, notably in the context of the renewal of the US – EURATOM agreement; improving the International Atomic Energy Agency (IAEA) systems of nuclear safeguards; setting up, improving and implementing export controls; dealing with the most difficult, proliferation-prone regions and countries, mainly in the Middle East and East Asia; and assessing the value of military means as an instrument to stem the proliferation of weapons of mass destruction (WMD).

In all of these cases, transatlantic disagreement was mitigated by factors of commonality. However, the common interest was most clearly borne out by the close and effective cooperation of the United States and Europe for the indefinite extension of the Nuclear Non-proliferation Treaty (NPT).

NON-PROLIFERATION IN THE TRANSATLANTIC RELATIONSHIP

The first two decades of US–European security cooperation after the Second World War were overshadowed by the nuclear proliferation problem. First, the United States abruptly cut the military nuclear collaboration with its wartime allies in order to prevent the further spread of nuclear weapons. Britain and France nevertheless 'proliferated', becoming the third and fourth nuclear weapon states. Sensing that a policy of denial was of limited utility, the United States offered its allies both a nuclear umbrella (within NATO) and broad civilian collaboration (by way of the 'Atoms for Peace' programme). This was used extensively by the Europeans, particularly after they formed the European Atomic Energy Community, or EURATOM, in 1958. From the mid-1950s to the completion of the NPT in the late 1960s, this cooperation was expanded to dissuade the Europeans, and the Germans in particular, from acquiring their own nuclear weapons. These efforts almost failed in 1957 when Germany entered an agreement with Italy and France to work on the bomb together. Only de Gaulle's coming to power prevented completion of this project. The multilateral nuclear force under the purview of NATO, later deemed incompatible with the NPT, was a further attempt to pacify the European non-nuclear weapon states' anxiety for their security. Finally, the NATO Nuclear Planning Group, a mere consultative and planning body, was created, and all European NATO allies non-nuclear weapon states ended up as parties to the NPT.[1]

Meanwhile, the Europeans installed their own non-proliferation policy process, first in the context of European Political Cooperation (EPC), an intergovernmental consultation and cooperation procedure to harmonize foreign policies, and, since 1993, in the context of the Common Foreign and Security Policy (CFSP) under the Maastricht Treaty. Working groups are dealing with nuclear, chemical and biological weapons non-proliferation. From the vantage point of CFSP, the task for the United States is therefore not to collaborate with 15 countries individually, but with a group of 15 that have set up their own common foreign policy-making process in the field of non-proliferation policy.[2]

However, in practice the situation is not quite as simple, particularly not in the field of nuclear non-proliferation. By nature of the diversity of EU membership, interests differ between the two European nuclear weapon states (France and Britain), and the 13 non-nuclear weapons states. These two groups tend to take different positions on issues such as disarmament, transparency of the nuclear weapons complexes, or the extension of IAEA safeguards in nuclear weapons states. Another division exists between those European countries with a strong nuclear industry – particularly those practicing plutonium recycling (France, Britain, Germany, Belgium, Spain) – and the more anti-nuclear-minded EU members (Austria, Denmark, Ireland). For this reason, the temptation of the United States to apply a 'divide-and-rule approach' to its European allies is rather strong.

A further complication is the role of the European Commission, which has broad competences in the peaceful uses of nuclear energy, including treaty-making power and the authority to verify nuclear material in peaceful uses in all member-states, the nuclear weapon states included. The

Commission is also to be 'fully associated' with the CFSP. However, some member-states, particularly France and the UK, watch jealously to ensure that Commission competences remain as limited as possible, while others would like to give it broader authority and freedom of action.

PROLIFERATION IN EUROPE: A SERIOUS POSSIBILITY?

When the NPT was negotiated, the industrialized states of Europe and East Asia were seen as the most problematic countries. After they all acceded to the NPT, Europe was no longer seen as a place where proliferation of WMD posed a significant problem. With the end of the East–West conflict, this certainty was seriously challenged.

The Proliferation Threat in the Former Soviet Union

Much has been said about the danger that the political revolution in Europe may lead to runaway proliferation on the continent.[3] In fact, the danger has been relatively well-contained, at least so far, though risks with regard to the security of fissile material in particular remain.[4] The acute risk that the decay of the Soviet Union could lead to 14, or at least four, new nuclear weapon states has not turned into reality: determined unilateral action by Russian authorities succeeded in bringing tactical nuclear weapons back from the other republics. And a well-orchestrated diplomatic campaign helped to persuade the three inheritors of strategic nuclear weapons outside of Russia – Kazakhstan, Ukraine and Belarus – to join the Lisbon Protocol to the START I Treaty and the Non-proliferation Treaty as non-nuclear weapons states, and to send the nuclear warheads on their territory back to Russia for dismantlement.

In this diplomatic approach the United States took the lead, but it did not act alone. Policies were closely coordinated with the European allies in three different bodies: in the North Atlantic Council, in the G-7, and in the semiannual meetings on non-proliferation which have become customary following the Transatlantic Declaration of 1990. The complementary nature of European and US policies were particularly useful in the most difficult case, that of Ukraine. While the Americans pursued a combination of sticks and carrots specifically aimed at the nuclear issue, the European Union pursued a policy of its own that complemented American arms-control efforts. The United States concentrated entirely on the nuclear question and sought to influence the Ukrainian decision with the help of security guarantees and direct financial contributions. The EU pursued a strategy whose political objective was the maintenance of an independent, economically and politically stable Ukraine as a buffer between Western Europe and Russia. In the framework of this strategy, the nuclear question was only part of the problem.[5] The Union worked out a package dealing with the whole spectrum of economic and political relations with Ukraine. The cooperation agreement brings Ukraine as close to the Union as is possible without promising membership; Ukraine's desire to be treated as an independent state was respected. The original intention to only negotiate or sign such an agreement once Kiev had acceded to the Non-proliferation Treaty was abandoned. Instead, the agreement was signed with all due ceremony, but its implementation deferred until such time as Ukraine completed the binding renunciation of nuclear weapons. Ukrainian politicians were able to see very clearly how advantageous this renunciation would be.

Meanwhile, the United States worked with Russia, France and the United Kingdom to produce the sort of country-specific security guarantees that the Ukrainian government had requested. Washington also provided a significant share of Nunn–Lugar funds to Ukraine to cover the costs of the removal of warheads from missiles and their transport to Russia, and for the dismantlement of missiles and silos. Also, the United States bore the brunt of the costs for opening an International Science and Technology Centre in Kiev, in addition to such a centre in Moscow. Finally, the US purchase of highly-enriched uranium (HEU) from Russia was shaped in such a way that part of the proceeds, supposedly proportional to the HEU share from dismantled warheads originating in Ukraine, paid for fresh Russian fuel to Ukrainian power reactors.

Most of European assistance to Russia was on a bilateral, national basis. France and Britain supplied some equipment for the safe transport, storage and dismantlement of nuclear weapons, while a larger number of European countries provided moderate assistance for physical security of nuclear materials and export controls. The European Commission helped to set up a training centre for Russian nuclear inspectors. The direct aid from Europe to Kiev in the disarmament field remained moderate (Germany helped with disposing of missile fuel, and Sweden added to the funds of the International Science and Technology Centre), but the European Union did put up a $2 billion package for nuclear safety.[6]

Clearly, this area was one where the interests of the transatlantic partners coincided, and the risk may be more in a duplication of efforts than in political discord between the two sides of the Atlantic. In order to cope with this problem, a couple of coordinating bodies work on optimizing assistance to the former Soviet Union. Such efforts go on within the G-8 group, following the Moscow nuclear summit in April 1996; the OECD which works on plutonium disposition options; and, most importantly, NATO's Group on Nuclear Weapons (GNW) that was, in May 1996, integrated into the Senior Political–Military Group on Proliferation (SGP), which is tasked with elaborating the Alliance's policy towards the whole spectrum of the proliferation problem.

Germany – A Resurgent Proliferation Problem?

As the Cold War ended, much speculation centred around whether a newly-united Germany could reconsider its nonnuclear status. It is significant that these speculations went on without any regard to the threefold renunciation of nuclear weapons by Germany – in the Protocol to the Brussels Treaty, in the NPT, and, most significant, in the Two-plus-Four Treaty that terminated allied privileges in Germany and instituted national sovereignty. The reasoning went that, with increased power and status and a more opaque security environment, Germany would strive to establish great power status through a nuclear weapon programme.[7]

This reasoning overlooks several important points. First, with the end of the East–West conflict, the major security motivation for Germany to consider nuclear weapons has disappeared. Second, Germany has become accustomed to non-nuclear weapons status to a degree that the aversion in the population against these weapons is considerable. An effort to change the status quo would cost any politician dearly, and consequently there is no political force in the country that supports this change. Thirdly, Germany is embedded in a network of international organizations with friends and partners, and these relations would be destroyed if Germany went nuclear. In fact, NATO would presumably not survive, nor would the EU. Indeed, political logic must turn the argument around: only in a Europe where NATO had crumbled, the EU disappeared, German–French friendship lay in shambles, and domestic upheavals had shattered the strong anti-nuclear consensus, would Germany ever consider acquiring nuclear weapons, if then. As long as NATO persists, that danger is mute.[8] The same reasoning applies to all other European countries. A special case is Turkey which today, like Germany during the Cold War, is most in need of credible security assurances. Turkey is located close to three major areas of unrest – the Balkans, the Middle East and the Caucasus. Again, the existence of NATO and the US guarantee is the best instrument to spare the Turkish government the agonizing necessity to consider a change in the nuclear status quo.

As a preliminary conclusion, the acquisition of weapons of mass destruction by the United States' European allies would have a destructive consequence on NATO and is conceivable only in a political environment where NATO would have ceased to exist a long time ago. To prevent proliferation in other parts of Europe, for example the Balkans, is obviously an interest shared by both the United States and Europe and would no doubt stimulate another round of intense preventative transatlantic diplomacy.

The 'European Option'

These considerations apply even to the implementation of the 'European option', that is the transformation of the British and/or French nuclear deterrent into a European force. The European Community's member-states jealously guarded this option, so when the NPT was negotiated they kept open this possibility quite explicitly in the statements that accompanied first signature and later ratification of the Treaty. The option has received renewed interest through the offer by the French government, somewhat clumsily inserted into the dispute over nuclear testing, to consider the 'Europeanization' of the French nuclear deterrent. The offer, one has to realize at the outset, was fairly limited and certainly did not include shared decision-making or even possession. Even so, the reactions were rather measured: from some friendly expression of interest by the German government, combined with a confirmation that NATO's guarantee covered satisfactorily foreseeable needs, to outright rejection by those anti-nuclear EU governments that are not bound to France by the same sort of ties as Germany. This lack of enthusiasm reflected a largely negative attitude of European publics to the idea of a European nuclear force, with vast majorities opposed in all non-nuclear weapons states, and simple majorities opposed in Britain and France. Given this political outlook, the prospect of geographical proliferation through 'Europeanization' can be left out of our considerations.

More to the point, under the terms of the NPT, only a federal European state could claim possession of and control over nuclear weapons as inheritor of what France and Britain possess. As long as CFSP remains in the realm of intergovernmental cooperation, this is not in the cards. And, judging by the provisions of the Amsterdam Treaty of 1997, it will remain so for a very, very long time. What can be expected is the emergence either of a trilateral forum to discuss nuclear matters, ranging from doctrinal issues to disarmament, between France, the UK and Germany, or – preferably – a forum open to all interested EU members. No basic change in the nuclear status quo is to be expected from such arrangements, and European–American cooperation in non-proliferation should thus remain largely unaffected by this issue.[9]

CIVILIAN USES OF TECHNOLOGIES OF WEAPONS OF MASS DESTRUCTION

Chemical, biological and nuclear technology all have important civilian applications, but the use and control of these

applications has proved to be a bone of transatlantic conten-
tion, particularly in the nuclear field.

The Civilian Uses of Weapons-usable Nuclear Materials

The core of US–European difference on this issue is the use of
weapons-usable material in the civilian fuel-cycle and in civilian
research. Since the 1970s, it has been US policy to prefer a
phasing-out of the recycling of plutonium and the employment
of highly-enriched uranium (HEU) in research reactors. On the
European side, some countries (notably France, the UK, Germany and Belgium) view matters differently. This has repeatedly led to acute controversy, most recently embedded in the
negotiations over a new agreement between Europe and the
United States.

The controversy concerned the US right of prior consent
for the uses and exports of those materials that were either
US-supplied or had been processed with relevant US equipment. The Europeans did not want to grant the United States
the right to give prior consent on a case-by-case basis. It was
feared that this could be used to impose US fuel-cycle preferences and to discriminate between the member-states of the
European Union, thus defying the principle of an integrated
market of fissile materials, one of the cornerstones of the
Rome Treaties, the 'European Constitution'. This latter aspect
rallied even those European governments behind the European negotiating position who had no interest in, or were
even outspokenly critical of, the policies of plutonium recycling.[10]

The matter was finally settled by granting programmatic prior
consent to the full area of the Union, and making withdrawal of
such consent contingent on a blatant breach of Europe's non-
proliferation commitments, in which case the full agreement –
and not only the bilateral relationship between the United States
and the state in question – would be hurt. This arrangement has
provoked strong criticism in Congress and parts of the US non-
governmental community that argue that this solution, while pleas-
ing the Europeans, deviates from core provisions of the US Nuclear
Non-proliferation Act of 1978. The precedence could be perni-
cious for prejudicing further policies towards Japan and, possibly

later on, countries with more doubtful non-proliferation credentials.

Despite these protestations, and after some intra-administra-
tion haggling, the agreement went through. It was accepted on
the European side only after some major discussions, too, as
France and other nuclear energy users discovered that in 1979
the European Commission had apparently given assurances to
the United States that were never authorized by the Council (the
highest intergovernmental decision-making organ of the European Community, now the European Union), and which had
not been included in the Commission's negotiating mandate for
the new agreement. Nevertheless these assurances were part of
the agreement reached between the Commission and its US
counterparts. This problem was also eventually sorted out,
enabling the agreement to enter into force, and preventing a far
more serious transatlantic rift than the few months without a legal
framework for nuclear commerce sustained in the first four
months of 1996.[11]

However, the issue of civilian uses of weapons-capable material is bound to continue to fuel transatlantic controversy. This
tension will be exacerbated by the decision of the German
government to support the construction of the first new
research reactor to use HEU since the late 1970s. Again,
Euratom has demonstratively backed the German position,
not least to accentuate the European independence from US
preferences concerning the civilian uses of nuclear energy.
Again, the US government, to the dismay of its NGO and
congressional critics, has indicated its aversion to risking a
nuclear trade war with both Russia and the EU over this
time. However, the deep differences in the perception of the
legitimacy – not the legality – of using weapons-capable material in civilian applications will remain a source of friction.[12]

IAEA Safeguards Reform

A different but related issue concerns the further development
of IAEA nuclear safeguards. The present reform, known as '93
plus 2', aims at enhancing the Agency's capability for detecting
unreported nuclear weapons activities. It would oblige non-
nuclear weapons states to report far more extensively about
all nuclear-related activities (rather than only about the fissile

material in their possession), and to grant access to IAEA inspectors to all sites where such activities are conducted (rather than only to those sites where fissile material is present).[13] Here, the rift did not cut exactly across the Atlantic, but divided the Europeans among themselves as well. Germany, Britain, Belgium and Spain were not enthusiastic about the IAEA proposals. Germany and Belgium were afraid of an additional safeguards burden for their industries that – in their view – would not help much to detect clandestine activities (because it relied on reporting in the first place). Moreover, they saw widening discrimination between the nuclear and non-nuclear weapons states. The United States and the majority of EU countries, however, believed that enhanced reporting would help the IAEA in discovering inconsistencies, and that enhanced access rights would give it the legal authority to follow-up these inconsistencies, considerably enhancing its abilities to detect clandestine nuclear weapons programmes.

From the fall of 1995 to the spring of 1996, differences escalated. The European dissenters complained about US arm-twisting and unwillingness even to consider legitimate concerns of close allies, and about US pressure on the IAEA secretariat to press through the US position regardless of objections. Simultaneously, the Europeans remained deeply divided, with strong misgivings building up in Germany and Belgium about what was perceived as the exploitation of nuclear-weapons state privilege by France.[14] Negotiations within the IAEA were thus initially rather confrontational and unproductive. However, the picture changed in January 1997 after the United States and Germany worked out their differences bilaterally. The negotiation group adopted a draft additional verification protocol in April 1997, and the IAEA Board of Governors approved it in June 1997. One of the most divisive rifts within the Atlantic Community during the last few years was thus successfully settled.

PROLIFERATION OUTSIDE EUROPE

Trade in Proliferation-prone Technologies

In the past, transatlantic cooperation with regard to export principles in the nuclear field had also suffered from substantial differences of approach as well as tactical disagreements. The United States has long pleaded for full-scope safeguards; that is, the termination of all nuclear exports to countries where not all fissile material was under supervision by the IAEA. While some European countries concurred, others did not, among them the major exporters: France, Germany, Belgium, Spain, Italy and the UK. Only at the beginning of the 1990s did this picture change, largely through a change of heart on the German side. By this time, it had dawned on the Germans that their liberal and over-cooperative export policy had led to results – in Pakistan, in Iraq – that were damaging the country's reputation and, after all, were not in Germany's own security interest. After Germany had turned to full-scope safeguards, the others followed rapidly and the issue was laid to rest as a source of transatlantic disagreement.[15] Today, the United States and Western Europe show a united front to Russian vacillations over export policies, and to Chinese refusal to play by the rules.

The United States and Western Europe work closely together in the major technology suppliers regimes; the Nuclear Suppliers Group (NSG), the Australian Group (dealing with chemical and biological weapons agents, precursors, and respective equipment and technology), and the Missile Technology Control Regime (MTCR). However, this collaboration is not always free from conflicts. In all cases the items under control are related to large and strategically important industries, and the problem of harmonization of policies and practices under continuing competition is confronting all participating states with a dilemma that is not always easy to work out.

Bearing in mind all necessary caveats, one can identify a common pattern across these export-control regimes: first, the United States is striving for more intensive control regimes close to the Cocom model that would afford Washington a considerable say over the decisions of its partners; the Europeans (led by the French) prefer regimes that coordinate while preserving strict sovereignty of decision for the participating parties. Second, the United States will, by and large, call for a broader range of items and technologies to be controlled, and for technical parameters that would cut deeper into the civilian side of the dual-use spectrum of controlled goods. The Europeans would rather restrict the number of listed items and narrow the parameters. Third, the United States demands tightened, embargo-like control practices against a handful of target countries, while the Europeans shy away from embargoes for all but the most extreme and evident cases.

These three levels of different style, if one can call them that, are exacerbated by the tendency of Congress (and certain US NGOs) to mistake the US government for world government, and thus to believe erroneously that the United States can impose any policies unilaterally on its hapless partners. While, admittedly, unilateralism has in the past sometimes served to call the attention of one or the other partner to its less than responsible practices, as a general line of policy it is bound to fail since export control regimes can function only on a consensual basis. The United States today does not have the necessary hegemonic resources in any of the areas subject to export control to run the show on its own. To extract its partners' effective collaboration, compromises are inevitable.[16] Policies towards Iran are a case in point. The United States has placed an economic embargo on Teheran and would very much like its partners to follow suit. For a combination of commercial greed and strategic disagreement – some do not want to isolate Iran and hope for a successful strategy of constructive engagement – Europe does not go along. While the Europeans are observing great caution in their licensing and do not permit transfers of direct-use materials and equipment usable for weapons of mass destruction, they prefer case-by-case scrutiny for dual-use transfers to a policy of outright denial. Given the degree of emotion that surrounds US–Iranian relations since the hostage drama in Teheran, European disobedience is not taken lightly by Congress, and the Clinton administration has been hard put to avoid unilateral sanctions against either companies or countries dealing with Iran.

This points to a deep-seated distrust by the Europeans of the US handling of international rules, including the case of the disputed fuel-cycle policies discussed above. That is, the Europeans view the United States as exerting leadership in establishing agreed rules for international conduct – in this case export controls – that the allies take to be the rules of the game for an extended period. The rules are hardly established when the US government, unilaterally and on the basis of national legislation, changes the rules as it sees fit, either because of alleged new insights into the problem in question, or for the sake of nationally-defined foreign-policy goals. The Europeans then find themselves in the role of the target and victim of such policies, rather than as collaborator and partner.[17]

Regional Non-proliferation Policies

Nuclear proliferation in other parts of the world has, of course, taken place, and some cases this has led to severe disagreements across the Atlantic. The grand picture, however, is one of consistent and continuing collaboration since the NPT entered into force.

In dealing with regional proliferation problems, it has become obvious that the weight of interests in Europe and the United States is not symmetrical. While both sides share the desire to avoid proliferation of weapons of mass destruction, US non-proliferation efforts are applied whenever proliferation concerns arise, whereas Europe's efforts are more regionally concentrated. The United States acts clearly as a global power, while the Europeans care far more for problems closer to home (Northern Africa, the Middle East and the former Soviet Union). This difference of intensity has been a source of conflicts. A considerable number of European countries, for example, feel that a more even-handed approach in dealing with the Middle Eastern proliferation scene would probably be helpful, while Washington continues to tilt in favour of Israel, the only nuclear weapon state in the region. The remarkable difference between softly spoken US admonitions to Israel to join the NPT, and the harsh treatment of would-be proliferators in the Arab world is telling. Europeans, notably Mediterranean countries, have frequently wondered whether a more determined request to Israel to make visible concessions would not considerably improve the willingness of the majority of Arab countries to support the international non-proliferation regimes. At the same time, Europe recognizes the special US–Israeli relationship, and it fully supports the US efforts to promote stabilization in the Middle East, including efforts to halt the spread and the probable deployment of weapons of mass destruction. This recognition very seriously limits Europe's ability, as well as willingness, to deviate too much from US non-proliferation policies in this region.

The major exception to European deference is Iran. The United States regards Iran as an outlaw state against which containment and isolation is the only policy that can be pursued. The Europeans, on the other hand, prefer a 'critical dialogue' that rests on the hope that the regime in Teheran might evolve under benign foreign influence. The brief interlude of the Mykonos incident, and the sentencing in absentia by a German court of leading Iranian politicians for their involvement in a terror act in Berlin, created the impression that US–European differences on Iran would give way to a common, more confrontational approach. However, the Europeans reacted to the election of Iranian President Khatami in May 1997 much more quickly and enthusiastically than did Washington; the 'critical dialogue' has been resumed under another name. Given strong American feelings about Iran, this issue holds the potential for a very serious transatlantic conflict, either because the Europeans are seen actively to support Iranian activities in the WMD area or are turning a blind eye to Teheran's encroachment on the Middle East peace process. Alternatively, the Europeans may gain the impression that Washington is needlessly provoking another threat to the world oil supply by risking an open confrontation.

On South Asia, the Europeans hardly pursue a non-proliferation policy worth talking about, with the exception of the full-scope safeguards policy that rules out major new supplies to both India and Pakistan. On East Asia, the potential for conflict between a fully-engaged United States and the detached and more abstract European approaches has become manifest in the dispute that occurred after the adoption of the 1994 'Framework Agreement' between the United States and North Korea. While Washington was gratified to have avoided a very dangerous escalation of the East Asian crisis and to have started down a path towards an eventual solution of the North Korean proliferation problem, some European governments (particularly France and Germany) complained aloud about US policy having compromised the IAEA and undermined the NPT. More tenacious bargaining, supported by a more determined stance on the part of the UN Security Council, they reasoned, could have extracted more concessions from Pyongyang. Needless to say, the United States had 37 000 soldiers on the ground while the Europeans had none; perspectives differed because escalation would have had to be borne by the United States rather than by its critical partners.[18]

Eventually, however, the EU did come around to support the Korean Energy Development Organization (KEDO), the mechanism set up to implement the US–North Korea Framework Agreement. The EU and United States started with a joint contribution of about $6.3 million in 1996, to be increased to $100 million over five years. In addition, some EU member states contribute funds on a national basis. The EU is now represented on KEDO's board by the Commission and the Presidency (the lead country that heads the Union for six months). It appears that with KEDO being the only game in East Asia, even the more critical European governments have been converted to the belief that opposition would be pointless. In this case, intense intra-European discussions – in addition to repeated transatlantic briefings on what KEDO was all about – had an evolutionary impact on the development of the EU position.[19]

Counter-proliferation

The constellation of hawkish Europeans against dovish Americans in the case of North Korea is somewhat curious, given the beginning of the debate about counter-proliferation; that is, using military measures to address proliferation. This term originated in Washington following the Gulf war, when it was realized that weapons of mass destruction might be confronted in a potential regional theatre of military operations. In addition, however, several political issues were added to this fundamental military rationale which tended to confuse the terms of the debate. Security analysts, military planners and defense contractors clutched on to counter-proliferation in order to secure the survival of defense programmes, projects and jobs under the umbrella of a new, fancy and fashionable mission. Ballistic missile defense-advocates easily grasped this new rationale for their old pet project. Newly-arrived officials in the Department of Defense also used counter-proliferation to put their own imprint on US policy and steal some turf from ACDA and the State Department, the lead agencies on non-proliferation, in the eternal turf battle between the Pentagon and Foggy Bottom.

As a result of this internal Washington debate, the issue of counter-proliferation was introduced into the transatlantic discussion with a momentum and a direction that disturbed and concerned the Europeans. The impression emerged that the United States wanted to replace non-proliferation diplomacy with preemptive military action. The Europeans were flabbergasted; their appreciation for the existing and emerging multilateral regimes was – and remained – high. In fact, supporting these regimes was one of the few uncontroversial cornerstones of their Common Foreign and Security Policy. Consequently, they staunchly refused to endorse the term 'counter-proliferation' in NATO, and insisted on an unambiguous priority for the diplomatic instruments of non-proliferation policy. On this they won, not least because the State Department was quite pleased to obtain this support in its intra-agency struggle.

Over time, the picture itself began to change. The United States clarified its understanding of counter-proliferation, giving it a less alarming and primarily defensive orientation, with prevention now portrayed very much as a last-resort and a highly remote possibility. At the same time, the Europeans developed a more differentiated approach. The Mediterranean countries are generally more supportive, given their proximity to the potential threat.[20] France, in particular, has become interested in the hardware questions, especially theatre missile defense. The majority of the Europeans have been convinced that, with out-of-area operations a possible and realistic mission for their troops under NATO auspices, it makes sense to protect their armed forces against a possible WMD threat, a consideration that led the UK, Germany and, until recently, France, to collaborate with the United States in developing theatre missile defense. Finally, the Europeans' worst fears have been mitigated by the clear priority given to diplomatic non-proliferation policies. This is affirmed in NATO documents, and it is also contained in the Joint Transatlantic Agenda and Action Plan of December 1995.[21] Working on the military responses to proliferation has meanwhile become a firm part of the NATO agenda, mainly due to the diligent work of the Senior Political–Military Group (SGP) and its military counterpart, the Senior Defense Group on Proliferation (DGP). The groups proceeded in three phases, starting with threat-analysis, proceeding to define military requirements, and finishing with defining shortfalls in Alliance equipment. This cycle was completed by 1997, and the Alliance has now integrated efforts for overcoming the shortfalls in its regular defense-planning cycle.[22] (For more details on the DGP, see Brad Roberts' chapter in this volume.)

Even so, differences in approach remain visible. The Europeans tend to favour the multilateral side of non-proliferation policy. For the United States, consideration of unilateral military steps meets far less resistance. This division between the European inclination for multilateralism and the US unilateral drive may become more divisive in the future, depending on whether the antipathies in Washington against multilateralism – as is the case for most of the Republican party – grows further and forces the government to act, or whether it is a transient phenomena that will soon cease.

The most dramatic indication of these differences emerged during the Iraqi crisis in fall 1997 and early 1998. For all its political and military work on dealing with military issues in the context of proliferation, NATO played no role in the crisis. Key NATO countries were deeply divided about the utility of a military response. The United States took the lead and the UK followed without hesitation. Others, such as Germany, Canada, the Netherlands and Portugal voiced more passive support. France, however, took the opposite stance, warning against a unilateral military strike and calling for a much more extended diplomatic effort. The other Mediterranean countries showed an ominous degree of indecision, ostensibly weighing the proliferation risks presented by Saddam Hussein against the dramatic deterioration of relations with their Arab neighbours that a military strike could entail.

COLLABORATION IN MULTILATERAL REGIMES: THE CASE OF THE NPT EXTENSION

Nevertheless, the transatlantic tandem can be successful working together in a multilateral environment. This was clearly demonstrated when, against many odds, in May 1995 the NPT was extended permanently and without a divisive vote.

In the US debate, this victory was often interpreted as a single-handed US success. This was not the case. The United States must be credited for its early promotion of indefinite extension and its vigorous and sustained campaign. However, the Europeans started discussing their own campaign in the fall of 1993, took a decision in the summer of 1994, and started with their diplomatic activities in the fall of 1994 in the form of a 'Joint Action' – the most powerful instrument available in their Common Foreign and Security Policy. This campaign had notable successes, particularly in black Africa and South America. It also helped provide a channel to Iran that was used successfully during the conference to convince the Iranian delegation that resistance against the consensus for extension would not be in its interest.

The campaign and activities during the extension conference itself were coordinated between the United States and the Europeans. This coordination took place through the regular exchange on non-proliferation under the Transatlantic Declaration of 1990, and through the Western Group in the preparatory committees and at the extension conference itself. However, during the preparatory phase there were complaints that the coordination did not work perfectly, that information was not flowing freely from Washington to the European capitals, and that, in fact, Europe's collaboration with a parallel Canadian/Japanese campaign worked much better.

Nevertheless, measured by the success, we should not complain. The early US determination to reach indefinite extension of the NPT helped to sway decisions in some European capitals where the issue of indefinite and unconditional extension was, for legitimate reasons, contested. In turn the softer style of European diplomacy helped to heal some wounds stricken by the very vigorous mode of US lobbying. European calls for patience and a consensus, or at least a very large majority, helped to dampen the US inclination to go for any majority that could be obtained, and not to care about the parties that might be disgruntled and alienated after a close vote.

The success of the campaign rested on several factors: a clear unity of purpose reached considerably before the event; US leadership particularly in the opening phase of the campaign; an effective, though probably not consciously devised, division of labour whereby each party played to its own strengths; and a meticulous coordination mechanism during the conference itself where practically each step was jointly considered among the major Western players as well as within the full Western group.[23] It is quite clear that these conditions are difficult to meet in areas that are not as clearly focused as the decision on NPT extension.

CONCLUSION

In drawing up the balance sheet on US–European coopera- tion and confrontation on nuclear non-proliferation issues, cooperation has the upper hand. Cooperation appears to be most successful – in the sense of achieving the agreed object- ive – when exercised in a division-of-labour mode: when Europe and the United States agree on the objective and the broad outline of the activities pursued, but each party plays to its own particular and specific strengths. However, when it comes to issues requiring the investment of resources, far closer coordination is needed; otherwise, there is a real risk of losses through duplication of effort or working at cross- purposes. Aid to the former Soviet Union in the nuclear field is a case in point. Efforts were pursued in a division-of- labour mode rather than in a coordinated way; coordination efforts were *ad hoc*, through the G-7, NATO and the Euro- pean Bank for Reconstruction and Development, but none of these organizations had a full overview of the whole problem. As a consequence, precious funds were not spent in the most economical way.

The parallel approach to cooperation (that is working for the same goal, but without effective consultation) holds less pro- mise in this issue area. The reason is that US and European positions on some issues are sufficiently divergent so that approaches that once could be pursued in parallel eventually diverged to a great extent. Nuclear export controls between 1977 and 1992–when the transition from a parallel to a coordinated approach was initiated – are a good example. Diverging approaches to proliferation in trouble spots has often been developed when different perceptions and interests exist, but there is no orderly approach to narrowing these differences. This situation contains a huge potential to drive the partners apart, with the risk of negative repercussions for the whole transatlantic relationship.

Ironically, differences might be as dangerous for transatlantic tranquillity when the Europeans are divided among themselves as when they are united. On the reform of safeguards, we witnessed strong rifts in the EU position and the potential for a detrimental transatlantic alienation between some European countries and the United States government. On Iran, the Europeans speak with one voice, but because of the particular relationship of the United States to Teheran, and the pressure engendered by Congress on this issue, the conflict must be regarded as fairly dangerous for the overall transatlantic relationship. On Iraq, the Europeans are divided again, but this does not much help transatlantic unity.

The combination of shared interests and divisive disturbances calls for an ever-closer fabric of consultation and coordination. It should go forward both in NATO and within the Transatlantic Action Plan framework. Particular emphasis should be placed on the continuous analysis of regional proliferation problems and the means to deal with them, since it is this kind of contingency that may require action in a crisis, and where transatlantic divisions could have the most damaging effects.

Notes

1. On the history, consult Bertrand Goldschmidt, *The Atomic Complex: A Worldwide History of Nuclear Energy* (LaGrange Park, Ill.: American Nuclear Society, 1982); David Fischer, *Stopping the Spread of Nuclear Weapons: The Past and the Prospects* (London and New York: Routledge, 1992), chapters II and III.

2. Harald Müller, 'West European Cooperation on Nuclear Proliferation', in Reinhardt Rummel (ed.), *Toward Political Union: Planning a Common Foreign and Security Policy in the European Community* (Baden-Baden: Nomos Verlas, 1992), pp. 191–210; and Harald Müller, 'The Export Controls Debate in the "New" European Community', *Arms Control Today*, vol. 23, no. 2 (March 1993), pp. 10–14.

3. Kurt M. Campbell, Ashton B. Carter, Steven E. Miller and Charles A. Zraket, *Soviet Nuclear Fission: Control of the Nuclear Arsenal in a Disintegrating Soviet Union* (Cambridge, Mass.: Center for Science and International Affairs, 1991).

4. William S. Potter, 'Before the Deluge? Assessing the Threat of Nuclear Leakage From the Post-Soviet States', *Arms Control Today*, vol. 25, no. 8 (October 1995).

5. *Europe*, no. 6339, 10 (October 1994), pp. 11–12.

6. As reported at the Petersberg Conference, 20/21 May 1996.

7. See, for example, John J. Mearsheimer, 'Back to the Future: Instability in Europe after the Cold War', *International Security*, vol. 15, no. 1 (Summer 1990), pp. 5–56.

8. Harald Müller, Wolfgang Kötter, *Germany and the Bomb: Nuclear Policies in the Two German States, and the United Germany's Nonproliferation Commitments*, PRIF Reports no. 14 (Frankfurt: Peace Research Institute, 1990).

9. On that issue, a useful reference is the Dossier France, 'Nuclear Deterrence and Europe', *Relations Internationales et Stratégiques*, no. 21 (Spring 1996), pp. 79–160.

10. For background cf. William Walker, *The US–EURATOM Disagreement*, discussion paper 55 (London: The Royal Institute for International Affairs, 1995).

11. *PPNN Newsbrief 30*, second quarter 1995, pp. 8–9; Ann MacLachlan, 'Impatient European Commission Gives US Assurances, Allowing Export of Parts', *Nuclear Fuel*, vol. 21, no. 6 11 March 1996), pp. 8–9; Kathleen Hart, 'Challenges to US-EURATOM Accord Fade as Congress' Review Concludes', *ibid.*, pp. 9–10; Kathleen Hart, – 'US – EURATOM Agreement Expected to Enter into Force in Early April', *Nuclear Fuel*, vol. 21, no. 7 (25 March 1998) pp. 15–16.

12. Cf. Annette Schaper, *Der geplante Forschungsreaktor in Garching – Rückfall in alte Sünderzeiten deutscher Nichtverbreitungspolitik?*, HSFK-Standpunkte, no. 3 (Frankfurt: Peace Research Institute Frankfurt, 1996).

13. Richard Hooper, 'Strengthening IAEA Safeguards in an Era of Nuclear Cooperation', *Arms Control Today*, vol. 25, no. 9 (November 1995), pp. 14–18.

14. *New York Times*, 4 June 1996; interviews by author in several European capitals.

15. The historical divergences are well-documented in Johan J. Holst *et al.*, *Blocking the Spread of Nuclear Weapons: American and European Perspectives* (Washington: Council on Foreign Relations 1986); for the change, consult Harald Müller, Matthias Dembinski, Alexander Kelle and Annette Schaper, *From Black Sheep to White Angel? The New German Export Control Policy*, PRIF Reports 32 (Frankfurt: Peace Research Institute Frankfurt, 1994).

16. For an overview of US–European differences on dealings with key states, see Philip Gordon's chapter in this volume.

17. Pierre Lellouche, 'Breaking the Rules Without Quite Stopping the Bomb', in George H. Quester (ed.), *Nuclear Proliferation: Breaking the Chain* (Madison: University of Wisconsin Press, 1981).

18. Mark Hibbs, 'Germany, Siemens Mulling Role in Implementing US – DPRK Deal', *Nucleonics Week*, vol. 35, no. 50 (15 December 1994), pp. 9–10.

19. *PPNN Newsbrief 32* (fourth quarter 1995), p. 12; *PPNN Newsbrief 33* (first quarter 1996), p. 11.

20. Harald Müller, 'Counterproliferation and the Nonproliferation Regime: A View From Germany', in Harald Müller and Mitchell Reiss (eds), *International Perspectives on Counterproliferation*, working paper no. 99 (Washington, DC, Woodrow Wilson International Center for Scholars, 1995), pp. 25–36; Harald Müller and Mitchell Reiss, 'Counterproliferation: Putting New Wine in Old Bottles', *The Washington Quarterly*, vol. 18, no. 2 (Spring 1995), pp. 143–54.

21. Robert Joseph, 'Proliferation, Counterproliferation and NATO', *Survival*, vol. 38, no. 1 (Spring 1996), pp. 111–30.

22. Jeffrey A. Larsen, *NATO Counterproliferation Policy: A Case Study in Alliance Politics*, INSS occasional paper 17 (Colorado Springs: US Air Force Academy, 1997).

23. Harald Müller and David Fischer, *United Divided: The Europeans at the NPT Extension Conference*, PRIF report 40 (Frankfurt: Frankfurt Peace Research Institute, 1995); and Lewis A. Dunn, 'High Noon for the NPT', *Arms Control Today*, vol. 25 no. 6 (July/August 1995), pp. 3–9.

8 The United States and the European Union in the Global Economy

Stephen Woolcock[1]

In Madrid in December 1995, the European Union and the United States agreed on a New Transatlantic Agenda (NTA) and an accompanying Action Plan for strengthening bilateral commercial relations. In this chapter, I discuss the NTA and other bilateral initiatives against the background of US and European responses to the current challenges posed by the global economy, such as increased interdependence or globalization. The approaches adopted by both the United States and EU in dealing with the growing importance of 'beyond-the-border issues' in commercial relations will also be considered, as will the effectiveness of each as actors in the global economy. I argue that both are seeking to adjust their respective roles in the international trading system. The EU is in the process of adjusting to a relative increase in its role, the United States to a relatively decreasing role. At present neither is able and/or willing to shape outcomes in the international economy alone, but together they can shape both agendas and outcomes. I conclude by considering whether efforts to strengthen bilateral cooperation will result in effective joint US and EU leadership of the global economy, and whether this would be a good thing.

THE CHALLENGES OF A GLOBAL ECONOMY

Although the challenges faced by the United States and the EU in the international economy have a lower political profile than immediate or direct threats to their security, US and EU responses to those challenges will have profound effects on bilateral relations, on the stability and nature of the international trading system, and thus ultimately on global security.

The challenges emanating from the international economy are threefold. First, there is the progressive increase in economic interdependence. The success of the post-1945, US-led liberal multilateral trade system in reducing tariff and non-tariff barriers to trade has provided the basis for a global system of trade and production. During the 1980s, liberalization of investment gave a boost to this process of 'globalization' and created conditions in which countries and regions now complete in the production of goods and services, as well as in attracting inward direct investment. In this competition, a range of national or sub-national regulatory policies on issues – ranging from food and product safety and environmental protection, to competition, investment and financial market regulation – have become important determinants of market access and thus the subject of commercial diplomacy. The 'globalization' process can be seen as moving from a form of 'shallow economic integration'[2] to a situation in which trade policy reaches 'beyond the borders' of sovereign states to touch on a range of domestic regulatory policies. Dealing with such interdependence in bilateral and multilateral commercial relations is the first major challenge for the United States and European Union.

A second challenge comes from widening of the established 'Western dominated' international order to include emerging markets that have been experiencing prodigious growth as well as from the transition economies, most notably China and Russia.[3] The integration of countries such as China, Russia and the other 'transition' economies is of special strategic importance. But neither the United States nor the EU are interested in widening World Trade Organization (WTO) membership if this means accepting lowest-common-denominator rules. If the aim is to deepen the coverage of multilateral rules to include issues such as investment or the environment, and thus keep pace with developments in increased interdependence, can this be achieved with more heterogeneous membership of the system? Striking the right balance between deepening and widening requires effective leadership of the multilateral system. To opt for widening at the expense of effective multilateral discipline is likely to precipitate greater use of unilateral or regional approaches. To push ahead with deepening could equally leave many developing and transition economies behind, and miss the strategic opportunity of establishing a genuinely global and liberal trading system.

A third, related, challenge is the freeing of commercial policy (trade and investment policies) from the self-restraint exercised during the Cold War on the development of competing trading orders. The removal of Soviet communism as a military and ideological challenge means that the security imperative for the West has changed, and commercial diplomacy has assumed greater importance.[4] This has been seen by some as providing 'open season' for trade wars because of the diminution of the need to avoid tensions or divisions within the Western Alliance. In reality the importance of US – EU commercial links is such that these have for some time provided a more than sufficient deterrent against transatlantic trade wars. The more likely effect of the greater freedom for commercial diplomacy in the post-Cold War era is on relations with third countries. The end of the Cold War diminished the perceived need for the Western security umbrella to be underpinned by a *single* liberal trading order. Competition to establish commercial links with third countries, either through regional or bilateral arrangements, therefore has a freer rein. As a result a more variable geometry in international economic relations is emerging.

Regional integration and trade agreements are among the forms that this variable geometry has taken. Regional agreements can be used to reap the benefits of removing regulatory and other barriers to trade within a smaller and thus more cohesive group. The European Union, of course, is based on such integration. But during the second half of the 1980s, the United States shifted from opposing such preferential agreements to a policy that embraces various forms of regional groupings, from the Canada – US Free Trade Agreement (CUSFTA) of 1988 and the North American Free Trade Agreement (NAFTA) of 1993, to the Free Trade for the Americas (FTAA) initiative of December 1993 and Asian Pacific Economic Cooperation (APEC). By 1994, it appeared that the only region excluded by the United States from active regional free trade negotiations was Europe. This fact, along with what proved to be an unjustified European concern that the United States might drift into an isolationist position after the end of the Cold War, led various European politicians to propose a Transatlantic Free Trade Agreement (TAFTA).[5]

While the prevailing view of regional agreements in the mid-1990s was that they have, at least to date, promoted rather than undermined multilateral trade,[6] a free trade agreement between the United States and EU could have profound systemic effects on the international trading order. The creation of the WTO in 1995 and the increased participation of many countries in that organization was seen as holding out the promise of a genuine multilateral order. A transatlantic free trade agreement at such a critical time could have undermined the credibility of the WTO. On the other hand, transatlantic economic interdependence is such that considerable gains could be achieved through the removal of regulatory and other non-tariff barriers to transatlantic trade and investment.[7]

THE STRENGTH OF THE BILATERAL COMMERCIAL RELATIONSHIP

The transatlantic commercial relationship remains the most important bilateral relationship in the global economy. Two-way trade accounts for ecu 355 billion (ecu 227 billion in goods and ecu 128 billion in services), and this trade has remained more or less balanced, unlike the case of trans-Pacific trade. Divergent growth rates and exchange rate fluctuations affect the balance of trade, but true to the expectations of liberal economic models, markets generally adjust to structural imbalances. Investment is at least as important as trade, with cross investment stocks (United States in the EU, and EU in the US) totalling ecu 720 billion in 1996. The EU accounted for over 60 per cent of total foreign investment in the US in 1996 (ecu 372 billion) and US investment for 44 per cent of foreign investment in the EU (ecu 348 billion) in 1996. Transatlantic investment has doubled over the period 1989–96.

This high level of interdependence in transatlantic commerce has not happened overnight, but developed over decades. Economic interest in stable commercial relations has deterred transatlantic trade wars. This deterrence effect was apparent in the 1980s with the dispute over the participation of Western companies in Soviet energy projects, such as the Urangoy gas pipeline.[8] The effect was equally clear during the debate over the impact of the EU's Single Market Initiative on the United States[9] and in the tensions over agriculture during the conclusion of the Uruguay Round in the early 1990s. The same effect is apparent in the handling of the contentious issue of those elements of the Helms – Burton and D'Amato acts aimed at EU businesses trading with Cuba, Iran and Libya. The mutual interest in commercial links is also reflected in the continued attempts to deepen transatlantic commercial ties, as reflected in the New Transatlantic Agenda of 1995, the establishment of the Transatlantic Business Dialogue (TABD) and the latest European Commission proposals for a New Transatlantic Marketplace Agreement.[10]

In the short and medium term, the strength of this bilateral relationship represents a powerful stabilizing factor. But what of the longer-term trends? Predictions that faster growth in the emerging markets in other regions would result in a reduction in the relative importance of the US–EU commercial relationship may have proven to be premature in the light of the 1997–98 Asian economic crisis. In the longer term, the critical factor will be how the United States and the European Union respond to the challenges described above. Domestic pressures or competition for access to third markets could result in divergent policies and a progressive drift in transatlantic commercial relations. If this is overlaid by a series of specific disputes over trade or economic policies, the pace of drift could be accelerated.[11]

THE GROWING EUROPEAN ROLE IN THE WORLD ECONOMY

The importance of the European Union in the global economy (or more accurately, the European Community since it is the EC which has competence for commercial policy) has increased progressively since the formation of the EEC in 1957. The impact of the EC is threefold: by virtue of its economic weight; as a model for accommodating national policy differences while removing non- tariff and regulatory barriers to trade and investment; and as an actor in commercial negotiations.

The Economic Power of the European Union

The European Union is at least a match for the United States in terms of economic power: the EU accounts for some 20 per cent of world trade. If one includes intra-EU trade, this figure rises to 44 per cent. As noted above, it is also a major source of foreign investment, and multinational companies based in the EU complete with US and Japanese companies in global markets.

The EU has added to its economic weight through enlargement, though also to its decision-making headaches. The latest enlargement brought in Sweden, Finland and Austria in 1995, and negotiations have now started with Poland, Hungary, the Czech Republic, Estonia, Slovenia and Cyprus. A deepening of integration within Europe has also added to the weight of the EU. During the 1970s and 1980s, EU competence was extended to include a wide range of non-tariff barriers, such as subsidies and technical barriers to trade. During the late 1980s and early 1990s, EU competence was further extended to cover many areas of environmental policy, cross-border services trade, sectors such as financial services and telecommunications, and most areas of government procurement. Furthermore, European competition policy was consolidated and extended to cover mergers and acquisitions as well as cartels.

Perhaps the most significant extension of EU competence is the introduction in 1999 of a single currency, and thus of European control over the euro's exchange rate and European Central Bank control over interest rates and money supply. For years US opinion of the single currency was influenced by Anglo- Saxon scepticism; as a result, all but a few individuals have failed to consider the implications of the euro for transatlantic economic relations or the potential for cooperation in macroeconomic policy.[12] If introduced successfully (and at the time of writing all but one of the EU member-states that had not opted out for political reasons – Britain, Sweden and Denmark – qualified for membership of the single currency in 1999), the euro could have a significant impact on transatlantic economic relations. The euro is not expected to replace the US dollar as a reserve currency, at least not for some time to come, but there is likely to be a progressive growth in its use. With a single currency, the EU will also be less susceptible to external adjustment pressures than were the individual member-states. This will mean a greater relative independence from macroeconomic fluctuations for the EU, which was one of the motivations behind the introduction of a single currency in the first place. This, together with the reduction in flexibility due to the need to reach internal agreement on exchange rate and monetary policy and the need to establish the credibility of European monetary policy, is likely, at least initially, to make the EU less amenable to international economic cooperation. Given that the United States has from time to time favoured cooperation, this will have an impact on US policy and perhaps even on US public opinion regarding US–EU cooperation in other areas.

The European Union as a Model

The EU also shapes the global economy by providing a model for economic integration. This factor has become more important as the global economy has moved towards integration. Thus as interdependence increases and more 'beyond the border' issues come to the fore, the potential influence of the EU increases. For example, in the GATT Uruguay Round, negotiations on services, technical barriers to trade and government procurement were affected by the approach adopted in the EU (and by that adopted in other regional agreements, including NAFTA). When it comes to the current new issues in commercial policy such as investment, competition, environment or social policies, the EU offers a functioning model in each case. The influence of the EU model can also be found in other agreements. For example, the concept of mutual recognition developed by the EU has been widely application in both other regional agreements and multilateral agreements.

It is not possible to describe the EU model in its entirety here, but the core elements are:

(a) an approach to policy differences based on mutual recognition and home country control, in which the regulation of goods and services is determined by the regulatory standards and control of the home country;

(b) harmonization of certain minimum essential requirements of regulation and standards, which is often a precondition for mutual recognition;

(c) a comprehensive approach to coverage, as reflected, for example, in the idea of a common or single market (that is, including all four freedoms: goods, services, labour and capital), which means that reciprocity does not figure in internal EU negotiations; and

(d) supranational institutions and the precedence of European law over national law.

The EC has often been seen as a process rather than a single actor. There is, indeed, constant negotiation on such issues as environmental policy, competition policy and social policy, with modifications being made all the time. These negotiations are also broadly-based, including governments as well as non-governmental bodies, business interests and trade unions.[13] It can be argued that as the global economy becomes more interdependent, concepts of economic integration and a process of constant negotiation become more relevant than rounds of trade negotiations between sovereign states. Thus, commercial diplomacy moves more and more into patterns of behaviour compatible with the European model.

The European Union as an Actor in Commercial Diplomacy

If the EU has become influential in commercial policy because of its economic weight and as a model or process, it has also been criticized for a lack of cohesion and consistency in commercial diplomacy. Some of the EU's trading partners, including in particular the United States, have tended to confuse an inability to agree on a common European position with an inability to agree on the position the United States wants. In the Uruguay Round, the EU agreed on a mandate for agriculture, and stuck with it, but the position was not one the United States or other WTO members were willing to accept.

The EU ran into difficulties when it came to deciding what concessions to make on agriculture in order to reach an agreement with the United States. Nevertheless, there are internal tensions within the EU which affect its role as an actor in commercial diplomacy.

The first tension concerns the *competence* of the EC, in distinction to that of the member-states. Although the Treaty of Rome (Article 113) granted exclusive competence to the EC for common commercial policy, it contained no exhaustive definition of commercial policy.[14] Therefore, as commercial diplomacy has evolved it has created controversy over EC competence, the most recent example of which was the question of whether the EC or member-states (or both) should ratify the results of the Uruguay Round. The European Commission argued that, as the Uruguay Round had been negotiated as a single package, it should be ratified as a package by the EC. The member-states, led by France and Britain, argued that these issues were national or mixed (national and EC) competence. In its November 1994 decision, the European Court of Justice tended to side with the member-states. This decision was in contrast to previous court decisions on competence in commercial policy, in which the Court had tended to favour Commission arguments in favour of greater EC competence.[15] It still remains unclear who will represent the EC in the WTO on issues of mixed national and EC competence. For example, negotiations took place in 1997–98 on a new multilateral agreement on investment (MAI), but without any agreement within the EC on the issue of competence in this policy area.

Disputes over competence have created internal tensions but have not generally had a detrimental impact on the ability of the EU to negotiate as a single actor. In cases of disputed competence, the member-states have adopted the practice of allowing the Commission to negotiate for the EU without, however, prejudicing questions of competence; but this means that competence issues must be resolved before ratification. In the Uruguay Round the EU negotiated with some effect and flexibility on the framework agreement for services, and even assumed a leadership role in the sector negotiations on financial services in June 1995, when the United States backed out of the talks. This was all done despite that fact that services were and remain an area of mixed competence. In contrast, agricultural trade was undisputedly on area of EC competence, but the EU had major difficulties developing a credible negotiating position.

Another important area in which competence is important is that of international economic cooperation. After the introduction of the euro, national governments will still retain fiscal powers, albeit subject to certain constraints set out in the Maastricht Treaty and the December 1996 Stability Pact. Responsibility for exchange rate policy of the euro will be shared between the European Central Bank (ECB), with responsibility for day-to-day operations, and the member-states in the Council of Finance Ministers, with responsibility for decisions on participation in exchange rate regimes. But there remains considerable scope for dispute over, for example, whether an exchange rate regime is a formal regime, in which case the Council determines policy, or an informal arrangement in which the ECB would have more control.

The second tension in EU policy concerns the *control* of policy and negotiations. According to the treaty, the Commission negotiates with the EC's trading partners on commercial policy on the basis of a mandate from the Council of Ministers. The General Affairs Council, composed of EU foreign ministers, then votes to accept or reject the resulting deal on the basis of a qualified majority vote (QMV). In practice things are much more complicated. There are often disagreements over how to interpret the mandate. This happened, for example, at a number of critical stages in the Uruguay Round. National governments, through the Council of Ministers, sometimes seek to exercise control over details of the EU's position and thus limit the scope for the Commission to negotiate. There is also a practice of seeking consensus rather than using QMV on matters of major importance to national governments (at least to the more important ones). As a result, hard bargaining and horse trading is often required before an agreement can be reached. Differences over who controls EU policy have created problems for the EU by undermining the credibility of the Commission as the single voice, and creating confusion among the EU's trading partners as to who is really making decisions.[16] Similarly, in exchange rate policy there will be scope for disputes over who is controlling EU monetary policy.

A third area of tension in EU policy, which is common to all countries, concerns the trade-off between *efficiency* and *accountability*. Compared with the United States, EU commercial policy can be characterized as 'technocratic', in the sense that key decisions are taken after negotiation between national and European officials in the so-called Article 113 Committee, the advisory committee of national officials with which the Commission is required to 'consult'. This has the advantage of being relatively efficient, since the Article 113 Committee is a collegial body of experts who are well aware of the constraints under which each has to operate, and there is a finely honed awareness of what is feasible in negotiations with trading partners. But it is not especially accountable. Neither European nor national parliaments have much effective scrutiny over decision-making. The European Parliament has no powers under Article 113 of the treaty, and national parliaments do not have the capability or inclination to follow detailed negotiations at two steps removed from their power base (that is, in Brussels, and then in Geneva or bilateral talks). In Europe the role of interest groups is also less formal and less pronounced than in the United States. The trade policy community, characterized by national and Commission officials, is also relatively insulated from political pressure. This technocratic approach may have been sufficient when trade was about tariffs and other 'measures at the border', but as commercial diplomacy intrudes upon more and more into domestic policy preferences, the tensions between efficiency and accountability can only increase.

The European Union's Approach to Multilateralism

What of the EU's general policy stance towards multilateral trade and the balance between rules and power in commercial policy? Before the Internal Market programme of the 1986–92 period, the majority of EC member-states favoured political negotiation of policy differences within the GATT, and eschewed the quasi-adjudicative approaches to the settlement of disputes sought by the United States. The implementation of EC legislation in the late 1980s, however, resulted in a significant reduction in the scope for national political discretion and consolidated strict adjudication of disputes by the European Court of Justice for almost all areas of intra-European commercial policy. Once national discretion had been ceded at a European level, the attitude of EU member-states to GATT/WTO adjudication changed. The EU co-sponsored (with Canada) proposals for the establishment of a stronger multilateral institution in the form of the WTO, and accepted a significantly more adjudicative GATT dispute-settlement procedure.

A further reason for this support for stronger GATT dispute settlement was the desire to bolster multilateral disciplines in order to contain United States unilateralism and 'fair trade' laws. As with most commercial policy issues, this is not new. The EU adopted a similar view during the Tokyo Round of the 1970s, although the focus was then on the narrower issue of countervailing duties, rather than the more general instrument of Section 301 of US trade law. In the Tokyo Round, the EU fought long and hard for the inclusion of a provision in the subsidies and countervailing duties code that required material injury to be shown before any countervailing duty action could be taken. It was believed that this would reduce the scope for such actions on the part of the US, but in reality it had little effect. It will be some time before it is possible to judge the effect, if any, of the enhanced dispute-settlement provisions agreed in the Uruguay Round. But the EU's use of WTO dispute settlement to challenge US sanctions against European companies under the Helms–Burton Act is evidence that multilateral rules can be used with some effect.

Compared to the previous policies of the individual European nation-states, EU commercial policy is also more inclined to support multilateral solutions to problems than revert to unilateral pressure. This is in part due to the absence of a tried and tested EU-level 'fair trade' instrument that could be used to bring leverage to bear on third countries, except for the defensive use of anti-dumping actions. The so-called New Commercial Instrument (NCI) introduced in 1985, although roughly modelled on the US Section 301, was much weaker, and there is no consensus among EU member-states on the desirability of using it. This may change following the adoption of a strengthened instrument in 1994 as part of the implementing package for the Uruguay Round. The Commission has also produced a paper on EU strategy on enhancing market access in third-country markets that envisages greater use of the revised measure.[17]

The EU has also shifted towards a more liberal position in negotiations, in part because the Single Market has resulted in a net opening of the European market.[18] In multilateral negotiations the EU has pressured for agreement, as in financial services in 1995 and 1997 when the United States was holding back because of a concern that agreement would not produce reciprocal market access. In 1997, the European Commission began pressing for a new multilateral 'millennium round' of trade negotiations, and was able to convince the member-states to support this position. This contrasts with the reluctance of the EU to enter into multilateral negotiations in the 1980s. In bilateral relations with the United States, the European Commission has been proactive in proposing a New Transatlantic Marketplace Agreement, including a Transatlantic Free Trade Agreement in services.[19] This latter proposal was attacked in some member-states, such as France, which argued that the Commission had exceeded its competence. Generally speaking, however, in the decade after 1988 the EU shifted towards a position favouring a liberal multilateral system. It remains to be seen whether this shift in policy is permanent.

THE US APPROACH: MULTILATERALISM VS REGIONALISM

The relative economic power of the United States may have declined as a result of the growth of Europe, Japan and now the dynamic emerging markets, but it still remains the single most powerful trading nation. Unlike the EU, the United States is not made up of 15 sovereign countries, and therefore finds it easier to develop and articulate commercial policies. Thus, it has tended to be the more proactive actor of the two in international negotiations. This section looks first at the US approach to multilateralism, before discussing the recent departure in US policy to pursue regional agreements. In so doing it will summarize the differences between the US and EU approaches to dealing with interdependence. Finally, it considers the internal tensions in US commercial policy-making.

Elements of US Commercial Policy

The US response to interdependence has been to pursue a three-pronged approach: unilateral, regional and multilateral. As a result, US support for multilateral solutions has become more qualified over the years. From 1973 onwards, concern about the deteriorating trade balance led to a strengthening of trade remedy law as a means of ensuring that US industries were compensated for 'unfair trade' practices. A major concern in the 1970s was the greater use of intervention, such as subsidies, by other governments. Thus, US law strengthened the ability to take countervailing duty actions.

This approach has been viewed by observers as unilateral and has become the subject of some debate.[20] The pressure for such action, however, stems from the nature of the US economy (and the structure of state regulation). The US domestic economy has long been characterized by transparency, limited discretionary intervention by the state, and a rules-based approach to internal regulation. The United States naturally sought to introduce this approach in the multilateral trade regime. As 'due process' regulated public intervention in the US market, multilateral rules designed to liberalize trade had a fairly immediate effect in opening the economy. This was not the case in other countries, such as Japan and many European countries, where state intervention was (until recently) more discretionary, less transparent, and thus less affected by multilateral disciplines. The adoption of multilateral agreements was therefore seen by more and more sectors of the US economy as resulting in a non-reciprocated opening of the market.

During the 1980s, pressure mounted to do something about this and to find more effective means of opening export markets for US producers. As a result, the balance of US policy shifted from seeking to strengthen multilateral rules and disciplines, to one aimed at achieving concrete results (that is, more open markets) by using the threat of 'fair trade' measures to close US markets to exporters from countries which did not cooperate. Towards the end of the 1980s, the objective moved beyond getting governments to desist from intervening and distorting 'fair' competition, to convincing governments to act (when they previously had not) to open markets to US exporters. For example, one of the main objectives of the US Structural Impediments Initiative targeted at Japan was to convince Tokyo to implement its anti-trust legislation. It was this pressure to make governments change their domestic policies that gave the US unilateralism of the 1980s its 'aggressive' character.[21] Whether this more aggressive approach is against the spirit, if not the letter, of multilateral agreements, has been the subject of considerable debate.

The Regional Departure

In the late 1980s and early 1990s, there was a major departure in US policy. Historically, the United States had opposed regional preferences in trade agreements, such as the EC, because they undermined the most-favoured-nation principles of the GATT. But then the US negotiated the Canada – US Free Trade Agreement (CUSFTA) between 1986–88, and the North American Free Trade Agreement (NAFTA) between 1990–93. These were followed by active US support for Asian Pacific Economic Cooperation (APEC), and the agreement in December 1993 in Seattle that APEC should work towards the long-term goal of free trade in the Pacific. In Bogor in 1994, the United States agreed to the specific target of free trade for developed APEC members by 2010 and 2020 for less-developed members. As in the case of NAFTA, the US objective was to tap rapidly growing dynamic markets, consolidate liberal trade policies, and encourage fuller compliance with WTO rules and obligations by the APEC countries. In Miami, in December 1994, a similar objective lay behind the US-supported aim of creating a free trade arrangement in the Western hemisphere by 2005. The Free Trade for the Americas Agreement would commit the whole of Central and South America and the

Caribbean, with the exception of Cuba, to rules-based liberal trade.

These regional agreements represent a response to increased economic interdependence. The US approach to such regional agreements has, however, differed in some important respects from that of the European model summarized above. The US approach is based on 'host-state control' and national treatment. In other words, regulation depends on the rules of the state in which economic activity takes place and is under the jurisdiction of the host-state authorities. National treatment provides the basis for non-discrimination, but errs in favour of respecting national sovereignty at the expense of removing regulatory barriers to trade and investment. National treatment is sometimes not effective in opening markets. For example, the maintenance of a public monopoly in telecommunications is consistent with national treatment because all potential new market entrants, whether national or foreign, are treated identically: they are all excluded from the market. The concept of mutual recognition has been introduced in NAFTA in terms of certification and testing, and is envisaged in APEC, but the US Congress has not yet accepted fully-fledged mutual recognition.[22]

The US approach also generally eschews harmonization, although there are some modest proposals for harmonization of regulations under NAFTA, such as in the areas of transport and telecommunications. Another characteristic of the US approach which is reflected in the regional agreements concluded by the United States, is a tendency to be less than comprehensive when compared to the EU approach. Market-opening is still negotiated on a 'request and offer' or selective basis, even if the more liberal negative lists (which contain only those sectors excluded from liberalization) have replaced positive lists (only those sectors to be liberalized), and the framework agreements cover all sectors. Finally, national law prevails and there is no supranational body to guarantee implementation of agreements. Chapter 19 of NAFTA introduces a tripartite dispute-settlement procedure, but the body asks only whether the national law implementing the agreement has been followed, rather than interpreting any supranational NAFTA legal provision.

The Multilateral Constant

The United States still supports multilateralism. It is argued by US officials, with some justification, that the United States has been behind most multilateral initiatives. In some cases, US unilateral pressure has precipitated multilateral negotiations, such as in the case of the intellectual property provisions in the Uruguay Round (although some developing countries argue that it is inappropriate for the WTO to require international standards for the protection of property rights). At least until the Uruguay Round (1986–94), the United States was more proactive in the launching of multilateral negotiations than was the EU. But in contrast to general US support for multilateral rules in the 1950s and 1960s, the pressure for multilateralism is now more common in those areas where the United States stands to gain most. In the 1990s, there has also been a trend towards favouring sector-by-sector negotiations in order to ensure reciprocal market-opening for US exporters and to prevent free riders. Thus, if concern for maintaining a liberal multilateral system – even at some cost to its own national interests – is a measure of economic leadership, the United States is no longer providing leadership for the multilateral system.

The United States as an Actor

One of the reasons the United States has been more focused, forceful and proactive in multilateral negotiations than the EU, is that it is more able to develop and articulate policy. This is to be expected given that the EC has to coordinate 15 member-states. But the distinction should not be exaggerated. Washington also has some internal tensions affecting commercial policy-formulation, which may increase in the future. There is also an issue of competence. In the United States there is a division of competence between the state and the federal government in a number of regulatory policy areas. Recent political trends suggest a move towards granting or returning more powers to the states. But it is the federal government that negotiates international commercial agreements. As commercial diplomacy reaches further beyond the borders it also reaches further into areas of state competence.

There have already been a number of cases in which state competence has complicated or limited the ability of the federal government to negotiate and conclude commercial agreements. For example, state competence in the area of public procurement and technical barriers to trade presented problems in the Uruguay Round of the GATT. State competence in the area of investment policy also prevented the federal government from concluding a binding national-treatment instrument for investment in the OECD in 1991, and was one of the factors blocking agreement on a Multilateral Agreement on Investment during 1996–98.

As in the EU, there is also an issue over control of commercial policy, with Congress and the administration in more or less constant dialogue. The Constitution grants the power to 'regulate commerce with foreign nations' to Congress, and in recent years the legislature has sought to tighten the rein it has given the administration in negotiating commercial agreements. This has happened primarily through trade legislation that reduces the discretion of the president. In the second Clinton administration, the refusal by Congress to grant 'fast-track' negotiating authority to the president severely curtailed the ability of the United States to pursue an active commercial policy, including negotiations for an FTAA. There is also a question concerning the degree to which US officials are in full control over the agenda and content of negotiations. In contrast to the EU, where the private sector is less focused, active private sector coalitions play a central role in shaping the US agenda. On the other hand, the ability of US multinationals to pursue their own active commercial policies means US private-sector interests also shape the international agenda. The intensive nature of links between the administration and Congress in commercial policy does mean, however, that the United States is addressing the ever-present tension between effectiveness and accountability.[23]

STRENGTHENING TRANSATLANTIC COMMERCIAL RELATIONS

Broadly speaking, the European Union and United States match each other in terms of economic weight. The United

States is more focused and proactive in some of its commercial policy, and this activism has, in recent years, been used more and more to promote a selective agenda that matches narrower national or even sectoral interests. The European Union is a powerful actor in the global economy, although internal tensions have to date limited its ability to articulate and project policies. The EU is also influential in that it offers a model for how to deal with integrating economies. But neither alone can offer the kind of leadership of the multilateral system that the United States provided in the years after 1945, and that may be needed again given the challenges facing the multilateral trading system. This raises the question of whether the United States and the European Union can jointly provide that leadership.

The idea of strengthening US–EU relations is, of course, not new. Previous efforts came in 1989–90 and culminated with the Transatlantic Declaration (TAD). At that time, the US interest in strong ties with Europe was stimulated by the dynamism of European integration, as reflected in the Single Market programme and efforts to create economic, monetary and political union in the 1991 intergovernmental conference (IGC). There was also a strategic motivation behind the stronger transatlantic ties proposed by Secretary of State James Baker in his November 1989 Berlin speech, just after the opening of the Berlin Wall, and followed by President Bush's May 1990 speech in Boston.[24] The United States wished to express its continued commitment to Europe and ensure that it retained a say in developments within the European continent. Although the outcome was not the new treaty floated by Secretary Baker, the Transatlantic Declaration codified existing contacts between the United States and the various European institutions and called for continued efforts to maintain and strengthen ties.

Despite the strategic motivation, the security provisions of the TAD were limited by the absence of a common European capability in security matters and a continued ambiguity in the Bush administration about greater European security cooperation. The Bush administration was concerned about the potential impact of a common European Defense Identity on NATO. This view was to change with the Clinton administration. More importantly, however, when the need for cooperation in European security arose as a result of the crisis in the former Yugoslavia, Europe could not respond adequately and the United States did not seek to participate in a common approach until late in the crisis. Political cooperation was an important feature of the TAD, and there followed a stream of common US–EU declarations on foreign policy. But, again, when concrete action was required, such as over international crime and drugs, no progress could be made because of a lack of EU competence in internal security issues (referred to as pillar three in the EU). This remained the case despite the fact that joint working groups were set up in late 1993 to address such issues.

In commercial relations the emphasis soon shifted from the TAD to efforts to complete the Uruguay Round, where the transatlantic debate was dominated by feuding over agricultural trade. Once the round was complete, however, there followed a period of relative stability in EU–US commercial relations, disrupted only by continental European dissatisfaction with yet another bout of neglect of the dollar as the United States, in European eyes, again moved to bring about domestic adjustment without considering the impact on Europe.

Since the Transatlantic Declaration, there have been several proposals for renewed efforts to strengthen transatlantic commercial relations. But these proposals raise a number of questions. First, would such efforts be worthwhile? As noted above, transatlantic commercial relations have been strong for some time, and there is little likelihood that developments in the world economy would do much to change this, at least in the short to medium term. Would it not be better instead to promote multilateral agreements on the current issues in commercial policy, especially given the importance of the EU and United States for the multilateral system? A formal US–EU agreement which did not cover all trade would also be incompatible with GATT provisions for free trade agreements (in Article XXIV). Although Article XXIV has been applied loosely in the past, for the EU and United States to bend the GATT rules just as the WTO is being initiated would seriously undermine the credibility of the WTO.

Second, what should be the substance of any transatlantic effort or agreement aimed at strengthening commercial relations? Should an agreement focus on the conventional issues of further tariff reductions and efforts to address non-tariff measures, as this is where progress would be easiest? But if progress is easiest on these, why not negotiate multilaterally rather than bilaterally? Should the sensitive issues, such as agriculture and audio-visual be tackled? Or would inclusion of such topics risk undermining the chances of success and therefore be better left to one side?

Third, should the United States and EU seek to go beyond the conventional tariff and non-tariff border issues and address the beyond-the-border agenda, including regulatory barriers to trade, and competition issues, or is progress in these areas limited by fundamental differences in approach to regulatory policy?[25]

The TAFTA Proposals

The main motivation behind the Transatlantic Free Trade Agreement (TAFTA) proposals of 1994 came from a European concern about a possible US trend towards isolationism and protectionism. In 1993, the new Clinton administration got off to a shaky start initiating a number of bilateral actions against the EU.[26] Despite early doubts, the administration lived up to the rhetoric of President Clinton's March 1993 speech in which he stressed there was no question of the United States turning inwards and adopting protectionist policies.[27] Indeed, the administration first pressed the NAFTA implementing legislation through a somewhat reluctant Congress, and then did the same with the Uruguay Round.

It was less tension about commercial relations and more concern over a deterioration in transatlantic security and political relations that lay behind the (mainly) European proposals for a TAFTA. The November 1994 mid-term elections brought to Congress a number of new legislators with little knowledge and even less interest in international affairs. At the same time there were important differences over Bosnia and NATO enlargement. European politicians concerned about the possibility of growing isolationist sentiment in Congress therefore proposed a major new initiative to consolidate

US–EU relations based on commercial relations.[28] If the United States was concluding regional agreements within America and with the Asia–Pacific region, why not negotiate such an agreement with Europe? There was also some concern in the United States over the danger of 'drift' in transatlantic relations.[29] But to affect political relations, galvanizing the attention of legislatures and attracting public interest, there needed to be a 'big idea'.

The private sector was also interested in strengthening commercial relations, and a treaty had been under discussion for sometime in certain business circles.[30] But for business and, above all, for officials on both sides of the Atlantic concerned with commercial policy, it was clear that there would be difficulties with a formal treaty. After seven years of heated agricultural negotiations, no trade official was keen to reopen that dossier. There was also concern about the message that a bilateral agreement between the two most powerful players in the trading system would have for their commitment to multilateralism. Business and trade officials therefore preferred a pragmatic, less-controversial, bottom-up approach which focused on removing barriers to market access by moving towards mutual recognition of standards, product-testing and certification. But this practical approach was difficult to reconcile with the pressure for a major initiative that would bring political benefits.

In June 1995, the US–EU summit of Presidents Clinton, Jacques Chirac (European Council) and Jacques Santer (European Commission) set up a High Level Group of Representatives to consider the way ahead. The ideas that emerged are interesting indicators of the prevailing thinking in Washington and Brussels at the time. In June 1995, Secretary of State Christopher made a speech in Madrid entitled 'An Agenda for Transatlantic Relations in the 21st Century'.[31] This favoured a cautious pragmatism over any major initiatives. The prevailing view in Washington was that EU–US commercial relations were sound, and that the initiatives taken by the US with others were aimed at bringing relations with these others up to the level of those with the EU, not at downgrading transatlantic commercial relations. Although the idea of a TAFTA was not discounted entirely, it was seen as a possible, but distant future prospect.

In July 1995, the European Commission produced a paper setting out the options from a European point of view.[32] This was also pragmatic but, in line with the interests of some member-states, was generally more enthusiastic about strengthening EU–US commercial links as a means of consolidating the transatlantic relationship than Secretary Christopher's speech had been. In an attempt to reconcile the political desire for a big idea and the realities of commercial diplomacy, the Commission picked up the idea of a Transatlantic Economic Area initially proposed by the Swedish Minister of Foreign Affairs and Trade.[33] This would bring together a series of pragmatic negotiations on technical issues under the umbrella of an integrating concept, while at the same time avoding sensitive sectors such as agriculture that would probably have to be considered in a free trade agreement.[34] There were differences within the Council on how ambitious to be in seeking to strengthen bilateral trade links. France, for example, was reported to be opposed to an ambitious initiative for fear that it would undermine multilateral approaches.[35] As in the case of the Christopher speech, the Commission paper and the Council position (adopted in October 1995) held out the possibility of a TAFTA but opted for a more cautious pragmatic approach.

The New Transatlantic Agenda

This pragmatism was reflected in the New Transatlantic Agenda (NTA) and the joint EU–US Action Plan agreed at the EU–US summit in Madrid in December 1995.[36] The NTA covers security, political and economic relations. It also makes explicit the link between security and political relations on the one hand, and commercial relations on the other, by stressing for example that the transatlantic 'economic relationship sustains our security and increases our prosperity'. Interestingly, for a document aimed at strengthening bilateral relations, the Agenda emphasises multilateralism, stating that the United States and European Union bear a special responsibility to 'lead and strengthen the multilateral system, to support the World Trade Organization and to lead the way in opening markets to trade and investment'. Rather than seek a TAFTA, the NTA aimed to create a New Transatlantic Marketplace

(NTM), a term which probably says more about the ingenuity of the drafters than it does about the content of commercial relations. But the NTM clearly put the emphasis on market-led developments rather than any policy-led treaty approach. The aim was progressively to 'reduce or eliminate barriers that hinder the flow of goods, services, and capital' between the US and the EU. To this end the NTA suggested a joint study of how and where to bring this about, regulatory cooperation, and a number of other ideas such as mutual-recognition agreements and the realization of a Transatlantic Information Society.

The Agenda and Action Plan recognized that the transatlantic dialogue was also in need of broadening. In the past when security issues predominated, it may have been sufficient to ensure cohesion within the 'security communities' on both sides of the Atlantic. But now that commercial relations reach beyond national borders, a wider constituency must be engaged if the transatlantic relationship is to continue to find support. Thus, the Action Plan set out to build new bridges across the Atlantic. The most concrete of these is the Transatlantic Business Dialogue (TABD) initiated in late 1994 by the US Secretary of Commerce Ron Brown and the European Commissioner responsible for external commercial policy and relations with the US, Sir Leon Brittan.[37] After some initial scepticism, the TABD developed into an effective instrument. The Transatlantic Declaration provided no means of monitoring whether the EU and US governments were acting on the proposals. But the TABD kept up the momentum, reviewing the work of officials developing the New Transatlantic Marketplace.

In 1995, neither Washington nor Brussels felt it was advisable to risk seeking a formal treaty; pragmatism and the caution of trade officials prevailed over more ambitious ideas. The fact that the NTA also stressed the 'special responsibility' of the United States and EU to support the multi-lateral system, reflected caution and a desire to ensure the continued growth of multilateral solutions, rather than the launching of major initiatives to strengthen bilateral links. At the same time, however, the detail of the Action Plan was oriented towards strengthening bilateral links. The work of the TABD created common agendas on both multilateral and bilateral issues.

In the period 1996–98 progress was made at bilateral and multilateral levels. On the bilateral level, mutual-recognition agreements (MRAs) were finally concluded in late 1997, although they were not as comprehensive in their coverage as the TABD had wished. There were also agreements on customs cooperation. These were low-profile issues, but when tariffs are low, the costs of technical barriers and customs procedures often exceed those of tariffs. There was also a strengthening in collaboration and dialogue on issues ranging from reducing unemployment and codes of conduct for companies combating exploitative child labour in developing countries, to the conclusion of a Science and Technology Agreement.

At the multilateral level, joint efforts facilitated the conclusion of a series of sector agreements. These included the 1996 Information Technology Agreement (ITA) which reduced tariffs on a range of IT products. In 1997 two sector negotiations in services – in basic telecommunications and financial services – were concluded under the framework of the General Agreement on Trade in Services (GATS). Both agreements were of strategic importance in that the sectors are important in the process of globalization of markets.

There were also failures and bilateral tensions. Negotiations on a multilateral agreement on investment (MAI) dragged on due to European reluctance to include audio- visual/broadcasting in its remit for fear that US products would adversely affect European culture. Washington also advocated a broad exemption for national security, which the Europeans believed would weaken the agreement. The United States also had difficulty providing a commitment to include the US states in the MAI disciplines. Food-safety issues created tensions, such as the EU ban on the use of hormones in beef, and European consumers threatened to create further problems by pushing for the explicit labelling of products containing genetically modified organisms. At the other end of the high politics–low politics spectrum, the Helms – Burton Act threatened to become a major transatlantic trade dispute until a ceasefire was called in 1998.

A New Transatlantic Marketplace Agreement (NTMA)

In March 1998 the European Commission proposed a redoubling of efforts to remove transatlantic barriers to market access. The Commission seems to have been motivated, in part, by a desire to ensure that the transatlantic relationship could focus on positive aims and thus be more able to absorb the negative impact of repeated disputes.[38] In its proposal, the Commission deftly avoided sensitive issues, such as agriculture, while producing proposals for bilateral liberalization that are consistent with the letter of the GATT provisions in Article XXIV and GATS Article V on preferential trade agreements. The proposals for a NTMA, which at the time of writing had not been adopted by the EU member-states, sought to extend the coverage of MRAs in order to tackle technical barriers to trade. The proposals also call for more bilateral liberalization in public procurement and investment, both of which are largely outside GATT rules.

The most radical proposal has been for the establishment of a Transatlantic Free Trade Agreement in Services. Again this is possible under Article V of the GATS and it could possibly be consistent with GATS rules even if sensitive sectors such as audio-visual and maritime transport are excluded. Although the GATS requires that substantially all trade be included in any preferential agreement, there does not appear to be wording that would require the EU and United States to include all service sectors. It may therefore be that the NTMA would be consistent with GATT rules, but a formal agreement between Washington and Brussels could still risk undermining multilateralism. Although the proposals are geared to match the interests of the TABD. It is unlikely, however, that the US would support a proposal which excluded agriculture, which is one of the reasons for French opposition to the NTMA.

This focus on the practicalities of commercial policy has led to some significant omissions in efforts to strengthen transatlantic economic relations. It has already been noted that some 'sensitive' sectors were omitted from the 1995 Action Plan. There has been the almost total omission of economic cooperation issues and exchange rate and monetary matters. Only one small paragraph in the 1995 document dealt with these issues, and it only committed Washington and Brussels to 'continue to follow' them. This reflected continued US indifference to the impact of its economic policy on other countries, and scepticism about EMU among Anglo-Saxon economists and politicians. The neglect of this issue does not reflect its potential as a source of transatlantic tension: exchange rate instability has already caused tensions in 1992 and 1995. Nor was there any debate on the potential impact of the introduction of the euro until it became clear that the Maastricht Treaty provisions would be implemented. There was a case to be made for talks on establishing cooperation on monetary and exchange rate policies, but by 1998 it was probably too late to have much impact on European opinion. If such an window of opportunity existed in 1995–96, it was missed.[39]

THE CHALLENGES AHEAD

Both the United States and the European Union face important challenges in commercial policy. In the short to medium term, bilateral commercial ties are strong and will provide a source of stability, despite changes in the security relationship. But in the longer term, divergent approaches to increased international economic interdependence could create problems. The United States now shows only qualified support for multilateral options. If it cannot get results in multilateral or regional negotiations, US commercial diplomacy could shift towards more unilateral solutions thus introducing an element of volatility and unpredictability into commercial policy. For its part, the EU continues to suffer from internal tensions which inhibit its ability to fill any leadership vacuum left by Washington. The EU failed to address the institutional sources of these tensions in the 1996 Intergovernmental Conference, even though the IGC was intended to make the EU more effective in its external relations.

Today, the EU and United States exhibit divergent approaches to regulatory policy issues and to the challenges of coping with market integration. Without efforts to bring about some form of policy approximation, these differences are likely to limit bilateral deepening of economic relations and could result in competing approaches to commercial relations with third countries. Combined with a relative decline in the importance of US – EU trade and investment as other regions grow, this could well result in drift and a weakening of bilateral commercial relations.

If this process is slow and takes place within a stable multilateral order there is little to be concerned about. But the WTO itself is unlikely to cope with these challenges without effective leadership, which neither the US nor the EU can provide individually. Hence the interest in strengthening bilateral relations to provide a 'pathfinder role' for the global economy. If Washington and Brussels are unable to cooperate in fulfilling such a multilateral role, it is unlikely that the WTO will be able to deepen its coverage of new issues. WTO rules would be limited to more conventional tariff and non-tariff barrier issues, and this would leave a vacuum in terms of international rules for trade and especially investment, which would probably be filled by regional agreements. Such an emphasis on regional agreements could, in the long term, limit the growth of multilateral agreements. Thus the long-term effect of a failure to cooperate would be a weaker multilateral system, even though, broadly speaking, it is in the interests of both to have a strong, rules-based, liberal trading system.

Notes

1. This chapter draws on research carried out at the London School of Economics' Centre for Research on the United States, as part of a project on 'subsidiary in the governance of the global economy' funded by the British Economic and Social Research Council's Global Economic Institutions initiative.

2. Robert Lawrence, *Multilateralism, Regionalism, and Deeper Integration* (Washington, DC: Brookings Institution, 1993).

3. See Renato Ruggiero, 'The Challenges Facing the WTO', speech at Harvard University *WTO Focus*, WTO, March 1995, Geneva.

4. Helen Wallace and William Wallace (eds.), *Policy Making in the European Union* (Oxford: Oxford University Press, 1996).

5. For details of what the substance of a TAFTA might be, see Bruce Stokes, *Open for Business: Creating a Transatlantic Marketplace* (New York: Council on Foreign Relations, 1996).

6. Organization for Economic Cooperation and Development, *Regional Integration and the Multilateral Trading System, Synergy and Divergence* (Paris: OCED, 1995); and World Trade Organization, *Regionalism and the World Trading System* (Geneva: WTO, 1995).

7. According to recent European Commission estimates, the removal of remaining tariff and non-tariff barriers to transatlantic trade could add some ecu 125 billion to the annual EU GDP, which would be broadly equivalent to the effects of the Uruguay Round. Further gains could be achieved through multilateral removal of remaining industrial tariffs.

8. Stephen Woolcock, *Western Policies on East-West Trade* (London, Royal Institute of International Affairs, 1993).

9. Gary Clyde Hufbauer, *Europe 1992: An American Perspective* (Washington, DC: The Brookings Institution Press, 1991).

10. European Commission, *Communication to the Council, European Parliament on the Establishment of a New Transatlantic Marketplace Agreement* (Brussels: 11 March 1998).

11. The Brookings Institution and Stiftung Wissenschaft und Politik, *Perspectives on Transatlantic Relations*, a report for the Forward Studies Unit of the European Commission, November 1995.

12. For a notable exception see Randall Henning, 'The Monetary Dimensions of a Transatlantic Agenda', paper presented to the conference on 'The US–EU Agenda for the 21st Century', Council on Foreign Relations, 27 September 1995.

13. Michael Smith, 'Economic Aspects of EU/US Relations in an Era of Change: The EU as a Strategic Partner?', paper presented at the International Studies Association annual conference, San Diego, April 1996.

14. Marc Maresceau (ed.), *The European Community's Commercial Policy after 1992: The Legal Dimension* (Dordrecht: Nijoff, 1994).

15. European Court of Justice, *Prise de position de la Cour*, 15 November 1994.

16. Michael Hodges and Stephen Woolcock, 'The European Union in the Uruguay Round: The Story Behind the Headlines,' in Helen Wallace and William Wallace (eds.), *Policy Making in the European Union*.

17. European Commission, *Communication from the Commission to the Council and European Parliament on the Global Challenge of International Trade: A Market Access Strategy for the European Union* (Brussels: 8 February 1996).

18. *Single Market Review* (Brussels: European Commission, 1997).

19. European Commission, *Communication to the Council, European Parliament on the Establishment of a New Transatlantic Market Place Agreement* (Brussels: 11 March 1998).

20. Jagdish Bhagwati and Hugh Patrick, *Aggressive Unilateralism: America's 301 Trade Policy and World Trading System* (Ann Arbor: University of Michigan Press, 1991).

21. *Ibid.*

22. It is important to distinguish between full mutual- recognition agreements as introduced in the EU, and mutual recognition of test results as used in NAFTA (with the exception of Mexico). Full mutual recognition means that country A receiving a good or service from country B,

recognizes that the product is safe to be sold in B and may therefore be sold in A. No approval by regulatory authorities in A is required, so that in effect country A recognizes the safety or environmental regulations of country B as equivalent. Mutual recognition of test results as used between Canada and the US and proposed for some sectors in APEC and transatlantic mutual-recognition agreements, means that the results of tests carried out in B to test a product against the requirements of country A will be recognized by country A's authorities. In other words this saves retesting by a laboratory in country A and thus reduces costs and duplication, but country A still retains sovereignty over which products may be sold in country A. A product satisfying the requirements of country B may still be rejected by country A if it has higher standards or changes its requirements. In the EU, once Germany, for example, approves a product, that product can be sold in all member-states.

23.   The idea of a fast-track procedure for the EU has also been proposed as a means of addressing the conflict between effectiveness in negotiations and accountability (see Stephen Woolcock, 'Trade and EU Commercial Policy' in *Crisis or Opportunity? The European Union and the 1996 IGC* (Centre for European Union Studies, University of Hull, 1995)).

24.   There were also initiatives taken by the European side, as illustrated by the meeting between the President of the EC Council of Ministers, Haughey, with President Bush in March 1990. Roy Ginsberg and Thomas Frellesen, *EU–US Foreign Policy Cooperation in the 1990's: Elements of Partnership*, CEPS paper no. 58 (Brussels: Centre for European Policy Studies, 1994).

25.   Stephen Woolcock, 'European and North American Approaches to Regulation: Continued Divergence?' in Jens van Scherpenberg and Elke Theil (eds), *Towards Rival Regionalism? US and EU Economic Integration and the Risk of Transatlantic Regulatory Rift* (Ebenhausen: Stiftung Wissenschaft und Politik, 1998).

26.   Michael Smith and Stephen Woolcock, 'Learning to Cooperate: The Clinton Administration and the European Union', *International Affairs*, vol. 70, no. 3 (July 1993).

27.   United States President Bill Clinton, at the American University, March 1993.

28.   Klaus Kinkel, 'Foreign Policy in the New Era: Forging a Transatlantic Approach', speech at the American Institute of Contemporary German Studies (Washington, DC: May 1995).

29.   Newt Gingrich, 'An American Vision for the 21st Century', speech at the Nixon Center for Peace and Freedom (Washington, DC: March 1995).

30.   *Towards a Transatlantic Partnership: A European Strategy* (Brussels: Transatlantic Policy Network, 1994).

31.   US Department of State, 'Charting a Transatlantic Agenda for the 21st Century', speech by Secretary of State Warren Christopher (Madrid: 2 June 1995).

32.   European Commission, *Europe and the US: The Way Forward*, communication from the Commission to the Council, COM (95) 411 final, 26 July 1995.

33.   Mats Hellstrom, speech at the European Institute (Washington, DC: May 1995).

34.   The GATT provisions in Article 24 require that substantially all trade is covered by free trade agreements and customs unions. It would have been difficult to justify excluding agriculture and still satisfy this provision.

35.   It is likely that concern about pressure to liberalize agricultural trade more, and to open the audio-visual market, also lay behind the French opposition to any idea of a free trade agreement. *Agence Europe* (European Daily Bulletin), October 1995.

36.   *The New Transatlantic Agenda and Joint EU–US Action Plan* (Madrid: December 1995).

37.   Glennon Harrison, *A New Transatlantic Initiative? US–EU Economic Relations in the Mid-1990s* (Washington, DC: Congressional Research Service, 95–983E, 1995).

38.   Sir Leon Brittan, 'The Future of Transatlantic Relations: Prospects for Stronger Economic, Commercial, and Political Ties', speech to the European Forum on Transatlantic Relations, (Germany: 1 February 1998).

39.   Randall Henning, 'The Monetary Dimension of a Transatlantic Economic Agenda', paper presented to the conference on 'The US–EU Agenda for the 21st Century', Council on Foreign Relations, 27 September 1995.

9 Reconciling Transatlanticism and Multilateralism: Great-Power Management of the World Trading System
Richard H. Steinberg[1]

In 1995, geostrategic demands and trade interests converged to refocus attention on transatlantic trade policy. With the fiftieth anniversary of the end of the Second World War and imminent plans for expanding NATO, geostrategists searched for trade policy initiatives that would reinforce the US commitment to Europe.[2] With fresh memories of ultimately successful European Union–US cooperation in closing the Uruguay Round and an awareness that transatlantic trade differences and rows had almost sunk the Round, trade policy strategists sought new ways to improve transatlantic relations.[3] That renewed interest in transatlanticism generated new trade initiatives and agreements between the European Union and the United States, statements of support for extensive transatlantic trade liberalization, and a formal dialogue between business leaders in the United States and Europe intended to generate new government-to-government trade agreements, as well as several new books on transatlantic trade relations.

This revived attention to transatlanticism also brought to the fore a discussion about how to reconcile transatlantic trade liberalization with another policy goal – the advancement of liberal multilateralism.[4] Various perspectives on the relationship between liberal multilateralism and transatlantic trade liberalization have been offered in discussions between representatives of the European Commission and the US government, in the business-led dialogues, and at policy institutes in the United States and Europe.[5] Among mainstream trade policy-makers in both the European Union and the United States, there remains a consensus favouring the pursuit of both policy goals. But there is disagreement, debate and a lack of confidence over how to simultaneously pursue them in a strategically consistent manner.

This chapter focuses on the logic of one approach to reconciling the pursuit of these two goals: the 'great-power management' approach. This approach, when applied to the contemporary world political-economy, stresses the importance of EU–US cooperation in using the bargaining power inherent in their combined market size to yield multilateral liberalization. The next section elaborates the logic of a great-power management approach to liberal multilateralism. Next, I consider obstacles to the modalities of transatlantic cooperation that are envisioned by the great-power management approach and ways to overcome those obstacles. I then evaluate contemporary transatlantic arrangements and four sets of recent policy proposals in terms of the great-power management approach. The conclusion considers the future of the multilateral system in terms of the great-power management paradigm, taking into account feasible transatlantic policies as well as regional and bilateral policies that the European Union and the United States are likely to continue to pursue.

GREAT-POWER MANAGEMENT AND THE LOGIC OF TRANSATLANTICISM

A traditional realist prescription for managing the multilateral trading system would suggest the importance of cooperation among the great trading powers – in the WTO, through transregional arrangements, and through negotiations between the great trading powers and third countries. By cooperating with each other, great trading powers with similar interests in liberalization could bring to bear the power inherent in their combined market size to yield global liberalization. Successful great-power management requires identifying which of the world's preferential trade regions could combine enough market power to pressure all (or almost all) other countries into liberalizing, and which regions have views of liberalization that are similar enough to make such transregional cooperation feasible.

Transatlanticism suggests itself as the obvious candidate for the job. Transatlantic cooperation in closing the Uruguay Round exemplifies the kind of cooperation contemplated by the great-power management approach. By withdrawing from the General Agreement on Tariffs and Trade (GATT) 1947[6] and joining the WTO (that includes GATT 1994), the transatlantic powers forced the rest of the world to join the WTO (and all the associated Uruguay Round agreements) or lose their guarantee of most-favoured-nation (MFN) access to Europe and the United States – something no GATT-contracting party could afford.[7]

The Power of Transatlanticism in Global Trade Negotiations

Market access has been the primary goal of trading nations in every round of trade negotiations since establishment of the GATT in 1947. The sovereign powers that have set the rules of that system have been those with the largest markets. Those powers have used access to their markets to coerce and compensate lesser powers into accepting rules of the system: they have compensated with promises of increased market access (few example, promising tariff reductions or elimination, and quota expansion or elimination) and coerced with threats of market closure (for example, threatening unilateral action by means of Section 301 of the Trade Act of 1974).

When it comes to setting the rules of international trade, the United States and the European Union are the world's greatest powers: they have the world's biggest markets. As a rough indicator of market power, consider that retained merchandise imports into the European Union and the United States in 1994 together accounted for almost 40 per cent of all such imports in the world, and that in 1994 the combined EU–US GDP represented nearly half the world's total. Japan is the next biggest market, but its 1994 GDP and retained merchandise imports were each less than half that of either transatlantic power. These may be only rough indicators of market power, but they provide a sense of the importance of the EU and US markets.[8]

The combined economic and political capacity of Europe and the United States – if employed cooperatively – could be used to provide incentives for multilateral adoption of liberalizing rules and principles agreed upon by the two powers. Transatlantic cooperation offers a greater probability of successfully resolving trade problems with third countries than does independent action of either power. Transatlantic cooperation in closing the Uruguay Round attests to that.

Transatlantic Interests in the Global Economy

Such cooperation is only possible if transatlantic interests are similar, and the transatlantic powers perceive a common external challenge. The European Union and the United States share a commitment to liberalization. But they also share a common interest in a *particular version* of liberalization and regulation that is derived largely from their Western style of capitalism and regulation. While the styles of capitalism in Europe and North America are not identical, they are more similar to each other then they are to the styles of capitalism in Asia, the transitional economies of Eastern Europe and the former Soviet Union, and the developing countries of Africa and Latin America. Compared to the policy positions of most third countries, those of the EU member-states and the United States are more similar to each other across a broad range of issues on the trade agenda – intellectual-property protection, competition policy, environmental protection, labour laws and services liberalization, to name a few.

The EU and US interest in a similar version of liberal multilateral outcomes may also be seen in legal-historical perspective. Just after the Second World War, with the world split into two blocs, and the United States dominant economically and militarily in the West, the United States was able to build a Western trading system in its image. The United States authored the text that became the GATT 1947, which provided a foundation for a liberal multilateral system, built largely on assumptions that the constituent economies were structured similarly to that of the United States and Western Europe – that they were Western liberal economies composed of price-sensitive, profit-maximizing firms with little government intervention except for purposes of solving market failures and engaging in modest income redistribution. GATT rules have acknowledged that state trading enterprises, anti-competitive behaviour and other non-liberal governmental intervention might play a role in some economies, but the GATT system did not contemplate that those features would be anything other than exceptions.[9] This system made sense as long as the constituent economies were essentially liberal, because liberal multilateral rules affected them similarly. But national economic systems structured very differently from those envisioned in the Western liberal model are increasingly important actors in the world trading system. Reflecting this development, the world trading system built in the Western image is suffering significant strains and lines of fracture.

To varying degrees, policy-makers in the European Union and the United States are likely to agree that several Asian economies, with industrial structures and government-business relationships that are fundamentally different from those in the West, pose challenges to the WTO system.[10] Strong industrial policies in Asian economies are seen by some as having denied benefits to the West that were expected from tariff concessions and other WTO guarantees.[11] And weak competition policies in these Asian economies, mirroring concentrated industrial structures and inaccessible distribution systems, have served to limit imports in favour of domestic production and to limit the 'contestability' of those markets.[12] Together, these policies have aided the development in Asia of sectors that many would consider strategic, and many see as having undermined the competitiveness of those same sectors in Europe and the United States.[13] In conjunction with macroeconomic savings and investment imbalances, some argue that these policies may also help explain chronic trade imbalances – particularly in specific sectors – between the United States and Europe on the one hand, and Japan, for example, on the other, regardless of the yen's value.[14]

At the same time, transatlantic trade policy-makers are likely to agree that WTO rules do not fully address developing-country issues. Many thoughtful policy-makers in the European Union and the United States want to integrate the developing countries more fully into the liberal trading system, largely for political purposes: to enhance the prospects for democracy and to 'lock-in' those countries while they are in the midst of economic and political liberalization. But this effort faces problems. Unstable macroeconomic histories in some developing countries limit EU and US business support for further integration. Many developing countries have a relatively weak administrative and legal infrastructure, making it difficult for them to administer and adjudicate customs issues, intellectual-property protection, environmental protection, labour protection, and other Western-style regulatory systems that are now seen as important trade- related issues by various groups in Europe and the United States. Moreover, their level of development affects the value that polities place on building and maintaining such systems.[15] At the same time, the GATT's MFN principle, combined with the developed countries' political need for reciprocity, makes it difficult for developing countries to bargain successfully for tariff concessions that favour their products.[16] As a result, North–South tension at the WTO persists and efforts to more fully open trade with developing countries face serious obstacles.

EU and US policy-makers also agree that the transitional economies of China, the former Soviet Union and Eastern Europe now entering the world trading system pose new challenges to the system. State or political party authorities, which still play an important role in most transitional economies, inevitably make decisions that are based on considerations other than price and may thereby defeat the GATT cornerstones of MFN, national treatment, tariff concessions and quota bans.[17] The relative weakness of legal systems and central government authority in the transitional economies makes compliance with WTO rules difficult. At the same time, political and social dislocations in those countries require a delicate balance between liberalization and continuity.

With so many different interests and national economic systems represented at the multilateral bargaining table, and with economic and political power more dispersed than it was at the founding of the GATT system, it is not surprising that progress through the traditional multilateral approach has been slower to face these broad, fundamental challenges than have regional liberalization efforts. Partly in reaction to frustration at the multilateral level, and partly in response to the preferences made possible by free trade agreements, many countries have turned to regional trading schemes. The consequent regional trade groupings and the emergence of competition between them are further straining the WTO system. The European Union has been joined by NAFTA, MERCOSUR, the FTAA initiative, APEC, and ASEAN's AFTA, each diverting (or threatening to divert) some trade and investment from countries outside its boundaries – much to the political chagrin of those countries.[18] While low MFN tariffs dampen the diversion effects of these arrangements, tariff peaks and other forms of protection still threaten diversion in certain sectors. Moreover, preferential rules of origin intended to enhance trade and investment-diversion exacerbate the associated political tension. Each time a free trade agreement is concluded or expanded, those left outside express concern and complain.

For liberal multilateralists, these are disturbing trends, yielding a system facing increasingly serious strains and fractures. Among the world's great powers, Europe and the United States uniquely share many of the same interests: solving problems with Asian economies whose industrial structures and government–business relationships are fundamentally different from those in the West; integrating the transitional economies into the world trading system; solving trade problems with developing countries; and reducing the trade-distorting effect of regionalism. As long as EU and US policymakers view their interests along these lines, perceiving these developments as a common external threat, there is a potential for strengthening liberal multilateralism through a transatlantic approach.

BUILDING SUCCESSFUL GREAT-POWER MANAGEMENT

Obstacles to Cooperation

While EU and US interests may be similar in some sectors or on some cross-sectoral issues, and their combined power great,

Europe and the United States face serious obstacles in attempts to advance free trade. At least three sets of obstacles demand attention.

The Structure of Trade Policy Interests and Opportunities in a Multiple-Nation Negotiation

The most consistent problems facing great-power management of the world trading system are related to the structure of EU and US interests and opportunities in a multiple-nation nego-tiation (i.e., any negotiation involving the European Union, the United States, and at least one other country). It is hardly surprising to find barriers to cooperation among great powers in a multipolar system. There are good reasons to believe that transatlantic cooperation will not be simple,[19] and recent history seems to bear that out. When transatlantic efforts have been made to solve third-country problems or system-wide problems, cooperation has frequently broken down. The analysis above suggested that US and European interests in third countries are similar; but they are rarely identical. Dif-ferences have often been exploited by third countries to drive a wedge into the transatlantic partnership. When EU and US objectives differ, there may not be enough common interest to cooperate.

For example, European and US auto-makers each want to further open Japan's new-car market, but they face different barriers to entry and different constraints on what they can demand of Japan. US auto-makers, which have not yet invested substantially in distribution and sales networks in Japan, are most concerned about closure resulting from ver-tical integration in Japan's auto distribution system. European auto-makers do not share that concern: they have already invested heavily to establish their own distribution networks in Japan; moreover, the European Commission has granted an EC Treaty Article 85 block exemption to European auto-makers to permit them to maintain their own vertically-inte-grated distribution system in Europe.[20] Thus, from 1994–95 the European Union and the United States each campaigned for further opening of Japan's automobile market. European auto-makers were most concerned about Japanese auto-parts testing requirements, border-inspection procedures that delayed and increased the price of importation into Japan, and other technical regulations.[21] In contrast, US auto-makers wanted changes in restrictive Japanese business practices to enable Japanese auto dealers to carry US cars.[22] The US government pressured Japan for these changes and Japan resisted. As US pressure mounted, Tokyo reached agreement with Brussels on changes which were of little value to US auto-makers, at the same time, the European Union backed Japanese diplomatic challenges and legal threats against US unilateralism. Eventually, Washington struck its own deal with Japan.[23] But there was no transatlantic cooperation in the automobile negotiations with Japan – while the transatlantic powers shared a common goal of liberalizing Japan's auto market, there was little similarity in terms of more immediate objectives.

Frequently, cooperation may break down when the transatlantic powers share identical objectives on a third-country issue, but the salience of those objectives (relative to those on other issues) differs. For example, US negotiators have complained that in the Uruguay Round negotiations on trade-related aspects of international property rights (TRIPs),[24] the transatlantic powers had agreed to jointly pursue enhanced protection for pharmaceuticals in the regulatory-approval pipeline, but the EU abandoned that position in exchange for other concessions from India that it considered more important; the US bargaining position on that issue was thereby ruined and the TRIPs agreement does not offer the enhanced protection.[25]

Even if there were complete agreement on transatlantic interests on a particular sectoral or cross-sectoral topic, a third country could almost always attempt to break up transatlantic cooperation by raising issues relating to a different sector on which transatlantic interests differ.

Transatlantic cooperation problems resulting from interests that are not identical appear endemic to many other sectoral and cross-sectoral topics.[26] Game theory analyses have long suggested these kinds of cooperation problems in multiple-nation negotiations. The problem in the preceding paragraph closely resembles what game theorists call a 'divide the dollar' bargaining game.[27] Although the conditions required for a third country to disrupt transatlantic cooperation are not found in all scenarios, it is often the case that the transatlantic powers seem to pursue liberalization on a preferential rather than a multilateral basis. This suggests that there is, in fact, room for such strategic moves by third countries.

Moreover in some circumstances, the transatlantic powers might prefer to liberalize on a preferential basis instead of negotiating through the WTO or on an MFN basis. The European Union may offer an attractive alternative to multilateral liberalization for some European producers, in so far as liberalization on that basis enables those producers preferential access to the third-country market. Similarly, for US producers, liberalization through NAFTA or on bilateral basis may be more attractive than multilateral liberalization. In short, this preferential alternative offers some producers in each great power more *absolute* gains than would be enjoyed if liberalization were to take place on a multilateral basis, and more gains *relative* to that of producers from the other great power. For example, the European Union's automobile arrangement with Japan, described above, could be seen as an attempt to secure improved access to Japan's market on a basis that would put Europe's auto-makers on a better footing than US auto-makers. Potentially more dangerous, the European Union and United States appear in some respects to be in competition to establish preferential arrangements to substantially liberalize all trade with third countries or regions: for example, while the United States is pursuing liberalization with Asia through APEC, the European Union has been arranging its own set of meetings with ASEAN countries, China, Japan and South Korea.

Transatlantic cooperation is also inhibited by a free-rider problem that results from providing negotiated results on an MFN basis. This may exacerbate the demand for preferential third-country negotiations. The European Union and United States face many trade problems with third countries which, if resolved on an MFN basis, would have the qualities of a public good. When one transatlantic power acts alone to resolve such a problem, and the resolution is on an MFN basis, the other power may simply free-ride on the result. For example, in 1994 the European Union refused US requests for help in negotiating improved intellectual-property protection in China. In 1995, US negotiators' unilateral tactics resulted in China agreeing to protect intellectual property on an MFN basis, and EU negotiators rushed to China to confirm that they would be able to free-ride off the US action.[28] This free-rider problem creates bilateral diplomatic resentment and is an incentive to fashion deals of interest to both transatlantic powers on a preferential basis.

Thus, it is not surprising that some Europeans have expressed concern that the United States may have concluded a preferential bilateral agreement with Korea on access for beef,[29] and with Japan on access for semiconductors.[30] Nor is it surprising that some Americans interpreted the EU Commission's 1995 green paper on ways to improve commercial ties with China as an effort by the European Union to achieve preferential access and relationships there.[31]

Divergent Views on the Property of Unilateral Ultimata
Normative differences between policy-makers in Brussels and Washington may explain differences in the tactics by which the European Union and the United States each negotiate with third countries on trade issues. The US government often uses Section 301, an approach that may culminate in the United States issuing an ultimatum to a third country to liberalize or face retaliation. European policy-makers disapprove of this 'unilateral' approach, deeming it contrary to WTO principles that favour the use of the multilateral dispute-settlement mechanism.

The European Commission usually opts instead for a less-directly-confrontational approach in negotiations with third countries. For example, instead of publicly threatening retaliation through tariff increases, the Commission may hint at proposals for directives or decisions that would have market-closing effects. Or the Commission may offer the third country greater market access in Europe, or technical aid, in exchange for concessions. Sometimes the Commission may work with large European companies to facilitate a large investment in the third country in exchange for concessions.

These tactical differences between the European and US approaches to third-country negotiations, and the normative views underlying them, might make it difficult to reach transatlantic agreement on an appropriate modality for trade negotiations with third countries. Thus, for example, one

analyst of international intellectual property issues acknow-
ledges the EU's interest in closer transatlantic cooperation
on intellectual property issues in third countries, but suggests
that cooperation will be unlikely as long as the US government threatens to act unilaterally.[32]

The Limits of Transatlantic Power
Finally, on some issues the market power of the United States
and Europe may not be sufficient to yield the bargaining outcomes they desire. As explained above, the great power management approach is premised on the notion that the combined
US and European markets are so important that implicit or
explicit threats of closure, or promises of increased access, can
be used decisively as bargaining leverage. While this premise
may be true generally, it is not true in every trade-related
negotiating context. For example, one analyst has argued that
EU and US negotiating leverage on raw materials eco-labelling
negotiations in Asia will be ineffective as long as it depends
solely on market power: Japan is such a huge consumer of
Asian raw materials that it might have to be added to a great-
power negotiation on that topic with any other country in Asia
if the negotiation is to succeed.[33]

Overcoming Obstacles to Successful Great-Power Management

These problems have constrained the combination of European
and American power necessary to solve third-country problems
and manage the world trading system. However, there are ways
to solve these problems.

Solving Cooperation Problems in Negotiations with Third Countries:
Building a Transatlantic Regime of Cooperation
Some cooperation problems can be solved through specially
designed mechanisms or regimes. The wisdom of any particular solution will vary depending on the transatlantic cooperation problem to be resolved. The central cooperation
problem identified above is the possibility that a third country
could drive a wedge between the transatlantic powers in a
negotiation on a particular sector or cross-sectoral topic,
offering enticing concessions or side-payments on issues of

interest to either the European Union or the United States in exchange for that power's 'defection' from the transatlantic effort. If it were possible for the transatlantic powers to commit to a particular cooperative regime, then they could solve this problem and advance cooperation in trilateral, plurilateral or multilateral negotiations by *packaging* several issues under a simultaneous negotiation process. Under such a regime, linkage can be maintained among all the issues which are negotiated jointly by the transatlantic powers. The benefits to be derived by each transatlantic power from successful negotiation of the package as a whole would be so great that each third country could not make an offer sufficient to entice either power into defecting from collaboration on the package. This prearranged interdependence across issues, and the fact that the two powers might otherwise be forced to pursue some of these issues on their own, would be enough to generate adequate incentives and assurance for both the European Union and the United States to adhere to a cooperative bargaining stance. For example, it might be useful for the United States to agree to back the European Union's efforts to end piracy of sound recordings in Central and Eastern Europe (a concern not as salient to US industry) in exchange for EU agreement to back US efforts to end piracy of software and films in Asia (a concern not as salient to European industry).[34]

An explicit linkage-strategy like that suggested above could also work in the context of a multilateral trade negotiation. EU–US agreement on a package of positions to take on third-country issues in advance of a multilateral trade negotiation offers an opportunity for such linkages. Such a package of positions could be established either through a specific transatlantic negotiation or through establishment of, for example, a transatlantic free-trade area that could institutionalize the convergence of EU and US positions on a host of issues.

Moreover, transatlantic cooperation on a *series* of topics with several third countries might be achieved even if these negotiations take place over time and there is no direct linkage among these issues. The transatlantic powers can avoid defection by each other by conditioning their future strategy on the behaviour of their coalition partner in the current negotiation. If transatlantic cooperation reduces the costs of a deal for both powers, then such 'tit-for-tat' strategies could be enough to induce cooperation, since both powers can move to mutually-beneficial outcomes over time. The crucial element is the transatlantic powers' clear understanding that they will be engaged in a series of negotiations over a long time horizon.

In short, this suggests that transatlantic agreement to pursue negotiations with third countries in a set or long series of issues will overcome the ability of third countries to easily drive a wedge into EU–US cooperation. And this conclusion holds regardless of whether such negotiations take place in a multilateral, plurilateral or trilateral context.

Overcoming the Normative Obstacle: Choosing a Modality for Cooperation

To the extent that the transatlantic powers agree to cooperate in the WTO context, there is unlikely to be a modality problem; the WTO negotiating process is considered legitimate and appropriate on both sides of the Atlantic. Cooperation with the European Union in the prosecution of WTO dispute-settlement claims should also be relatively straightforward, since this process is also considered legitimate and appropriate. Moreover, the US government's domestic authority to engage the WTO dispute-settlement process, Section 301, requires Washington to abide by the results of the dispute-settlement mechanism, ensuring that related US action will be consistent with the WTO. The European Commission also has the institutional authority to cooperate with the US government in WTO dispute-settlement actions pursuant to the Trade Barriers Regulation.

The norms problem is serious, however, in the context of efforts to engage in trilateral US–EU–third country negotiations, or in pairs of bilateral (US–third country and EU–third country) negotiations, given US attachment to the Section 301 approach (which may culminate in an ultimatum to a third country) and Europe's disdain for it. But there may be a way to overcome this problem in a trilateral context. Washington and Brussels could establish a 'Transatlantic Action List' that includes topics and countries that are the subject of trilateral negotiation. With respect to items on that list, the US government could declare either that it will not use, or will suspend the use of, Section 301 during a specified period (perhaps 12 months) when the European Union and the United States are effectively participating in the trilateral negotiations. The USTR could certify on a regular basis (perhaps every four months) that the trilateral negotiation on a particular topic is producing positive results; failure to so certify would then cause the USTR to consider treating the problem under Section 301. This approach could probably be adopted by means of agency action, requiring no formal congressional action, but key congressional leaders should be first convinced that the approach is worth a try.[35] Both the European Union and the country that is the focus of the liberalization effort would have incentives to make the negotiations work, because they both dislike the Section 301 approach.

Transcending the Limits of Transatlantic Power
If transatlantic power in a particular negotiating context is insufficient to yield an effective bargaining outcome, there are at least two sets of solutions. First, the European Union and the United States could create linkages across topics. For example, the transatlantic powers could expand the parameters of a negotiation, demanding progress on the topic on which they lack leverage (for example, natural resources eco-labelling in Asia) in exchange for concessions on another topic on which they do have leverage (for example, increased Asian access to the US and European apparel markets). More broadly, they could create a package of market-access opportunities for a third country in exchange for concessions by that third country on the topic where the transatlantic powers otherwise lack sufficient bargaining leverage.

Second, the transatlantic powers could bring into the game another powerful player with interests similar to theirs. This obvious solution is suggested by the great-power management approach. For example, in negotiations on raw material eco-labelling issues in Asia – a topic on which EU and US threats to act together appear relatively ineffective[36] – the European Union and the United States could add another powerful country – Japan – to the concert so that combined power is adequate to yield a negotiated outcome. Similarly, EU–Japan–US cooperation on fourth-country issues might be appropriate on investment-policy issues in certain Asian countries (since Japan has been such an important source of investment in Asia). Hence, this solution suggests using plurilaterals instead of trilaterals on some topics.

TRANSATLANTIC TRADE POLICY AND PROPOSALS

Having identified the parameters of a successful great-power management strategy, it is useful to evaluate contemporary transatlantic trade policy and proposals. Is that policy consistent with a great-power management strategy? What would alternative policies look like? Are these feasible, especially given the kinds of cooperation problems identified above?

The State of Play: Current Transatlantic Trade Policy

For the past few decades, Europe and the United States have organized their trade relations and cooperation on common trade problems through summit meetings (now regularly scheduled twice annually); transatlantic cabinet meetings (which used to be regularly scheduled); relatively frequent ministerial and sub-cabinet meetings; normal diplomatic channels; *ad hoc* bureaucratic contacts; and plurilateral vehicles such as Quadrilaterals, G-7 meetings and OECD activity. This approach has constituted a broad transatlantic trade dialogue that has often successfully resolved trade issues. But, in 1995, leaders on both sides of the Atlantic began championing initiatives to deepen EU–US trade relations. Some called for increasing joint work by civil servants and ministers in Washington and Brussels on specified EU–US trade issues; others called for the negotiation of a Transatlantic Free Trade Agreement (TAFTA); and still others for a EU–US 'economic space' or 'New Transatlantic Marketplace' (NTM) that would progressively eliminate tariff and non-tariff barriers to trade, and would presumably address deeper trade-related policies such as standards, subsidies, intellectual-property protection, investment measures, services and competition policy.[37]

Two main rationales have been offered for this flurry of proposals. Several supporters of transatlantic deepening –

including former U.S. and European officials like Warren
Christopher, Malcolm Rifkind, Margaret Thatcher and Henry
Kissinger – have offered a geostrategic rationale.[38] Many of
them perceive or fear a 'transatlantic drift' in light of the
dissolution of the Cold War glue that helped bind together
Europe and the United States. They hope new economic
arrangements could infuse the bilateral relationship with a
dose of formal cooperation. Most of them have argued that
the increased political commitment by the United States to
Europe implicit in NATO expansion will require an economic
counterpart. And many of the Americans among them have
suggested that efforts at deeper economic integration will help
provide a broad context in which to generate US domestic
political support favouring NATO expansion. All of these individuals have endorsed negotiation of a Transatlantic Free
Trade Area (TAFTA), although former Secretary Christopher
later backed off from his endorsement.

In contrast, several trade and commerce government officials
– including Mickey Kantor, Ron Brown, Sir Leon Brittan, Roy
Maclaren and Jacques Santer – have focused their arguments
for deepening transatlantic economic relations on potential
bilateral trade benefits (while acknowledging and supporting
other arguments as well).[39] Their trade-policy recommendations have usually been less ambitious than those of the geostrategists. Economic policy analysts Clyde Prestowitz, Lawrence
Chimerine and Andrew Szamosszegi have estimated that direct
static gains from EU–US free trade would approximately equal
a 0.5 per cent increase in the GDP of both the United States
and the EU – a modest figure.[40] Yet, US and EU trade and
commerce ministers have not been willing to commit to the
serious bilateral negotiations that would be required to realize
even these modest gains. To most veterans of the Uruguay
Round, calls for negotiating a TAFTA need to be sobered by
the reality of serious domestic political barriers, particularly in
sectors like agriculture, broadcasting and maritime services.
Nonetheless, trade ministry officials do see some potential for
concluding transatlantic trade arrangements on topics where
there is likely to be agreement between businesses on both
continents.

The net result of these policy discussions has been the
development of a relatively modest programme for action in

the short term, and more ambitious talk about what might be possible in the longer term. At the December 1995 Madrid Summit, the European Union and the United States agreed to a New Transatlantic Agenda,[41] one part of which commits the parties to 'Contributing to the Expansion of World Trade and Closer Economic Relations'.[42] The New Transatlantic Agenda launched several bilateral trade activities, many of which had been recommended by the Transatlantic Business Dialogue (TABD), a group of business leaders convened at the behest of EU Commissioners Brittan and Bangemann and the late US Commerce Secretary Ron Brown. Specifically, the transatlantic powers agreed to support the negotiation of an Information Technology Agreement, which has now been successfully concluded; to reduce technical and non-tariff barriers to trade associated with business regulations in Europe and the United States, including the conclusion of mutual-recognition agreements on conformity-assessment, one of which has now been concluded;[43] to conclude a bilateral customs cooperation and mutual-assistance agreement; and to establish a joint working group on employment and labour issues.

More broadly, instead of immediate negotiation of a TAFTA, the New Transatlantic Agenda called for the creation of a New Transatlantic Marketplace (NTM) that would 'progressively eliminate' transatlantic tariff and non-tariff barriers. But the parties were conveniently vague about the time-span for completing liberalization, and which barriers will be eliminated. Moreover, some policy-makers seem to envision a piecemeal negotiation in which the NTM is built slowly over the course of a decade or more, with successive arrangements concluded issue-by-issue as solutions become feasible.

Since the Madrid Summit, work on these areas has moved steadily forward. Yet, for the most part, little of magnitude in the NTM has been concluded. The brightest lights have been conclusion of the ITA and the mutual-recognition agreement, and the extent of consensus reached among business leaders engaging in the TABD, reflected most clearly in their May 1996 Progress Report which offers dozens of recommendations for reducing transatlantic trade barriers. Even these modest accomplishments may overstate the extent to which cooperation has succeeded and may succeed under the New Transatlantic Agenda. Moreover, in 1998, establishment of an NTM was blocked by France, so the European Commission and the US government are now backing still another plan – liberalization of a few sectors or on a few cross-sectoral topics, which they are calling the 'Transatlantic Economic Partnership' (TEP).

These may be useful efforts, reducing bilateral tension and slowly encouraging transatlantic convergence on some trade issues of multilateral interest. But the great-power management paradigm suggests that transatlantic trade relations should be structured to address common problems with third countries more effectively and directly, and to manage the multilateral trading system. By late 1998, transatlantic policies – and the associated debates over reorganizing transatlantic trade relations – had not fully articulated a relationship between transatlanticism and multilateralism. Several policy proposals, which are variants of proposals that have been floated in the last few years, should be evaluated with the great-power management paradigm in mind.

Policy Proposal One: A Transatlantic Deep Integration Package, Quickly Negotiated

Deep transatlantic integration could serve as a cornerstone of enhanced cooperation, and if properly structured could advance liberal multilateralism. 'Deep integration' entails substantially liberalizing all transatlantic trade in goods and services. It includes not only the elimination of *international* trade barriers, such as tariffs and quotas, and the conclusion of agreements on anti-dumping and countervailing duties issues, but would also address topics often considered *domestic* in nature, such as product standards, domestic regulatory policies, environmental policies, intellectual property, rights of establishment in manufacturing and services sectors, other investment rules, competition policy, and other domestic trade-related measures.[44] Some proposals for a TAFTA seem to have had transatlantic deep integration in mind.[45] Through liberalization, integration could offer not only increased efficiency and welfare, but also a substantial decrease in trade and investment diversion associated with the powers' respective regional free-trade arrangements. Perhaps most significantly, such an exercise would likely improve transatlantic cooperation in third country negotiations, and could be structured to maximize the chances that EU–US deep integration arrangements may become multilateral rules.

The process of negotiating deeper transatlantic integration could offer a means of resolving outstanding bilateral trade disputes that otherwise may be exploited in subsequent EU–US negotiations with third countries. It would also entail the simultaneous negotiation of outstanding bilateral trade issues, potentially transforming the transatlantic dialogue from a serial bilateral dialogue to a dialogue with cross-issue linkages. This might make it possible to resolve several bilateral problems that had been unsuccessfully addressed on an individual basis. Resolution of outstanding EU–US trade disputes would not only permit EU and US diplomats to refocus their attention on more serious strains on the multilateral system, it would also eliminate divisive issues that third countries might otherwise be able to exploit in subsequent negotiations with the transatlantic powers.

More broadly, a transatlantic deep integration package would help make it easier for the two powers to cooperate in efforts to liberalize trade with the rest of the world. The European Union and the United States would have established a linked set of issue positions that would also be employed in subsequent negotiations they could hold with third countries. By reaching agreement on most major trade issues, the two powers would have effectively agreed on trade-liberalizing treaty language that could serve as the basis for third-country treaties. And, after implementation of a transatlantic deep integration package, the European Union and the United States would have approximated many relevant rules and regulations.

A transatlantic deep integration package could then be used to build a similar multilateral deep integration package in a relatively passive, non-aggressive manner by making the package open for accession through negotiation to any country willing to adopt all the arrangements' obligations. This would be an offer to effectively end the risk of trade diversion from the giant transatlantic market in exchange for transforming other national economic systems into conformity with the Western liberal model implicit in the transatlantic package. To be consistent with current WTO rules, a transatlantic deep integration package could offer conditional MFN treatment (that is, MFN treatment only to signatories who undertake its obligations) only to the extent that the trade package meets the criteria of GATT Article XXIV, that the services package meets the criteria of Article V of the General Agreement on Trade in Services (GATS), and to the extent not otherwise inconsistent with WTO rules. Since a central goal of any transatlantic deep integration package should be the establishment of deep integration on a multilateral basis, the European Union and the United States should take into account the position of countries outside the transatlantic region before agreeing how to resolve each issue.

Ultimately, a transatlantic deep integration arrangement could serve as a means of ratcheting regional liberalization towards multilateral liberalization through joining the world's two most important sets of 'hub and spokes' trade regimes. It is possible to see US regional negotiations helping to liberalize the Western hemisphere, while EU regional negotiations would help to liberalize Central and Eastern Europe, the Mediterranean and parts of Africa. A transatlantic deep integration package might eventually be shaped to serve as a vehicle for merging the two sets of regimes. In other words, a solution to the apparent contradiction between multilateralism and regionalism might be provided by great-power management.

But a deep integration arrangement between the European Union and the United States will not be successfully concluded in the short term. The biggest problem is in goods, particularly in agriculture. EU intransigence on the issue in the Uruguay Round, France's apparent willingness to invoke the 'Luxembourg compromise' to block substantial agricultural liberalization,[46] and the EU–US 'peace treaty' on agricultural issues through 2004 (embodied in Article 13 of the Uruguay Round Agreement on Agriculture) all suggest the difficulty of agreeing on transatlantic agricultural liberalization in the short term. While it is not certain that agriculture needs to be fully liberalized in a deep integration package to satisfy GATT's requirements for a 'free trade area', it is certain that agricultural issues create a transatlantic political problem that is not easily solved. A deal without agriculture would probably not be acceptable to the US Congress, and a deal with agriculture would probably not be acceptable in Brussels. This does not mean that eventual negotiation of a transatlantic deep integration package is hopeless. Continued US pressure on the subject may help, and as Central European countries join the European Union – especially Poland – the continued viability of the Common Agricultural Policy (CAP) will be questioned. Further long-term decline in the value of the dollar would put additional pressure on the CAP. Eventually, the agriculture problem may become more easily solved; however, in the short-term, conclusion of a deep integration package that includes a transatlantic free trade area in goods is of questionable feasibility.

Policy Proposal Two: A Transatlantic Deep Integration Package, Negotiated 'Progressively'

Some policy-makers, recognizing the political constraints on agreeing now to eliminate tariff and quota protection on transatlantic trade in goods completely, are considering deepening transatlantic integration in stages, element-by-element over time, with no clear establishment of a free trade area in goods at the outset. This appears to be what some policy-makers had in mind when they endorsed the negotiation of an NTM that would 'progressively eliminate' transatlantic tariff and non-tariff barriers. And it may be what some hope for when they back the TEP.

Current proposals for element-by-element transatlantic integration fall into two categories. One set of policies and proposals is aimed at piecemeal liberalization of trade in goods, and many of these have been recommended by the TABD. They will reduce transatlantic tension, facilitate trade, and could be considered part of a 'progressive' deep integration process. For example, the effort to reach agreements on mutual recognition of conformity-assessment has been successful for some product groups and beneficial to both the European Union and the United States. The same may be said of efforts to negotiate 'rules of the road' on relatively technical issues, such as on-going sectoral efforts to harmonize certain technical standards, and on-going negotiations on customs matters.[47] Agreements on these topics should be relatively easy to negotiate (compared to a topic like agriculture), which is another attraction of the element-by-element approach to deep integration.

But these efforts to liberalize transatlantic trade in goods through mutual-recognition agreements, harmonization of technical standards, and so on, do not obviously advance the agenda of liberal multilateralism. These efforts preclude evaluating when the transatlantic package of liberalizing agreements would constitute a free trade area as defined under GATT Article XXIV. A series of transatlantic arrangements, negotiated piecemeal, does not meet the terms of GATT Article XXIV until it schedules the liberalization of 'substantially all trade' between the EU and United States. Until then, it could not offer preferential treatment for EU and US production; most piecemeal-negotiated outcomes would have to be offered to other WTO members on an MFN basis. The resulting free-ride would make it difficult to conclude a transatlantic free trade area in goods in this manner; many in the United States would be loath to continue engaging in a process that would allow free-riders. Moreover, to the extent of the free-ride, the transatlantic powers would not be using their market power to yield multilateral solutions.

Notwithstanding this criticism, an element-by-element approach could advance liberal multilateralism to the extent that it resulted in preferential agreements that could be opened for accession by third countries willing to assume the agreements' obligations. Specifically, the transatlantic powers could negotiate agreements on important topics not yet fully covered by the WTO, and try to use those agreements as a basis for further liberalization of world trade and investment. To the extent that they are not inconsistent with WTO rules, each such agreement could offer MFN and national treatment to third countries only on the condition that they agree to accede to the instrument and undertake its obligations.

Perhaps the most attractive element to pursue would be the establishment of a free trade area in services, pursuant to GATS Article V.[48] In contrast to the GATT's relatively stringent Article XXIV requirement that a free trade area in goods must liberalize 'substantially all trade', GATS Article

V provides that a free trade area in services must have 'substantial sectoral coverage'. Thus, the GATS language would probably permit the establishment of a transatlantic services free trade area, even if it were to exclude politically sensitive sectors from coverage. A transatlantic free trade area in services could therefore legally discriminate against third-country services-providers to the extent not inconsistent with GATS-scheduled national treatment commitments or services commitments in other arrangements such as NAFTA. Discrimination in services sectors against third countries by the European Union and the United States might be bad policy, but the absence of a legal obligation prohibiting it would provide an incentive for third countries to commit to national treatment to European and US services-providers in exchange for commitments by the transatlantic powers not to discriminate against their services-providers.

The OECD Multilateral Agreement of Investment (MAI) negotiations seemed to offer an analogous opportunity: Europe and the United States were, until late 1998, negotiating an agreement with others in the OECD that they intended to use as a basis for later WTO negotiations on the subject. However, the effectiveness of this effort in providing incentives for non-OECD members to join was limited because the MAI could have denied the benefits of its liberal investment rules to WTO members only to the extent permitted by the GATS MFN obligation, and TRIMs constraints in particular. Although the MAI talks have foundered for now, the transatlantic powers are sure to consider again how to create incentives for third countries to liberalize their investment rules.

Similarly, a transatlantic agreement on competition policy would resolve many EU–US differences on the topic. Such an agreement would also coordinate a position that Brussels and Washington could use as a basis for negotiation with third countries, and that would serve as a basis for action against anti-competitive behaviour throughout the world.[49] The transatlantic powers could build off the EC–US Cooperation Agreement to consider whether a new agreement should embody provisions establishing rules on the extraterritorial application of competition policy, define as impermissible specific types of anti-competitive behaviour faced by both EU and US exporters, establish special obligations for the extra-jurisdictional

production of evidence in competition- policy cases, and establish certain presumptions where evidence is not produced or
otherwise difficult to obtain. However, the US government
would probably have to modify its anti-dumping laws in
exchange for a meaningful agreement on competition policy.

Each of these arrangements on non-goods topics – a transatlantic free trade area in services, the MAI approach, a transatlantic agreement on competition policy – has intrinsic merit
and could be used to varying degrees to help liberalize third-
country trade.

Policy Proposal Three: Trilaterals and Other Arrangements Aimed Largely Third-Country Issues

In an effort to reduce strains on the liberal system, the European
Union and the United States could consider launching a *set* or
series of trilateral negotiations in which the transatlantic powers
would cooperate in resolving trade tensions they have with various third countries. These negotiations could complement or
substitute for the other strategies described above. A programme
of trilateral negotiations would have three elements: (1) identification of topics and countries with which the transatlantic
powers should jointly negotiate; (2) identification of linkages
across various trilateral negotiations in an effort to enhance
the prospects for transatlantic cooperation; and (3) an effective
modality for coordinated action. Initial topics might include:
access to Japan's automobile parts and electronics consumers;
competition-policy issues in certain countries; bringing China
into the WTO; piracy of intellectual property; accelerated
implementation of the TRIPs agreement in certain developing
or transitional economies; or liberalization of investment measures in third countries. The potential of these topics to become
the focus of trilateral negotiations may be inferred from the
substantial agreement among TABD participants that they are
third-country issues in which European and US businesses have
similar interests.[50] A simultaneous or serial negotiation on
several topics may help ensure continued cooperation between
the transatlantic powers should either be tempted otherwise to
cut its own preferential arrangement with a third country.

The hardest part may be agreement on an appropriate
modality for coordination, given US use of Section 301 and
Europe's disapproval of that approach. The analysis above

suggests a few modalities that might be politically and legally acceptable on both sides of the Atlantic, such as a US decision to refrain from using Section 301 on a specified topic and country during the time in which the European Union and the United States are effectively engaged in a trilateral negotiation with that country. Although trilaterals would be the norm, transatlantic cooperation in plurilateral negotiations might be appropriate in some cases, particularly where a sector operates or a product is made across more than one country, or when a third country, like Japan, holds significant power with respect to a fourth country.

Where the transatlantic powers cannot agree to jointly solve a common problem in a third country, they could have 'rules of the road' to ensure that they do not undercut each others' initiatives there. To assure adherence by the European Union and the United States, any such transatlantic arrangement would need to provide means of assuring that agreements with third countries were concluded on a non-discriminatory basis, otherwise each transatlantic power could be enticed by the third country into concluding a discriminatory agreement. And any such arrangement would need to cover a long or indefinite series of EU-third country and US – third country negotiations, because in the absence of an expected long stream of pay-offs from continued cooperation each transatlantic power might be enticed by the third country into defection from the transatlantic arrangement. Thus, these rules might include: a commitment to conclude agreements on an MFN basis; a promise to support the goals of a negotiation, even if they disagree on methods; and a commitment make public all such agreements (so as to provide a means of assuring that the agreements were non-discriminatory).

Policy Proposal Four: Transatlantic Cooperation in the WTO
Europe and the United States might consider reorganizing their cooperation in the WTO on a basis consistent with the great-power management paradigm. Their activity could focus on third-country problems, which would require deciding the same three issues raised in the context of trilateral negotiations outside the WTO: (1) the topics on which they could cooperate in the WTO, such as China's accession; competition policy rules; and accelerated application of TRIPs to developing countries;

(2) linking or sequencing negotiations on those topics so as to reduce the chance that third countries could entice one of the great powers into breaking ranks with the other; and (3) the appropriate modality of coordination.

The most ambitious modality would be initiation of a 'deep integration' trade round, probably building from a transatlantic deep integration understanding.[51] Recent proposals by the European Union to launch a new 'millennium round' have received substantial support in the WTO, and, in early 1999, Washington announced its support for a new round. From the great power management perspective, it is important that the European Union and the United States should specify from the start a set of specific third-country objectives that they will pursue jointly. In addition, Brussels and Washington should agree from the outset to close the deep integration trade round in much the same manner that they closed the Uruguay Round: withdrawing from GATT 1994 (thereby disengaging from its MFN obligation), and signing a new GATT with its MFN obligation and an associated deep integration package.

In the longer term, the European Union and the United States might consider alternatives to the WTO consensus decision-making practice. The consensus tradition does not reflect the underlying power of the European Union and the United States in world trade affairs. Moreover, it slows the process of further multilateral liberalization and necessitates the kind of power play inherent in withdrawing from GATT and joining the WTO – used to conclude the Uruguay Round – and suggested above as a means of concluding a deep integration trade round. Creation of an executive committee could provide a useful forum for regularized management of the WTO,[52] and adoption of a UN Security Council-style voting system[53] (majority rule, with specified members having a veto) could speed up the decision-making process and formalize efficient governance of the WTO.[54] These approaches recognize that the multilateral system has been managed effectively in the last 20 years only through close transatlantic cooperation and coordination. However, such a change is likely to be resisted by third countries that would lose formal power under such rules and by bureaucrats from the WTO and some member-states who are wed normatively to the consensus decision-making practice.

CONCLUSIONS: ALTERNATIVE FUTURES FOR POLICY AND THE WORLD TRADING SYSTEM

The great-power management approach to liberal multilateralism, described in this chapter and explored in the current policy context, is based on the dual premise that the European Union and the United States are the only great powers that share a Western view of what liberal multilateral rules should be, and that acting together they have market power sufficient to facilitate adoption of such rules. This suggests that transatlantic cooperation is crucial to advancing liberal multilateralism. While there are significant barriers to transatlantic cooperation, these can be overcome.

Yet this analysis of current transatlantic trade policy suggests that the European Union and the United States have not been pursuing strategies likely to substantially advance liberal multilateralism. Instead, their efforts have focused on incrementally lowering barriers to transatlantic trade in goods. At the same time, each power has been pursuing its own regional and bilateral policies with third countries, as well as exploring single-issue multilateral liberalization efforts in the WTO. This policy has resulted in both transatlantic partnership and competition.

In this context, a range of alternative futures for the world trading system may be posited as anchored by two extremes: competitive regionalization or great-power management. Under one extreme scenario, transatlantic cooperation does not move forward; EU–US trade relations become strained increasingly due to continuing competition for preferential advantage in negotiations with third countries, and by finger-pointing over the slow pace of success in the WTO. The failure of the European Union to help the United States advance liberal multilateralism will leave US trade policy with little choice other than a unilateral and regional strategy. The multilateral trading system fractures into competitive regionalism.

Under a more promising scenario, the transatlantic powers will combine their power in the pursuit of liberal multilateralism, perhaps by launching a new WTO trade round aimed largely at third country problems. The European Union and the United States could work towards establishing a preferential free trade area in services, open to accession by third countries willing to undertake its obligations. The transatlantic powers could engage in trilateral negotiations on a set of third-country problems, agreeing first on appropriate topics and modalities for such negotiations. And the European Union and the United States could complete the negotiation of a deep integration package and present it (subject to fine-tuning) as a *fait accompli* to the rest of the world, either as the basis of a WTO deep integration round, or as open to third countries willing to undertake its obligations. EU–US cooperation would thus become the basis of deeper liberalization on a multilateral basis, and would diffuse or eliminate the tension associated with interregional competition. In the future, the transatlantic powers might also champion changes in WTO decision-making rules to reflect transatlantic power.

Thus, this analysis suggests the importance of refocusing the ways the European Union and the United States can cooperate to advance liberal multilateralism. But it also suggests the difficulty of establishing and sustaining the cooperation required to do so.

Notes

1.   I am grateful for the comments on earlier drafts from Benedicte Callan, Stephen S. Cohen I. M. Destler, Eileen Doherty, Ellen Frost, Julius Katz, Mohan Penubarti, Arthur Rosett, John Setear, Bruce Stokes, Phillip R. Trimble and Alan Wm. Wolff. Support for research on this topic was provided by the German Marshall Fund of the United States.

2.   See, for example, Malcolm Rifkind, 'Practical Steps to Take Toward Global Free Trade', *Wall Street Journal*, 30 November 1995, sec. A; Warren Christopher, 'Charting a Transatlantic Agenda for the 21st Century', address at Casa de America, Madrid, Spain, 2 June 1995, in US Department of State Dispatch, 5 June 1995, pp. 467–70; and 'Germany Suggests Euro-NAFTA Trade Zone', *The Reuters European Community Report*, 19 April 1995.

3.   See, for example, Leon Brittan, 'The EU–US Relationship: Will It Last?', speech to the American Club of Brussels, Brussels, 27 April 1995; Michael Kantor, 'Talking Points to American Chamber of Commerce', address to the American Chamber of Commerce, Brussels, 22 May 1995, Roy Maclaren, 'The Occident Express: Toward Transatlantic Free Trade', address to the Royal Institute of International Affairs, London, 22 May 1995. See also Bruce Stokes (ed.), *Open for Business: Creating a Transatlantic Marketplace* (New York: Council on Foreign Relations Press,

1996); Miles Kahler, *Regional Futures and Transatlantic Economic Relations* (New York: Council on Foreign Relations Press, 1995); Ellen L. Frost, *Transatlantic Trade: A Strategic Agenda* (Washington, DC: Institute for International Economics, 1997).

4. Kahler, *Regional Futures, op. cit.*; Jagdish Bhagwati, 'Aggressive Unilateralism: An Overview', in *Aggressive Unilateralism*, ed. Jagdish Bhagwati and Hugh T. Patrick (Ann Arbor: University of Michigan Press, 1990). For illustrations of an approach that supports a process of 'competitive liberalization' as a means of achieving multilateral outcomes, see Jeffrey J. Schott, 'More Free Trade Areas?', in *Free Trade Areas and US Trade Policy*, ed. Jeffrey J. Schott (Washington, D.C.: Institute for International Economics, 1989).

5. For examples of two of these perspectives, see Kahler, *Regional Futures, op. cit.*, and Frost, *Transatlantic Trade, op. cit.*

6. General Agreement on Tariffs and Trade, 30 October 1947, 4 U.S.T. 639.

7. For more detail on this power play, see Richard H. Steinberg, *Trade–Environment Negotiations in the EU, NAFTA, and WTO: Regional Trajectories of Rule Development, American Journal of International Law*, vol. 91 (1997), p. 241.

8. World merchandise trade import shares are from World Trade Organization (WTO), *International Trade: 1995 Trends and Statistics* (Geneva: WTO, 1995) table II.3 p. 26. The 1994 GDP figures are from CIA, *The World Fact Book 1995* (Washington, DC: CIA, June 1995), except for the EU GDP figure, which is from WTO, *International Trade: 1995 Trends and Statistics*, table III. 30, p. 54.

9. Clair Wilcox, *A Charter for World Trade* (New York: Arco Press, 1949).

10. For analyses of Japan's trade and industrial policies and their relationship to world trade, see Chalmers Johnson, *MITI and the Japanese Miracle: The Growth of Industrial Policy, 1925–1975* (Stanford: Stanford University Press, 1982); Laura Tyson, *Who's Bashing Whom? Trade Conflict in High-Technology Industries* (Washington, DC, Institute for International Economics, 1991); Alan Wm. Wolff and Thomas R. Howell, 'Japan', in Thomas R. Howell, Alan Wm. Wolff, Brent L. Bartlett, & R. Michael Gadbaw (eds.), *Conflict Among Nations: Trade Policies in the 1990s* (Boulder, Col.: Westview Press, 1992), p. 45.

11. See, for example, Tracy M. Abels, *The World Trade Organization's First Test: The United States–Japan Auto Dispute, UCLA Law Review*, vol. 44 (1996), p. 467; and Eastman Kodak Company and Dewey Ballantine, 'Privatizing Protection: Japanese Market Barriers in Consumer Photographic Film and Consumer Photographic Paper (Memorandum in Support of a Petition Filed Pursuant to Section 301 of the Trade Act of 1974, May 1995).

12. On 'contestability' in the trade policy context, see Robert Z. Lawrence, 'Towards Globally Contestable Markets', in *Market Access After the Uruguay Round* (Paris: OECD, 1996), p. 25.

13. See, for example, Stephen S. Cohen, 'Geo-Economics: Lessons From America's Mistakes', in Martin Carnoy *et al.* (eds), *The New Global Economy in the Information Age* (University Park, Penn.: Pennsylvania.

State University Press, 1993), pp. 97, 99–105. But also see Paul Krugman, 'Competitiveness: A Dangerous Obsession', *Foreign Affairs* vol. 73, (March–April 1994), p. 28.

14. See Johnson, *MITI and the Japanese Miracle*, *op. cit.*

15. Aaron Wildavsky, *Searching for Safety* (New Brunswick: Transaction Books, 1988).

16. Ian Goldin, Odin Krutsen, and Dominique Van Bermensrugge, (eds), *Trade Liberalization: Global Economic Implications* (Paris: OECD, 1993).

17. See John H. Jackson, 'State Trading and Non-Market Economies', in *The World Trading System* (Cambridge, Mass.: MIT Press, 1989), pp. 283, 283–98. See also Donald C. Clarke, 'GATT Accession for China?' *University of Puget Sound Law Review*, vol. 17 (1994), p. 517.

18. See Richard H. Steinberg, 'Antidotes to Regionalism: Responses to Trade Diversion Effects of the North American Free Trade Agreement', *Stanford Journal of International Law*, vol. 29 (1993), p. 322–5.

19. For example, hegemonic stability theory and game theory suggest the instability of coalitions in a multi-polar system. See, for example, Stephen Krasner, 'State Power and the Structure of World Trade', *World Politics*, vol. 27, (1976) p. 317, and Kenneth Waltz, *Theory of International Politics* (Menlo Park, CA: Addison-Wesley, 1978).

20. Winfried Ruigrok and Rob Van Tulder, *Exploring the Potential for US–EU Trade Cooperation in Asia in the Automobile and Auto Parts Industries*, Working Paper no. 120 (Berkeley: Berkeley Roundtable on the International Economy, 1998).

21. Bureau of National Affairs, 'Brittan Says EU, Japan Reach "Breakthrough on Auto Imports"', *International Trade Reporter*, vol. 12 (1995), p. 970.

22. Bureau of National Affairs, 'US, European Executives Views Differ on Framework Agreement', *International Trade Reporter*, vol. 12 (1995), p. 1769.

23. Bureau of National Affairs, 'Brittan Says EU, Japan Reach "Breakthrough on Auto Imports"', *op. cit.*; Bureau of National Affairs, 'EU Threatens Complaint in WTO if US, Japan Agree on Import Plan', *International Trade Reporter*, vol. 12 (1995), p. 918; Bureau of National Affairs, 'US Report on Auto Accord, Say Dispute is Now Removed from WTO', *International Trade Reporter*, vol. 12 (1995), p. 1176.

24. Agreement on Trade-Related Aspects of Intellectual Property Rights (15 April 1994), reprinted *International Legal Materials*, vol. 33 (Washington, DC: American Society of International Law) p. 1197.

25. Julius Katz, former Deputy United States Trade Representative, interview with author, Washington, DC, May 1995.

26. See for example Ruigrok and Van Tulder, *Exploring the Potential for US–EU Trade Cooperation*, *op. cit.*; Francois Bar and Emily M. Murase, *The Potential for Transatlantic Cooperation in Telecommunications Services Trade in Asia*, Working Paper no. 108 (Berkeley: Berkeley Roundtable on the International Economy, 1998).

27. The general problem was suggested in an early game theoretical analysis of the three-person 'majority rule' game. See John von Neumann and Oskar Morgenstern, *Theory of Games and Economic Behavior*, 2nd edn

(Princeton: Princeton University Press, 1947), pp. 220–37. For 'divide the dollar' games, see, for example, Hans Haller, 'Non-Cooperative Bargaining of $N \geq 3$ Players,' *Economic Letters*, vol. 22 (1986), pp. 11–30.

28. Bureau of National Affairs, 'China to Apply US Agreement Equally to All Trading Partners, Brittan Says', *International Trade Reporter*, vol. 12 (1995), p. 741.

29. The agreement is focused on 'high quality beef', the definition of which has the effect of including most US beef and excluding most EU beef. Letter and Record of Understanding from Tong-Jin Park, Ambassador for the Republic of Korea, to Carla A. Hills, United States Trade Representative (26 April 1990), on file with author; Letter and Record of Understanding from Carla A. Hills, United States Trade Representative, to Tong-Jin Park, Ambassador for the Republic of Korea (27 April 1990).

30. Arrangement between the Government of Japan and the Government of the United States Concerning Trade in Semiconductor Products (2 Sept 1986), reprinted *International Legal Materials*, vol. 25, p. 1409. For the EU view of the Japan–US semiconductor arrangements, see 'Brittan Says US–Japan Chip Pact Must Go Before ITA Can Arrive', *European Report*, 24 April 1996 (http://www.lexis-nexis.com, Nexis library, EUR-COM library, EURPRT file).

31. The green paper is described briefly in Bureau of National Affairs, 'China to Apply US Agreement Equally', *op. cit.*

32. Benedicte Callan, *The Potential for Transatlantic Cooperation on Intellectual Property in Asia*, Working Paper no. 116 (Berkeley: Berkeley Roundtable on the International Economy, 1998).

33. James Salzman, *Product and Raw Material Eco-labeling: The Limits of a Transatlantic Approach*, Working Paper no. 117 (Berkeley: Berkeley Roundtable on the International Economy, 1998).

34. Callan, *The Potential for Transatlantic Cooperation on Intellectual Property in Asia, op. cit.*

35. Convincing Congressional leaders of the worthiness of the approach is likely to be a political prerequisite to trying it. Before adopting its creative interpretation of 'Special 301', the US Trade Representative consulted carefully with Congressional leaders. Michael Brownrigg, former Chief of Staff to US Trade Representative Carla A. Hills, interview with author, Los Angeles, California, 4 April 1997.

36. See Salzman, *Product and Raw Material Eco-Labeling, op. cit.*

37. For examples of this flurry of proposals, see Rifkind, 'The Occident Express: Toward Transatlantic Free Trade', *op. cit.* 'EU/US: Action Plan Fine-Tuned Before Transatlantic Summit', *European Information Service*, 5 December 1995; Steven Greenhouse, 'US to Seek Stronger Trade and Political Ties With Europe', *New York Times*, 29 May 1995, sec. A.

38. See sources in note 2; and also, Peter Brimelow, 'Tafta?', *Forbes*, 1 July 1996, p. 52.

39. See sources in note 3.

40. Clyde Prestowitz, Jr, Lawrence Chimerine, and Andrew Z. Szamosszegi 'The Case for a Transatlantic Free Trade Area', in Bruce Stokes (ed.),

Open For Business: Creating a Transatlantic Marketplace (New York: Council on Foreign Relations Press, 1996).

41.   US Information Agency, *The New Transatlantic Agenda* (visited 18 November 1997), <http://www.state. gov/www/regions/eur/ european union agenda.html>

42.   *Ibid.*

43.   The June 1997 mutual-recognition agreement covers six product areas – medicinal products, medical devices, telecommunications terminal equipment, electromagnetic compatibility, electrical safety equipment, and recreational boats. See Bureau of National Affairs, 'US, EU Agree on Mutual Recognition of Electronic Products, Official Says', *International Trade Reporter*, vol. 13 (1996), p. 1016. Commission of the European Communities, 'EU Reaches Agreements to Cut Red Tape With United States and Canada', *RAPID Press Release*, 13 June 1997.

44.   See, for example, Lawrence, 'Towards Globally Contestable Markets', *op. cit.*

45.   See, for example, Rifkind, 'The Occident Express: Toward Transatlantic Free Trade', *op. cit.*

46.   See Bureau of National Affairs, 'EC Ministers Instruct Negotiators to Clarify Blair House Accord With US', *International Trade Reporter*, vol. 10 (1993), p. 1564

47.   See generally, Bureau of National Affairs, 'Business Leaders Draft Proposals for US–EU Trans-Atlantic Summit', *International Trade Reporter*, vol. 13 (1996), p. 884. and Bureau of National Affairs, 'US, EU Agree to Move Ahead with Information Technology Pact', *International Trade Reporter*, vol. 13 (1996), p. 1016.

48.   In early 1998, the European Commission proposed such an initiative to the Council; see speech by Sir Leon Brittan, 'The New Tiger? The Shape of Tomorrow's Global Economy', delivered at the Kennedy School of Public Policy, Harvard University, Boston, Mass., 18 March 1998.

49.   Howell and Wolff, *US–EU Cooperation in Competition Policy in Asia*, *op. cit.*

50.   See Transatlantic Business Dialogue, *Progress Report* (Brussels, 23 May 1996).

51.   See Brittan, 'An Open Europe in an Open World', speech delivered to the Netherlands Trade Federation, Scheveningen, Netherlands, 16 November 1996.

52.   Proposals for an 'executive committee' or 'advisory council' of powerful contracting parties or member-states to lead decision-making in the GATT/WTO were made in 1990–91 in bilateral proposals by the United States to the European Community, and by the United States meetings between members of the Quad group. See Katz interview, *op. cit.*

53.   Such a system was proposed to high-level EU negotiators by high-level US negotiators in 1990–91 bilaterals, but was rejected. See Katz interview, *op. cit.*

54.   In contrast to the WTO's consensus decision-making rule, the International Monetary Fund and the World Bank employ weighted voting, which reflects underlying power more accurately.

10 The United States and Europe: The Emerging Regulatory Framework for International Capital Markets

Beth A. Simmons

During the past two decades or so, capital controls have been lifted, national capital markets have been liberalized and international capital markets have exploded among the advanced industrial economies and beyond. As major players with significant stakes in the smooth operation of international capital markets, the United States and Europe have common interests in the emergence of a regulatory framework that enhances market stability, minimizes systemic risks, and allows for the efficient operation of markets. Yet despite the growth in cross-border capital movements, regulatory cooperation is at times plagued by differences in national approaches and preferences, difficulties coordinating rules where multiple regional or international organizations are involved, and regulators' reluctance to cooperate fully with foreign jurisdictions.

As a result, cooperation among financial regulators in Europe and North America has been intense but uneven since the late 1980s. It has assumed a variety of forms – multilateral, regional and bilateral – that are closely related to the nature of the problem regulators are trying to tackle and the market forces at play. Few have doubted the need to address in some fashion regulatory problems that arise with the internationalization of capital, but the politics of regulatory harmonization have been driven by concerns about defection and the regulatory scope necessary to assure regulatory effectiveness. And, increasingly, decisions made outside of the North Atlantic region influence financial stability within that region, as the instability that started in late 1997 in Asia has graphically illustrated.

A single chapter cannot do justice to the range of rules and agreements that have been made among the banking and securities regulators of Europe and America over the past decade. Rather than strive for exhaustiveness, this chapter selects three issue areas that illustrate particular dynamics of rule development: capital adequacy standards for internationally active banks; anti-money laundering efforts; and international accounting standards for foreign listings on local stock exchanges. There are two key dimensions that these cases illustrate: the problem of *defection* (which demands stronger rules of surveillance and sanction than mere coordination problems), and the issue of the *scope* of agreement (systemic problems demand multilateral solutions).

The remainder of this chapter is organized as follows. The first section presents evidence of the growth in international capital flows that motivate much of the concern to coordinate a regulatory response. Next, I explore the rationale for US–European cooperation in regulating these growing markets. Section three discusses the international organizational context in which US–European relations take place in this issue area. Then I examine three areas of regulation, and characterize the process of rule development in each. Finally, in the concluding section, I offer policy implications for transatlantic coordination with respect to the regulation of international capital markets.

THE GROWTH OF INTERNATIONAL CAPITAL MARKETS

There is little doubt that the relatively recent burst of concern within the Atlantic community for fashioning some kind of common regulatory regime for international capital markets has been the result of the fantastic growth in these markets over the past decade. Balance of payments statistics indicate that cross-border transactions in bonds and equities for the G-7 rose from less than 10 per cent of gross domestic product in those countries in 1980, to over 140 per cent in 1995.[1] International bond markets have reached staggering proportions: by the end of 1995, some \$2.8 trillion of international debt securities were outstanding worldwide. Capital flows, largely from Europe and the United States, but also from

Japan, to developing countries and countries in transition grew from $57 billion in 1990 to over $211 billion in 1995.[2] Foreign lending in the form of international syndicated credit facilities has surged since the 1980s, to over $320 billion at the end of 1995. Foreign exchange transactions – which represent the world's largest market – reached an estimated average *daily* turnover of nearly $1.2 trillion in 1995, compared to $590 billion daily turnover in 1989.[3]

Several explanations have been advanced for such phenomenal growth. Competitive deregulation, foreign policy pressures, and the exogenous development of technology are prominent themes in the literature.[4] Governments' need to tap international markets to finance growing debts also figure prominently.[5] Many studies have noted the central role played by neo-liberal economic thought and the resurgence of conservative political ideology.[6] But whatever the reason, capital controls have dropped drastically throughout Europe and North America over the past two decades.[7] Consequently, as Figure 10.1 illustrates, foreign investment and capital flows have mushroomed as a proportion of total economic activity for these countries.

At the microeconomic level, this exposure to international markets creates a host of new potential risks, which firms and other investors have tried to reduce through the use of derivative instruments. Exchange-rate and interest-rate volatility have especially contributed to the risks investors face in overseas markets. As a result, the annual turnover in derivatives contracts – defined as financial agreements which derive their value from the performance of other assets, interest or currency exchange rates, or indexes – doubled between 1990 and 1995, from 635.6 million contract trades in 1990 to over 1.2 billion in 1995. The value of these contracts tripled from $3.4 trillion in 1990 to over $10.6 trillion in 1995.[8]

INTERNATIONALIZATION OF CAPITAL AND THE RATIONALE FOR COOPERATIVE REGULATION

In the 1990s, the speed with which international transactions take place, the complex structure of many financial contracts, and the complicated network of branches and affiliates

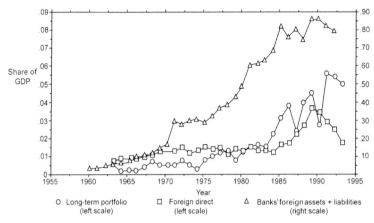

Figure 10.1   The growth in cross-border capital movements: portfolio investment, foreign direct investment and deposit banks' foreign assets plus liabilities, each as a proportion of GDP for the OECD countries, 1960–93

Sources:

Foreign direct investment is calculated from *Balances of Payments of OECD Countries* (Geneva: OECD)

Portfolio investment is calculated from *Balances of Payments of OECD Countries*, supplemented by IMF *Balance of Payments Statistic Yearbook*, (Washington, DC: IMF) detailed transactions tables:

> portfolio outflows are calculated from lines 53 (government bonds), 56 (corporate bonds), and 59 (corporate equities);
> portfolio inflows are calculated from lines 55 (government   bonds), 58 (corporate bonds), and 61 (corporate equities).

Deposit banks' foreign assets and liabilities: IMF, *International Financial Statistics Yearbook* (world tables), various years.

Total flows are calculated as the absolute value of the sum of these inward and outward flows.

through which they pass often makes it difficult for national authorities to properly supervise and regulate financial markets. Increasingly, it is difficult to promote behaviour that is reasonably prudent and fair, without significantly cutting into the efficiency of the market or the jurisdiction of another national regulator. National regulators are also wary of creating a domestic regulatory environment that raises costs for nationally-based firms or that encourages legitimate capital to migrate to jurisdictions with more favourable regulations.

Yet the traditional reasons for regulating capital markets remain.[9] The reduction of systemic risk, the need to protect consumers of these services from flagrant fraud, and the desire to crack down on related illicit activities that use capital markets to launder profits, have increasingly preoccupied regulators across the Atlantic and around the world. Financial liberalization and integration has in many ways complicated their regulatory tasks. Liberalization has increased competition in banking, which in turn has encouraged some firms to take on more risk, potentially threatening systemic stability. A plethora of innovative financial instruments and varying accounting and reporting standards across jurisdictions has reduced transparency. And as capital controls have been lifted, the opportunity to use international markets for illicit activities has increased.

Since the late 1980s, there has been a flurry of activity among national decision-makers, regulators, standard-setters, and law-enforcers in Europe and the United States to stitch together a set of rules for international capital market participants. Financial-market rule development has tended to involve small numbers of national regulators or supervisors, working briefly but intensively on relatively narrow issues, and producing non-binding agreements. It is easy to see why this is so: financial markets are changing so rapidly that drawn-out, legalistic negotiations among a large number of participants would produce agreements that would be obsolete long before they were ever implemented. For example, in thinking about how much capital should be kept on hand to guard against risk, regulatory focus has shifted rapidly from *credit risk* to *market risk*, a concept which itself mutates as quickly as financial instruments and strategies proliferate. This fact has placed the EU, with its relatively cumbersome legislative process, at something of a disadvantage compared to less-formal entities in regulating market risk.

Finally, there is the issue of the concentration of power and the conscious decision among regulators in the largest markets in the United States and Europe to minimize the role played by minor players or the growing number of extra-regional regulators. After all, the largest internationally-active banks are still disproportionately from the G-10 countries; the world's largest stock exchanges are in the United States and London; and some 85 per cent of world foreign exchange transactions involve the US dollar. Moreover, the 25 biggest foreign banks in the world keep roughly 5.6 per cent of their assets in the United States, or about $536 billion.[10] In addition, though difficult to quantify, much of the world's regulatory expertise with respect to finance is concentrated in the major financial centres of the United States and Europe. As a result, the lead regulators in the transatlantic region have approached regulatory harmonization as though the rest of the world has little to contribute and can only slow things down. Increasingly this idea is being challenged, but it is a direct function of shifts in financial power away from Europe and towards Japan, Hong Kong and Singapore. The exception is in anti-money laundering efforts, where smaller jurisdictions' cooperation has been essential to achieve US and European goals.

Overall, the process of rule development has been shaped by the fact that financial markets – and, even more so, financial transactions – are swiftly-moving targets whose supervision and regulation requires streamlined decision-making and a tremendous amount of technical expertise.

The International Organizational Setting

One of the complicating aspects of US–European cooperation is the organizational architecture that deals with cooperative international financial regulation. As will become clear below, many aspects of this cooperation involve parallel harmonization, but there are four significant organizations involved in various aspects of regulatory cooperation (see Figure 10.2).

The first of these is the G-10 group of countries, which makes up the Basle Committee on Banking Supervision (sometimes called the Basle Committee or the Banking Committee) of the Bank for International Settlements. This group is widely recognized as the principal international forum for developments in international banking supervision. (See Table 10.1 for a description of the Basle Concordat System.) The Banking Committee makes decisions by consensus, moving quite swiftly when an issue is viewed as urgent. But the

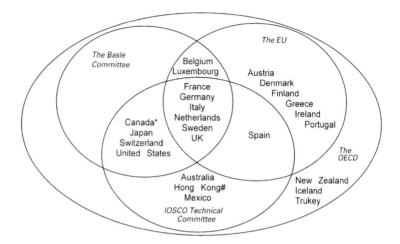

Figure 10.2   Overlapping organizational memberships: the OECD, European Union, Basle Committee, and the Technical Committee of IOSCO

*Canada is represented at the Basle Committee by the Bank of Canada, and at IOSCO by the Ontario and Quebec securities commissions.

#Hong Kong is the only country represented here that is not a member of the OECD.

Source: Adapted from IMF, *International Capital Markets* (Washington, DC: IMF, 1996), p. 145.

Committee has no enforcement power; implementation of its decisions takes place through national regulatory structures. The focus of this group has been to provide standards and general principles to insure adequate supervision of internationally active banks, typically promulgating guidelines that reflect minimum standards to which the member countries are willing to adhere.

Securities regulators have formed their own International Organization of Securities Commissions (IOSCO). The organization as a whole is highly inclusive (95 per cent of the world's stock exchanges are claimed to be represented), but the most important regulatory work is done in the Technical Committee, which is overwhelmingly American and European. Like the Basle Banking Committee, this group also

Table 10.1   The Basle Concordat System

The Basle Concordat of 1975: *Report of the Governors on the Supervision of Banks' Foreign Establishments*. Guidelines for cooperation between national authorities for supervisory authority over foreign banks (branches, subsidiaries, joint ventures).

The Basle Concordat of 1983: *Principles for the Supervision of Banks' Foreign Establishments*. Recommended that parent and host supervisors communicate to determine whether either is unable to supervise a foreign office effectively. Parent supervisor should take over if the host supervisor's level of supervision is deemed inadequate, and vice versa. Parent supervisor is responsible for ensuring that holding companies and their subsidiaries are adequately supervised.

Supplement to the Concordat, 1987/90: Emerged from a joint report by the Basle Committee and the Offshore Group of Banking Supervisors, issued in August 1987. Provided recommendations concerning the removal of secrecy constraints; noted that national secrecy laws designed to protect the legitimate interests of bank customers can be an obstacle to information-exchange among supervisors and banks.

The Capital Adequacy Accord, 1988: *International Convergence of Capital Measurement and Capital Standards*. Provided for a common definition of capital. Established a risk-weighting framework which ties capital requirements to the credit risks of assets and off-balance-sheet activities; and a standard that internationally-active banks must maintain a capital base equivalent to at least 8 per cent of their risk-adjusted assets by the end of 1992.

The Minimum Standards Statement, 1992: *Minimum Standards for the Supervision of International Banking Groups and their Cross- border Establishments*. Lays down standards of supervision. Recommends that supervisors have the right to gather information from cross-border banks or groups for which they are the home-country supervisor.

Source: *International Currency Review*, vol. 22 no. 3–4, 1993/94, p. 99.

makes decisions by consensus; for example, they have recommended endorsement of some of the International Accounting Standards proposed by the International Accounting Standards Committee (referred to in more detail below). The group has also actively encouraged bilateral cooperation

among regulators to curb and punish securities fraud, and in
the wake of the Barings crisis are disseminating recommendations on procedures for identifying large exposures and sharing this information among regulators.[11] Once again, the
decisions of this group are non-binding, and there is a significant disparity among the members with respect to implementation.[12]

The most authoritative international organization dealing
with financial market regulation is without doubt the European
Union. The EU formally entered the banking supervisory
arena in 1977 with the enactment of the 'First Banking Directive'. Of course, in contrast to either the Basle Banking Committee or the Technical Committee of IOSCO, EU directives
are binding on the member-states. The EU has implemented a
'single passport' concept in European financial services, which
permits EU incorporated banks and investment firms to provide cross-border services without further authorization by the
host country. Common rules have been established for capital
adequacy for EU banks, and the EU has made an effort to
extend similar supervisory regimes to banks and securities firms
alike.

The very authoritativeness of the EU has placed it at somewhat of a disadvantage in international financial regulatory
affairs. Because it is crafting legislation, the EU's decision-
making process is far less flexible than that of the G-10's
Banking Committee. For example, the EU's Capital Adequacy
Directive took nearly three years to be adopted after the
proposal had been approved by the Commission. By contrast,
the Banking Committee proposed a common method of measuring capital and it was endorsed by all central bank governors
within seven months, creating the 1988 Capital Accord. As will
be discussed below, the slow pace of EU decision-making has
created further problems in adapting to both the demands of
market conditions and changes in rules by the G-10 supervisors, increasingly rendering the EU a follower rather than
an initiator in banking supervision.

Political organization is only one aspect of the process of
developing a regulatory regime for international capital,
and arguably it is not the most important. Even more crucial
to understanding US–European relations within this issue area
is the central role of market forces that cause interests to

converge or diverge, that create pressures for harmonization or defection, and that create incentives to develop bilateral solutions, or even take unilateral actions, rather than negotiate multilaterally. The cases discussed below highlight the interaction of decision-making and market reaction, thus providing a sense of the context in which cooperative arrangements are made, implemented within the region, and promulgated to the rest of the world.

CASES

The Case of Capital Adequacy Rules

One of the most significant international banking agreements of the past decade has been the decision of the G-10 countries to coordinate their rules on how much capital their nationally-chartered banks are required to hold against credit or other risks. In December 1987, central bankers from the G-10 countries adopted guidelines for evaluating the adequacy of capital in their international banks and agreed to reach an established minimum level by 1992. Worried by a trend towards capital deterioration despite growing financial risks associated with internationalization and liberalization – and the initially serious concern that differential approaches to capital requirements would constitute a competitive disadvantage for banks chartered in countries with more stringent requirements – the United States Federal Reserve and the Bank of England initially struck a bilateral agreement. That accord provided for a common definition of capital, adoption of a risk-weighting system for each class of assets, the inclusion of 'off-balance-sheet' items in risk-determination, and a formula for calculating specific capital requirements for individual banks, based on their weighted-asset risk profile.

The bilateral agreement between the two largest players sparked intense negotiations among the G-10 to adopt a common approach to capital adequacy. By some accounts, Japan, Germany and France accepted the US/UK framework (with some changes) because they were concerned that their banks might be excluded from those markets.[13] More plausible, however, is the reluctance of the G-10 central bankers to cede leadership in this area to the United States and the United Kingdom. A more likely impetus to the broader accord was worry of being perceived as underregulated. The dynamics of capital adequacy harmonization since 1988 have largely been one of *voluntary rule adoption and compliance*, despite early predictions that 'rigorous enforcement' of the rules would be necessary.[14] By the end of 1993, internationally-active G-10 banks had capital ratios that *exceeded* the prescribed minimum.[15] By the mid-1990s the European Union had followed suit. Increasingly, emerging markets around the world have adopted elements of a common approach to capital adequacy: the Czech Republic, Poland and Hungary, for example, have all adopted Basle capital-adequacy standards, and banks in their jurisdictions typically exceed the 8 per cent rule, often by significant margins.[16]

This pattern of concentric waves of harmonization has been influenced by the perceived systemic nature of the risks and low value of defection inherent in this issue area. Despite initiation by the US and the UK, there was never any doubt that a common definition of capital adequacy would have to be applied, at a minimum, across the G-10. The globalization of banking has increasingly meant that any bank involved in the increasingly dense network of interbank relations can potentially transmit its weaknesses – such as problems of liquidity or solvency – to the interbank market and throughout the system. It is for this reason that individual bank failures such as the Herrstatt Bank in 1975, the Italiano Banco Ambrosio, and the scandal and collapse of the Bank for Credit and Commerce International (BCCI) have stimulated *collective* responses – creation of the Basle Banking Committee, promulgation of the G-10 principles of consolidated supervision, and international agreement on minimum standards of home-country supervision, respectively.[17] Prudential banking regulation, of which capital-adequacy standards are just one example, are explicitly intended to 'protect the safety and stability *of the system as a whole*'[18] from risky activities that could originate in any number of institutions in the system.

On the other hand, there are no major net advantages to undercutting a well-established capital adequacy standard. In increasingly complex and highly internationalized financial markets, private actors often depend on the regulatory environment to provide information on the quality of an institution as a counter-party to an agreement. Where the reputations of firms are crucial and information asymmetries provide an opening for opportunistic behaviour, the advantages of providing a well-regulated financial environment generally outweigh those of lowering regulatory standards and competing on price alone. A regulatory race to the bottom is conceivable in the absence of any obvious focal point, but once one has been established there is very little incentive to reduce standards and thereby risk developing a reputation as 'poorly regulated'. Appropriate prudential regulations in fact are a competitive advantage that other jurisdictions have an incentive to copy, for, in the words of the chairman of the Federal Reserve Bank of Australia:

> [o]nce standards or requirements of these [capital adequacy requirements] are adopted by the Central Banks in G-10 countries, there is considerable pressure on others to follow – otherwise their banks risk being perceived as somewhat inferior institutions in competitive situations.[19]

The combination of a systemic problem and low incentives to defect has meant that capital adequacy rules have been negotiated first among the most important financial centres, and then gained adherents *without the pervasive use of political pressure*. The European Union has used the G-10 guidelines as a basis for the Capital Adequacy Directive (CAD) which came into effect in January 1996. This has not been without some complications for the EU, since they are in the business of creating binding directives with which national legislation must be brought into conformity, a process that can barely keep up with the changes in regulatory recommendations coming out the group of G-10 central bankers. Harmonization has also been complicated by the fact that the G-10 focuses its attention on large money-centre banks, while the EU necessarily crafts directives for large and small banks that comprise national banking systems. Nor does adoption of the G-10's approach resolve the issue of the 'level playing field' for the European countries, since some banks have much larger trading books than do others, and these are now taken into account in calculating value at risk according to the G-10 rules. But despite what might be construed as difficulties, harmonization with respect to capital adequacy has proceeded rapidly from the G-10 to the EU.

Capital adequacy standards have become more rigorous and more widespread than a model of competitive regulatory laxity would suggest. The standards have emanated from the most important financial centres, notably the United States and the United Kingdom. They have spread among the G-10, throughout the EU, and beyond through multilateral efforts organized by bank supervisors in the major financial centres, who have defined the problem as systemic. Market pressures to match international standards have been far more important than political pressure, in sharp contrast to the case of anti-money-laundering efforts discussed below.

The Case of Anti-Money Laundering

Money-laundering is the transferring of illegally obtained money or investments through an outside party to conceal the true nature of the source. The Financial Action Task Force (FATF), created by the major industrial countries of the OECD in 1989, estimated that by 1990 about $122 billion was being laundered in Europe and the United States every year (or about $85 billion net after 'expenses').[20] By some estimates, $1 billion of criminal profits finds its way into the world's financial markets *every day*.[21] Lifting capital controls has made laundering easier by reducing the scrutiny given to international transactions.[22] Money-laundering has become a global phenomenon: as North American and European regulators have stepped up enforcement efforts, sometimes with notable success, illicit funds have moved on to Eastern Europe, the former Soviet Republics, the Middle East and parts of Southeast Asia.[23]

International initiatives to control money-laundering have come primarily from the United States, in alliance with the United Kingdom, France and increasingly Australia. As recently as 1986, the United States was the only country in the world to have criminalized money-laundering, and it remains by far the leader in prosecutions.[24] Relatively few prosecutions have actually taken place in Europe, though regulations have tightened significantly as a result of an EU directive on money-laundering.

Money-laundering cannot be handled effectively on a unilateral or bilateral basis. Significantly different rules across jurisdictions invite the shifting of business to countries with weaker controls.[25] For example, when the United States passed the Bank Secrecy Act of 1970, which tightened reporting requirements for cash transactions over $10,000, illicit money moved to Europe where most banks were not required to collect information on large cash deposits.[26] Even cooperation among the major financial centres is insufficient to pose a significant barrier to determined criminals. As the rules have tightened in the industrialized countries, illegal-source money is increasingly directed towards jurisdictions where regulations are more lax (Eastern Europe and the former Soviet Republics, the open economies of the Gulf and Mediterranean regions, and the emerging economies of Asia)[27] or to non-bank institutions where stockbrokers are much less likely than bankers to know their customers.[28] One Bank of England official has reportedly said fighting money-laundering is like squeezing a balloon – you simply displace the activity to wherever there is the least resistance.[29] To yield significant benefits, near-global cooperation is a virtual necessity.

However, individual jurisdictions may face incentives to resist international agreements to control money-laundering. Banking secrecy is often considered essential in attracting legitimate business; rules that require extensive inquiry into the source of funds are likely to push funds offshore.[30] Private banking, as it has been practiced in Switzerland, Liechtenstein and Luxembourg, for example, has proved a lucrative financial niche. The business of managing the funds of wealthy clients provides a third of the Swiss Bank Corporation's very stable profits. Some estimates suggest that private assets managed in Switzerland total SFr20 000 billion, or about a third of all money placed by wealthy individuals in banks outside their home countries.[31] These funds also provide the basis for the country's relatively large capital and securities market. Swiss officials have long recognized that bank secrecy has contributed significantly to the high standard of living and thus 'at least indirectly concerns substantial economic interests of the state'.[32] In Liechtenstein, even mild rules regarding 'due diligence' – which require bankers to report suspicious activities to authorities – 'pose a direct threat to Liechtenstein's basic competitiveness', according to bankers in Vaduz.[33]

Other motives also discourage cooperation. Cost may be one; extensive financial reporting systems are expensive.[34] Tradition and idiosyncratic domestic political constraints in some countries may even be a factor. Austria's unwillingness to give up its traditional anonymous savings accounts has led to a dispute with the EU about whether Austria has fulfilled its obligations under the 1991 directive on money-laundering. Unlike the interest financial institutions may have in developing a reputation for safety, 'it is not necessarily in the direct financial interest of financial institutions to adopt anti-laundering behaviour'.[35] Anti-money laundering efforts provide no clear economic payoff, and may in fact exact immediate costs.

As a result, *international political pressure* has been the driving force behind harmonization to date[36] (for a list of major international anti-money-laundering conventions and agreements, see Table 10.2). The earliest initiatives came from the

*Table*10.2   Major US and European anti-money-laundering initiatives

---

Group of Ten; Committee on Banking Regulation and Supervisory Practices[a]

'*Basle Statement of Principles*'; *Prevention of Criminal Use of the Banking System for the Purpose of Money Laundering* (December 1988).

- Establishes a minimum set of operating standards and management principles by which all banks in the IMF member countries should operate.
- Includes standards on customer identification, and adherence to national laws and policies intended to prevent money- laundering.

Financial Action Task Force (FATF)[b]

'*Financial Action Task Force on Money Laundering Report: Forty Recommendations*' (February 1990).

- Establishes a framework of comprehensive programmes to address money-laundering and facilitate greater cooperation in international investigations, prosecutions and confiscations which the FATF wants all countries to follow (not just its own membership).
- Calls for each country to define money-laundering and make it a criminal offense; recommends that countries extend the definition to

'knowingly' having laundered, and to the proceeds from all illegal activities, not just drug proceeds.

- Recommends that financial institutions do not keep anonymous accounts or accounts in fictitious names. Financial institutions should establish the principal owners and beneficiaries of all accounts.
- Financial institutions should be permitted or required to report suspicious activity to the competent authorities.

Council of Europe[c]

'*Convention on Laundering, Search, Seizure, and Confiscation of the Proceeds of Crime (Strasbourg Convention)*' (November 1990).

- The main purpose of the convention is to coordinate policies with respect to investigation of suspected money-laundering and confiscation of the property and proceeds associated with illegal activities.
- The convention creates an obligation to provide other parties the 'widest possible measure of assistance in the identification and tracing' of property and proceeds, including providing and securing evidence to establish its existence, location, nature, and so on.

European Union

'*Directive on Prevention of the Use of Financial System for the Purpose of Money Laundering*' (June 1991).

- Obliges credit and financial institutions to require proper identification for all their customers when beginning a business relationship, when a single transaction or linked transactions are conducted exceeding ecus 5000, or when money-laundering is suspected.
- Allows member-states to put stricter rules in place than those provided in the directive. These should be coordinated by and communicated to a 'contact committee' to be established by the European Commission.

---

[a] G-7 countries plus Austria, Switzerland and Luxembourg.
[b] The original FATF consisted of G-7 members, eight other industrialized nations, and the European Commission.
[c] Membership currently includes 25 nations from Western Europe, and several Central and Eastern European nations.

United States, when Congress passed the Kerry Amendment,[37] which required the Treasury to negotiate with foreign countries with the objective of having foreign banks record all cash deposits over US$10,000 and to provide information to US authorities in the event of a narcotics-related investigation. Should a bank fail to agree, the amendment gave the President the power to deny that bank access to the US clearing-house system, in an effort to isolate it from world trade. For a number of reasons – including the universal nature of the problem, opposition from Treasury,[38] the fear of stimulating foreign alternatives to US clearing facilities, and the fear of retaliation against US banks – this unilateral approach has fizzled with few tangible results.

Since 1988, political efforts have had a broad regional or multilateral focus. The United States was central in the drafting of the 1988 Vienna Convention Against Illicit Traffic in Narcotic Drugs and Psychotropic Substances,[39] which specifies 'intentionally' laundering drug profits as a criminal activity.[40] Such a designation is meant to assist in information-sharing to further prosecution, since mutual legal-assistance agreements usually specify that the activity under investigation must be a crime in both the requesting and the receiving country.[41] The US also brought the issue of money-laundering to the initially unenthusiastic G-10 banking supervisors, where it met with reluctance on the part of the French and especially the Germans to draw bank supervisors into what were widely perceived as law-enforcement efforts. Indeed, there was some suspicion that congressional pressure underlies the Federal Reserve's interest in the matter. Nevertheless, as the wrongdoing at BCCI was beginning to unfold, both the Swiss and Italian regulators were won over to the idea that the Basle Banking Committee should make some kind of statement that financial systems must not be allowed to be used to aid criminal activity.[42] In December 1988, the G-10 bank supervisors came up with a 'statement of principles' recommending that banks cooperate with investigators and limit their dealings with customers if they believe the funds are either derived from illegal activity or to be used for illegal purposes. But this agreement noted explicitly that bank supervisors in the G-10 have very different roles and responsibilities in this area, that this was *not* a legal document and *not* in any way intended to supersede national legal approaches.

The centre of multilateral political pressure is not in Basle, but in Paris, where the FATF is headquartered. The FATF is comprised of experts from government ministries, law-enforcement authorities, and bank supervisory and regulatory agencies from the OECD countries. The FATF regularly employs peer pressure and potentially a graduated set of sanctions to review and influence the policies of its own members and those of non-members to follow the spirit of its 'Forty Recommendations' promulgated in 1990. These recommendations call for states to ratify the 1988 Vienna Convention, to adopt effective seizure and forfeiture laws, and to prohibit anonymous accounts, endorsing the Basle group's 'know your customer' guidelines.

The FATF employs a system of mutual review in which each member's laws and efforts are scrutinized by an FATF team and then assessed by the full membership. Members can be sanctioned for making no effort to adhere to the Forty Recommendations. The mildest sanction is a letter from the president indicating shortcomings in a particular country; the harshest sanction is expulsion. Turkey has been sanctioned; it is the only country in the FATF that until recently had failed to make money-laundering a crime.[43]

The EU is also a source of pressure to control money-laundering. Removal of capital controls – and the potential danger of importing criminal activity from Eastern Europe – has helped to forge a strong consensus that money-laundering rules must be stringent and harmonized across the market. The EU Directive on the Prevention of the use of the Financial System for the Purposes of Money Laundering (1991) applies to all credit and financial institutions, including insurance companies. The rules require the identification of customers, data-recording and storage, an obligation to report suspicious transactions, and internal control mechanisms and staff training. The rules have entailed costly adjustments, for example in Luxembourg,[44] and have influenced a major 1995 overhaul of the Spanish penal code, encompassing money-laundering and corruption.[45] But the most contentious case has been that of Austria, which, despite significant reforms, ran into trouble with the Commission over anonymous bank accounts.[46] In 1996, the EU indicated that continued Austrian non-compliance could mean legal action before the European Court.[47]

The convergence across national jurisdictions since 1986 has been significant, but hard fought and hardly complete. The United States and every European country agrees that money-laundering should be considered a crime, although there is continuing disagreement on the 'precedent offenses' that produce illicit gains. Furthermore, few countries have embraced the US approach of comprehensive reporting of all cash transactions above $10 000 and extensive record-keeping for all international wire transactions (most banks have lobbied their governments hard to reject US-style record-keeping and reporting).[48] Recent rules in France, however, will bring that jurisdiction closer to the American standards.[49] The traditional European approach – leaving it to the banks to know their customers and to report suspicious activities – has found much more favour worldwide, and in fact is currently the basis of the FATF recommendations.

In short, harmonization with respect to money-laundering depends on pressure from a financial centre or centres and, because the problem is systemic, steps must be taken multi-laterally. The benefits of remaining outside of a tight regime tempt many jurisdictions to defect, and encourages the major financial centres to press hard for cooperation. Because the issue area so clearly involves dilemmas of collective action, international fora have been directly involved in rule-development, surveillance, and even enforcement.

The Case of Accounting Standards

Cross-border flows of portfolio investment have grown ten-fold as a proportion of GNP in the G-7 countries since 1980. Yet equity markets remain highly-segmented internationally. Investors favour domestic equities over foreign ones, despite the fact that they could benefit from further international diversification.[50] Stock exchanges are heavily dominated by domestic listings.[51] This may be due to informational barriers and incompatibilities that encourage firms to list at home and investors to buy stocks of the better-known nationally-based firms.

Accounting rules that provide the basis for the information on which investment decisions are made are determined by the national jurisdiction of the exchange on which the stock is listed. Tremendous advantages could be realized by using a single accounting language for cross-border listings worldwide. Investors would be better able to reduce risk and increase returns through informed portfolio diversification at drastically reduced information costs. Firms would be able to list on any exchange in the world on the basis of a single set of reporting rules. In the absence of a widely accepted international standard, information costs may be a significant deterrent to investors who otherwise might diversify their holdings and firms that would otherwise seek foreign listings.[52]

The difficulties are especially serious for cross-border listings between jurisdictions with very different accounting standards. This partially explains why it is, for example, that no German firm had ever traded on a stock exchange in the United States before 1993. When Daimler Benz reconciled its accounts based on 'United States Generally Accepted Accounting Principles' (USGAAP) as a condition of listing on a US exchange, potential investors were stunned to learn that Daimler's *DM615 million profit* in 1993 under German accounting rules dissolved into a *DM1.8 billion loss* using USGAAP for the same period.[53] The episode serves to illustrate that widely varying accounting rules add to transactions costs, potentially deter cross-border listings (as of early 1996, Daimler was still the only German firm listed on the NYSE), and confuse investors.

There is little disagreement that internationally accepted accounting standards would contribute to more efficient securities markets. The politics – which pits the United States and United Kingdom against much of the rest of Europe – revolve around *which* standard, and therefore *who* adjusts. As in all areas of finance, the struggle is among unequal contenders, given the dominance of the New York and London markets, and the insistence of the SEC that any firm listing in the US must use USGAAP.

The coordination of accounting standards across jurisdictions has been broadly regional, decentralized and evolutionary in nature. Perhaps because securities markets were originally organized around time zones,[54] there are significant advantages to coordinating national requirements with those of a major nearby capital market even if there is far from universal agreement on an 'international' standard. Thus, Canada's standards tend to resemble those of the United States,[55] New Zealand's those of Australia, and the Scandinavian countries' those of Germany. Such coordination is useful in the absence of global or even G-10 agreement. In contrast to anti-money-laundering efforts, bilateral coordination *does* produce significant benefits; in contrast to capital adequacy, lax accounting rules may result in allocative inefficiency but *do not generate serious systemic risks*. As international markets grow, the demand for comparability in financial reporting among countries and across regions increases.[56] Ultimately, the political struggle for international preeminence is likely to develop between two or more emerging regionally-based standards or approaches.

The harmonization of accounting standards is also characterized by very low incentives to defect from an obvious focal point. Disagreements emerge over which rules should be the international standard, but no one has the incentive to differ radically from a major market, and, once accepted, there are virtually no incentives to defect. For internationally-active firms, the transactions costs of keeping up to speed on multiple standards are likely to exceed the one-time adjustment costs to a widely-used standard no matter what its 'nationality'. Indeed, many firms have prepared their statements voluntarily in order to maximize their access to international capital. Thus, in the 1960s Sony adopted US accounting rules in order to tap the US capital market, and in the last few years there has been a trend by Swiss, French and Belgian companies to adopt USGAAP or the less-stringent International Accounting Standards (IAS) currently under development by the International Accounting Standards Committee (IASC).[57] Stock exchanges themselves want to attract as much high-quality foreign business as possible, making them strong proponents of international standards.[58] Indeed, the decision of the newly-established EASDAQ (European Association of Securities Dealers Automated Quotation – the European equivalent of the US NASDAQ market) to use the American system of reporting, indicates the strength of the incentives to fall in line with the dominant system.[59] As is the case with prudential regulations regarding bank capital, harmonization is reinforced by market pressures; once the adjustment costs are paid, there is no reason to buck the regulatory trend.

The most distinct accounting divide among the major capital markets is between the 'Anglo-American' versus the 'continental' approaches, which in turn have histories rooted in the way firms have traditionally been financed. The former stresses the shareholders' need for information about earnings and profitability, and is common where capital markets have traditionally provided the major source of external financing for firms. Countries in this school include the United States, United Kingdom, Australia, New Zealand and the Netherlands.[60] On the other hand, a number of countries, especially in continental Europe, use their tax books as the basis for financial reporting, which tends to mingle signals about a firm's profitability with its tax accounts. This is the method of accounting that has developed where firms' capital needs have traditionally been supplied by banks, which in turn are in a much better position to monitor a firm's true financial position than are decentralized stockholders. The emphasis using this method tends to be on capital maintenance and the mini-mization of distributable income – a purpose which better suits the interests of bank creditors since it focuses on the long-run source of income rather than profitability *per se*. Countries with accounting standards that fit this description include Germany, the Scandinavian countries, France, Bel-gium, Italy and Spain.[61]

Harmonization of accounting standards revolves primarily around which of these conceptual models should prevail, and secondarily over a myriad of details on exactly how calcula-tions should be made to achieve the broad purpose of the standard. In a competitive market, the Anglo-American approach has two tremendous advantages: first, and most obviously, it is the approach governing the jurisdictions of the world's two largest securities markets. But secondly, it may be inherently more suited to globalized equity markets. It sends clearer signals to international investors, without mingling these with noise regarding national fiscal policy or other objectives. Competing on the basis of the 'usefulness' of the information to the market, the Anglo-American approach is more likely to gather adherents.

Continental accounting ideas are most firmly rooted in countries of the EU, with the crucial exception of the United Kingdom. Britain has therefore opposed standardizing accounting rules at the European level. The EU has instead pursued a policy of mutual recognition,[62] which has left the Europeans somewhat disunited in their effort to influence international accounting standards. The European Commission has formally given up any effort to create a European Accounting Standards body.[63] Their strategy is now to try to influence the work of the IASC,[64] which is politically more palatable than accepting USGAAP without any pretense of multilateralism. The IASC appears to be making progress, but the progress it is making looks increasingly American to many.[65] The IASC knows its standards have little credibility unless the SEC accepts them, and, as one might expect, those rules that the SEC has accepted have been quite close to US practices anyway.[66]

Meanwhile, the Anglo-Americans continue to press for investor-oriented accounting on a number of fronts. Unilaterally, the SEC continues to require that any cross-border listings within the US be *quantitatively* reconciled to USGAAP, which encourages foreign firms to adopt American standards and undercuts the bargaining position of the Europeans. In April 1996, Germany's fourth largest company, Veba, an energy and industrial conglomerate now moving into telecommunications, adopted USGAAP, its CEO explaining, 'It is a global capital market, and we all have to play by the same rules'.[67] A raft of European multinationals, and most of corporate Germany including Bayer, BASF and Hoechst, and many companies awaiting privatization, including Deutsche Telekom, may seek New York listings and may have to opt for USGAAP standards before IASC standards are complete.[68] They do not want to wait for a long fight in the IASC only to find out that the SEC decides in the end to continue to demand USGAAP. This has greatly increased the willingness of the Europeans to make concessions in multilateral talks. And the signals coming out of the SEC are usefully ambiguous: while in the past the SEC has stalled multilateral work on accounting standards by opposing them in the technical committee of IOSCO,[69] in the spring of 1996 it began to show signs of interest in furthering the work of the IASC, signalling possible willingness to 'fast track' acceptance of accounts lodged in accordance with international standards by foreign companies listed on US stock exchanges.[70]

All the while, tighter regional coordination among the Anglo-Americans remains a live, indeed a thriving option. American standard-setters, notably the Financial Accounting Standards Board (FASB) remain deeply skeptical of the IASC, and continue to nurture the Anglo-American accounting alliance through the 'Group of 4+1' countries – the US, Britain, Australia and Canada, plus an IASC representative (who reportedly never contributes much) and sometimes New Zealand (when their travel budget permits). This group was created as an informal forum for discussion in 1994, but in the spring of 1996 became somewhat more organized with the election of its first chairman, David Tweedie of the UK's Accounting Standards Board.[71] In the view of American standard-setters, it is crucial to continue a dialogue with this group of 'like-minded' standard-setters, and not to count on progress at the IASC, which is far more likely to promulgate stretchy rules which would allow for outcomes unacceptable to the US.[72] The strategy of US standard-setters is to make as much progress as possible in the Group of 4 so that the Europeans are persuaded to participate essentially on Anglo-American terms.[73]

The process of harmonization of accounting standards has had a distinctive dynamic: two alliances relating to two schools of thought have developed over the past several decades and now are vying to influence the emerging global standard. Because accounting harmonization is characterized by divisible benefits, the roots of cooperation have been local or regional. In the absence of significant advantages to defection, these loose alliances of like-minded standard-setters have grown and are now facing-off for global dominance. Political power will determine the winner; market forces will ensure compliance once a clear standard emerges.

CONCLUSIONS AND POLICY IMPLICATIONS

Capital markets have developed so rapidly over the past decade that regulators everywhere have had to struggle to keep up with the changing markets and institutions they are charged to supervise. Internationalization of these markets has added a dimension that was not present only two decades ago: national markets are sufficiently integrated with one another that national rules cannot effectively achieve the regulatory goals of reducing systemic risk, protecting customers, and other related social objectives. All across the regulatory spectrum, from bank supervision to accounting requirements to anti-money-laundering efforts, national authorities are finding that the ability to achieve their objectives at a reasonable cost is influenced by the action (or inaction) of their counterparts in foreign jurisdictions. This is especially true in the North Atlantic region, where barriers to international capital mobility are virtually nil, markets are highly sophisticated, and capital flows have exploded in real terms over the past two decades.

Across the Atlantic region, national approaches to regulating capital markets are far more similar in the late-1990s than they were only ten years ago. Market pressures have cut both ways in the process of regulatory harmonization, reinforcing some aspects of financial regulation but sharpening dilemmas of collective action in others. For the most part, the convergence of rules regarding capital adequacy has been far more 'natural' than many would have predicted, due to the advantages of being viewed as matching 'global standards' with respect to prudential banking practices. The contrast with anti-money-laundering is stark: central political pressure exercised by the United States, the FATF and the EU has been necessary to counter market pressures that encourage defection in this issue area. The development of international accounting standards illustrates yet a third process. Regional practices have gained adherents, until globalization has led to demands for a single widely-accepted standard for stock-exchange listings. Anglo-American rules now vie with a more 'continental' approach for status as the global standard.

Convergence across these issue areas – whether through multilateral negotiations, regional approaches or unilateral actions – has not been without significant challenges, which may have important implications for future cooperative efforts. As markets continue to grow and change technologically, potential problems include the following:

Coordination among international organizations. One of the great challenges for the United States and Europe is to deal with what in many ways is an unnatural division of organizational responsibility and authority. The problem has two dimensions, one jurisdictional and the other intersectoral. The recent uncertainties over capital adequacy rules resulting from the Basle committee and the EU illustrate the difficulties of coordinating across these organizations despite significant overlap in their membership. More generally, one can wonder whether the decision-making process of the EU is well-suited to dealing with the intricacies of regulating the rapidly moving target of capital markets. The EU needs to refine regulatory decisions with respect to banking supervisions in a timely manner, or else should cede standard-setting to the G-10.

The second dimension of the coordination problem among international organizations is intersectoral, and reflects the traditional (in the US context, anyway) separation of securities and banking business. As these functions continue to merge, there will be an increasing need to coordinate the work of the G-10 bank regulators and the securities regulators meeting in IOSCO. Bank regulators have traditionally been much more focused on systemic risk than have securities regulators, whose attention has been centred on customer protection and market fairness. The distinction is increasingly untenable, as banks increasingly trade securities for their own accounts, and securities firms make deposits that constitute significant proportions of liabilities within particular banks. There is some evidence of movement towards intersectoral coordination, such as in the area of regulating financial conglomerates, but common approaches to capital adequacy for securities and banking institutions, for example, remain illusive outside of the EU itself.

Addressing the divergence between agreement and fulfillment. While it is easy to point to significant international regulatory output over the past decade, the true test will remain the extent to

which politically challenging agreements are actually implemented. In the North Atlantic regime, this is scarcely a
problem for capital adequacy where meeting international
standards of prudent operation is a competitive advantage;
or for accounting standards, where there are strong incentives
to coordinate on a single standard for purposes of international listings. Such is not the case, however, with respect to
anti-money-laundering efforts. Suspicions have arisen in the
United States that despite the harmonization of law, there has
hardly been a harmonization of zeal to enforce, prosecute
and punish. The task is not complete merely because the
law is on the books, and continued perceptions of uneven
commitment can create a certain degree of political friction,
even among allies in a common cause. This will have to be
kept in mind as the FATF continues to develop more specific
policies (and possibly go beyond 'recommendations') in the
future.

The shift of financial power beyond the Atlantic region. The most
significant challenge for US–European cooperation with respect
to the regulation of cross-border capital is that the market is a
global one, and even a well-coordinated regional approach will
eventually prove inadequate to the task. According to a recent
report by the Bank for International Settlements, Singapore
and Hong Kong are now the fourth and fifth largest foreign
exchange trading centres in the world. A group of 26 emerging
economies (plus Australia and New Zealand) whose total non-
gold reserves were less that 50 per cent of those of the G-10 in
1987, had reserves in 1995 that were nearly 90 per cent of that
group's total reserves. This same group had a stock-market
capitalization in 1987 that was 6 per cent that of the G-10,
but over 15 per cent of that group's total stock-market capitalization by 1995.[74] This constitutes good evidence that capital
markets are growing much more quickly outside of the major
economies of America and Europe than they are within the
region.

Regulatory decisions made within Europe and the United
States have in the past largely been accepted by countries
outside of the region as 'international standards'. Regulatory
cooperation and harmonization can be expected to meet
significant resistance, however, where major players outside

the region are expected to make costly adjustments to their regulatory approaches. This problem is especially stark with respect to anti-money-laundering efforts. Outside of Japan, Singapore and Hong Kong, money-laundering is not a crime in much of Asia. Furthermore, despite encouragement and even pressure from the United States, Europe and Australia (who was willing to commit their own forfeiture funds for the development of a secretariat for the FATF in Asia), Asian support for some version of the FATF for the region has not been forthcoming.[75] Increasingly, Europe and the United States will have to devise policies that provide the proper incentives for global cooperation. At a minimum, they should anticipate discussions that broach the question of greater extra-regional representation in the centres of regulatory decision-making, if Asian cooperation is to be forthcoming.

Regardless of these continuing and future challenges, by almost any standard, it is fair to say that Europe and the United States are closer than ever to the liberal ideal of regulatory harmonization with respect to international financial markets. Standards will continue to evolve as market (and black market) conditions and technologies change, but if the United States and Europe work to adapt regional decision-making arrangements to the global arena, and if this can be done without sacrificing the speed, flexibility and standards of technical expertise that have been the hallmark of transatlantic cooperation, these adapted institutions should be able to address with some degree of success a more genuinely global regulatory regime for international finance.

Notes

1. Figures exclude the United Kingdom. Cited by William White, 'International Agreements in the Area of Banking and Finance: Accomplishments and Outstanding Issues', paper presented at the conference 'Monetary and Financial Integration in an Expanding (N)AFTA: Organization and Consequences', organized by the Center for International Studies at the University of Toronto, Toronto, 15–17 May 1996, p. 3.
2. International Monetary Fund, *World Economic Outlook* database.

3. Bank for International Settlements, *Central Bank Survey of Foreign Exchange and Derivative Market Activity* (Basle, Switzerland: Monetary and Economic Department, May 1996), p. 5.

4. Jeffrey A. Frankel, *The Yen/Dollar Agreement: Liberalizing Japanese Capital Markets* (Washington, DC: Institute for International Economics, 1984); 'Measuring International Capital Mobility: A Review', *AEA Papers and Proceedings*, vol. 82, no. 2 (1992), pp. 197–202; Jeffry Frieden, *Banking on the World* (New York: Basil Blackwell, 1989); Ethan Kapstein, 'Resolving the Regulations' Dilemma: International Coordination of Banking Regulation', *International Organization*, vol. 43, no. 2, (19..) pp. 323–47; Peter B. Kenen, 'Macroeconomic Theory and Policy: How the Closed Economy was Opened', in Ronald Jones and Peter Kenen (eds), *Handbook of International Economics* (Amsterdam: North Holland, 1985); Michael Porter, *The Competitive Advantage of Nations* (New York: The Free Press, 1990); Robert Reich, 'Who is Us?', *Harvard Business Review* (January–February 1990), pp. 53–64; and Jonathan W. Moses, 'Abdication from National Policy Autonomy: What's Left to Leave?', *Politics and Society*, vol. 22, no. 2, (June 1994), pp. 125–48.

5. Philip G. Cerny, 'The Deregulation and Re-regulation of Financial Markets in a More Open World', in P. G. Cerny (ed.), *Finance and World Politics: Markets, Regimes, and States in the Post Hegemonic Era* (Aldershot, England: Edward Elgar, 1993), pp. 51–85. On the Japanese case see Robert Alan Feldman, *Japanese Financial Markets: Deficit, Dilemmas, and Deregulation* (Cambridge, Mass.: MIT Press, 1986); James Horne, *Japan's Financial Markets: Conflict and Consensus in Policy Making* (London: Allen & Unwin, 1985). On the French case: Philip Cerny, 'The Little Big Bang in Paris: Financial Market Deregulation in a Dirigiste System', *Journal of European Research*, vol. 17, no. 2 (March 1989), pp. 162–92.

6. See Ton Notermans, 'The Abdication from National Policy Autonomy: Why the Macroeconomic Policy Regime has Become so Unfavorable to Labor', *Politics and Society*, vol. 21, no. 2 (June 1993), pp. 133–67.

7. The most authoritative source is the International Monetary Fund, *Annual Report on Exchange Arrangements and Exchange Restrictions*, published continuously since the 1950s.

8. Bank for International Settlements, *International Banking and Financial Market Development*, various issues, and ISDA statistics.

9. Richard J. Herring and Robert E. Litan, *Financial Regulation in the Global Economy* (Washington, DC: Brookings Institution, 1995), p. 50.

10. 'Who's Counting on the US', *International Banking Regulator*, nos 96–30 (29 July 1996), p. 4.

11. *International Securities Regulation Report*, 11 April 1996, pp. 15–17.

12. Interview with Eduard Canadell, Secretary General of IOSCO, *International Securities Regulation Report*, vol. 8, no. 22 (October 1995), pp. 1, 10.

13. Kapstein, 'Resolving the Regulations Dilemma', *op. cit.*, pp. 340–1.

14. *Ibid.*, p. 345.

15. Tommaso Padoa-Schioppa, 'Banking Supervision in a Global Market', Vienna, October 1994.

16. *The Banker*, February 1997, p. 42; *The Banker*, January 1997, p. 43; Michael S. Borish, Wei Ding and Michael Noble, *On the Road to EU Accession: Financial Sector Development in Central Europe*, World Bank Discussion Paper no. 345 (Washington, DC: World Bank, 1996), p. 92.

17. See for example, Richard Dale, 'Regulation Goes Global', *Financial Regulation Report*, April 1996, p. 1; John Walker and Brendan Gormley, 'Multinational Banks Face Tougher Scrutiny', *International Financial Law Review*, March 1996, pp. 41–4. For a related argument see Beth Simmons, 'Why Innovate? Founding of the Bank for International Settlements', *World Politics*, vol. 45, no. 3 (April 1993), pp. 361–405.

18. E. Gerald Corrigan, Statement (with Appendices) before the United States Senate Committee on Banking, Housing and Urban Affairs, 3 May 1990, as quoted by Yasushro Machara, 'Comments', in Herring and Litan, *Financial Regulation of the Global Economy*, *op. cit.*, p. 154 (emphasis added).

19. Mr B. W. Fraser, Governor of the Reserve Bank of Australia, to the 24th Conference of Economists, Adelaide, 25 September 1995. Reprinted in the *Reserve Bank of Australia Bulletin*, October 1995. Fraser's reference to pressure alludes to economic, not political pressure.

20. Henry Harrington, 'Go East – or Bust', *The Banker* (January 1993), pp. 15–17. The Task Force included the G-7 plus Austria, Australia, Belgium, Luxembourg, the Netherlands, Spain, Sweden and Switzerland.

21. Estimate given by Eduardo Vetere, head of the Crime Prevention and Criminal Justice Branch at the opening sitting of the European Regional Preparatory Meeting for the 9th UN Congress on Crime Prevention and the Treatment of Offenders, 28 February 1994, Vienna.

22. See testimony in April 1989 of the Governor of the Bank of Italy, quoted in Gurwin, *Global Finance*, *op. cit.*, p. 48. See also Vito Tanzi, 'Money Laundering and the International Financial System', International Monetary Fund: Fiscal Affairs Department, Working Paper 96/55, May 1996.

23. Harrington, 'Go East – or Bust', *op. cit.*, p. 15; Raymond Colitt, 'Survey of Ecuador', *Financial Times*, 27 July 1995, p. 28.

24. Adam Courtney, 'The Buck Never Stops', *The Banker* (November 1994), p. 825.

25. Ron Noble, immediate past president of the FATF, *Financial Regulation Report*, March 1996.

26. Larry Gurwin, '1992 Means a Single Market for Crime, Too', *Global Finance*, vol. 4, no. 1 (January 1990), pp. 46–50.

27. Jimmy Burns, 'MPs Urge Money Laundering Crackdown', *Financial Times*, 26 July 1995, p. 8. Harrington, *op. cit.*, pp. 16–17; Scott B. MacDonald, 'Asia–Pacific Money Laundering', *International Currency Review*, vol. 22, no. 2 (October–December 1993), pp. 30–4.

28. Courtney, 'The Buck Never Stops', *op. cit.*, pp. 88–9.

29. *Ibid.*; Johannes Dumbacher, 'The Fight Against Money Laundering', *Intereconomics*, vol. 30, no. 4 (July/August 1995), pp. 177–86.

30. Lisa Troshinsky, 'Ex-NatWest Lawyer Fears "Know Your Customer"' Fallout', *International Banking Regulator*, no. 96–31 (5 August 1996), pp. 1, 6.

31. Ian Rodger, 'Survey of Swiss Banking', *Financial Times*, 26 October 1995, p. III.

32. This statement is a translation of official Swiss federal government policy, quoted in M. Aubert, P. J. Kernen and H. Schoenle, *Das Schweizerische Bankgeheimnis* (Bern, 1978), p. 59 (translation provided in a summary generously supplied by an official of the International Monetary Fund). Recent changes in Swiss bank secrecy law now give banks the *right* – but *not the obligation* – to report suspicious clients. See articles by Frances Williams and Ian Rodger, 'Survey of the Swiss Banking System', *Financial Times*, 26 October 1995, p. iv, v. See also Thurston Clarke and John J. Tigue, *Dirty Money: Swiss Banks, the Mafia, Money Laundering, and White Collar Crime* (New York: Simon & Schuster, 1975).

33. Liechtenstein offers a level of banking secrecy that is even tighter than that of Switzerland; bankers there are not required to know the identity of the account's ultimate beneficiary as would be required in Switzerland. 'So Far but no Further', *Euromoney*, July 1996, p. 151.

34. In the US, approximately 10 million Currency Transaction Reports (CTR) for cash transactions exceeding $10,000 were filled out in 1993. Estimated costs for the financial institutions per report were between $15–17. Additional costs include training, recording and storing the data. Dumbacher, 'The Fight Against Money Laundering', *op. cit.*, p. 181. Some industry sources place the cost of CTR preparation alone as high as $136 million annually. Robert Powis, 'Money Laundering: Problems and Solutions', *The Banker Magazine* (November/December 1992), pp. 52–6.

35. Peter J. Quirk, 'Macroeconomic Implications of Money Laundering', Working Paper 96/66, Monetary and Exchange Affairs Department (Washington, DC: International Monetary Fund, June 1996), p. 24.

36. Dumbacher, 'The Fight Against Money Launderers', *op. cit.*, pp. 180–1; see also 'Falling Out with Uncle Sam', *The Economist*, 16 March 1996. See the comments of R. D. Fullerton, Chairman and CEO, Canadien Imperial Bank of Commerce, Toronto, Canada, 'Clearing out the Money Launderers', *The World of Banking* (September–October 1990), pp. 5–7.

37. Section 4702 of the 1988 Omnibus Drug Bill. See also Thomas Crocker, 'Bankers, Police Yourselves', *International Financial Law Review* (June 1990), p. 11.

38. Treasury's lack of enthusiasm for this approach is described in 'Drug Money Laundering, Banks, and Foreign Policy', a Report to the Committee on Foreign Relations, United States Senate, by the Subcommittee on Narcotics, Terrorism and International Operations (USGPO), 101th Congress 2d session, February 1990, p. 28. This opposition was also confirmed in an interview with a Treasury official, 7 August 1996, Washington DC.

39. The Vienna Convention (20 December 1988). Twenty ratifications were needed for it to enter into force, which it did in 1990; 100 ratifications had been deposited by the end of 1994.

40. Article 3, section 1, (b) (i) and (ii).

41. T. Crocker, 'Bankers, Police Yourselves', *International Financial Law Review* (June 1990), pp. 10–11.

42. Telephone interview with a Federal Reserve official who was involved in the drafting and negotiation of the 1988 agreement, Washington DC, 8 August 1996.

43. Interview with a Treasury official, 5 August 1996, Washington, DC. Dumbacher, 'The Fight Against Money Launderers', *op. cit.*, p. 183.

44. Financial services account for an estimated 20 per cent of Luxembourg's GDP, four times the proportion in most other European countries. Philip Eade, 'Facing up to Harder Times', *Euromoney*, May 1996, pp. 132–43.

45. David White, 'Spain Overhauls Penal Code', *Financial Times*, 9 November 1995, p. 3.

46. In Austria, the 1994 Banking Act revisions had put in place a strong set of measures, including an obligation to report any 'suspicious' dealing or clients. Austria's anonymous numbered bank accounts remain (though foreigners are not allowed to use them). 'Survey of Austria', *Financial Times*, 12 December 1995, London, page III.

47. F. Schwank, 'EU Threatens Anonymous Banking in Austria', *International Financial Law Review*, vol. 15, no. 7 (July 1996), p. 332.

48. R. D. Fullerton, Chairman and CEO, Canadien Imperial Bank of Commerce, Toronto, Canada, 'Clearing out the Money Launderers', *The World of Banking* (September–October 1990), pp. 5–7.

49. Andrew Jack, 'France Might Force Banks to Disclose Transfers', *Financial Times*, 23 December 1995.

50. K. French and J. Poterba, 'Investor Diversification and International Equity Markets', *American Economic Review* (March 1991); I. Cooper and E. Kaplanis, 'Home Bias in Equity Portfolios, Inflation Hedging, and International Capital Market Equilibrium', *Review of Financial Studies* (Spring 1994); and L. Tesar and I. Werner, 'Home Bias and High Turnover', *Journal of International Money and Finance* (August 1995).

51. For example, at the end of 1993 only about 7 per cent of the companies listed on the New York Stock Exchange were foreign; the comparable figure for the London Stock Exchange is about 17 per cent, and that for Tokyo about 6 per cent. The foreign share on continental European exchanges, which tend to serve the regional market, are much higher: about 22 per cent for Paris, and about 46 per cent for Amsterdam and the German stock exchange. The *Euroclear IFR Handbook of World Stock and Commodity Exchanges, 1995* (London: IFR Publishing, 1995). See also Andrew Sobel, 'Breaching the Levee, Waiting for the Flood: Testing Beliefs about the Internationalization of Securities Markets', *International Interactions*, vol. 19, no. 4 (1994), pp. 311–38.

52. According to an official at the New York Stock Exchange, differences in accounting requirements across jurisdictions were the single most important obstacle to the integration of equities markets, and,

specifically, the most important obstacle to attracting foreign firms to list on the NYSE; interview, 8 November 1995, New York City.

53.   'Europe Finance: Region Pushes for New Accounting Standards', *The Economist Intelligence Unit*, NewsEDGE LAN, 13 May 1996. See also Ferdinand Protzman, 'Company News: Daimler Benz Reports Sizable Loss', *New York Times*, 16 December 1993; Floyd Norris, 'Market Place: Daimler Benz Paves the Way for Other German Companies', *New York Times*, 31 March 1993, section D, p. 8.

54.   Jean-Francois Theodore, Chairman and Chief Executive, SBF-Paris Bourse, 'The Emergence of Transnational Financial Zones and Prospects for Harmonization', presentation at the 20th ISOCO Conference, Paris, 11–13 July 1995, p. 1.

55.   Associate Chief Accountant, Securities and Exchange Commission, interview by telephone, Washington DC, 13 August 1996. See also Paul Pacter, 'Turning the Multinationals Inside Out…' *Financial Times*, 30 May 1996, London edition p. 28.

56.   Michael Sharpe, 'Is it Possible to Evaluate a Company Objectively?', presentation to the 20th IOSCO Conference, 12 July 1995, Paris.

57.   *Ibid.*

58.   Certainly this has been the position of the New York Stock Exchange, which has relentlessly pressured the Securities and Exchange Commission to adopt the rules being developed in the International Accounting Standards Committee (IASC), even though in many ways they deviate from USGAAP. Interview with James Shapiro, Research and Planning, New York Stock Exchange, New York City, 8 November 1995.

59.   Dirk Tirez, 'EASDAQ Benefits from European Framework', *International Financial Law Review* (November 1997), pp. 11–15.

60.   Cummins, Harris, and Hassett, March 1994.

61.   *Ibid.*

62.   For example, mutual recognition of disclosures made in public-offer and listing prospectuses. See Mario Monti, 'The Establishment of Regional Financial Areas and Perspectives on Regulatory Harmonization', presentation at the 20th Annual Meeting of IOSCO, 13 July 1995, Paris.

63.   'Europe Finance: Region Pushes for New Accounting Standards', *Economist Intelligence Unit*, NewsEDGE/LAN, 13 May 1996; Jim Kelly, 'Cautiously Counting Lucky Stars in Europe…', *The Financial Times*, 6 June 1996, p. 29.

64.   See the comments of Mario Monti, 13 July 1995, *op. cit.*; Karel Lannoo, 'IOSCO Annual Conference', *Financial Regulation Report* (July/August 1995), p. 9.

65.   *Financial Regulation Report* (July/August 1995), p. 8. A draft of IASC's Work Program for harmonizing international accounting standards can be found in *International Securities Regulation Report*, vol. 8, no. 16 (3 August 1995), p. 4.

66.   Interview, 8 November 1995.

67.   'German Finance: Large Corporations Turn to Global Capital Markets', The Economist Intelligence Unit, NewsEDGE/LAN, 15 April 1996.

68.   Economist Intelligence Unit, NewsEDGE/LAN, 13 May 1996.

69. This is the International Organization of Securities Regulators, the body which would endorse (or not) the accounting rules coming out of the IASC as appropriate (or not) for securities listings. Decisions of the group are, however, non- binding.

70. *International Securities Regulator* (25 April 1996), p. 7; 'Global Finance: Europe–USA Explore Uniform Listing Standards', *Economist Intelligence Unit*, NewsEDGE/LAN, 25 April 1996.

71. Jim Kelly, 'UK Aims to Influence Search for Global Accounting Code', *Financial Times*, 22 April 1996, London edition, p. 26.

72. One standard-setter expressed strong doubts that there could be any serious 'harmonization' with the Germans and Japanese, who have a completely different view of the purposes for providing information. Interview by telephone with Vice-Chairman of the Board, FASB, Norwalk, Conn., 15 August 1996.

73. *Ibid.*

74. International Finance Corporation, *Emerging Stock Markets Factbook*, various issues.

75. Discussion with officials from the US Treasury and FINCEN, 5–8 August 1996.

11 Cooperation in US–European Relations

Frances G. Burwell[1]

Since the end of the Cold War, the United States and Europe have struggled to find a new basis for partnership. The demise of the Soviet Union radically changed the context of the transatlantic relationship, including the threat it faced and the environment in which it operated. The *raison d'être* of the partnership – to deter Soviet aggression and provide security in Europe – seemed to have been achieved. And, the international arena no longer appeared riven by the bipolar contest, with local tensions exploited to advance the superpowers' cause. Instead, it was hoped, the dangers of the Cold War would be replaced by relative peace and prosperity.

Yet, it quickly became clear that the world was far from secure. The Gulf War and the violent breakup of Yugoslavia were only the most prominent examples of continuing international instabilities. Indeed, those conflicts demonstrated the wide range of threats facing the United States and Europe in the post-Cold War era, including the proliferation of weapons of mass destruction; the eruption of ethnic conflicts; the outlaw behaviour of the so-called 'rogue states'; resource shortages and environmental devastation; and even armed violations of sovereign territory. They also faced the need to integrate the former command economies into the global economic system, even while launching the WTO; and to help the Central European countries and newly-independent states as they embarked on the uncertain path towards democracy.

In this new environment, the transatlantic partnership confronted a fork in the road. In one direction, the Alliance would remain focused on the security and prosperity of Western Europe. In this case, the United States and Europe would act separately and distinctly outside Europe, in accordance with their own interests and perspectives. Given the Alliance's past difficulties in dealing with 'out-of-area' issues, such an approach had a certain logic. Also, given the pressure on the US and European governments to focus on domestic issues, there was little incentive to undertake broad new initiatives against international threats that seemed quite distant.

In the other direction, however, the United States and Europe would expand the scope of their Cold-War partnership and work together to address the new set of threats before them. And indeed, both Europe and the United States had a significant interest in doing so. Most of the emerging issues had the potential to disrupt the international order that the transatlantic partners had fostered for so long. The spread of weapons of mass destruction, the frustration of democracy in Central Europe and the former Soviet Union, the outbreak of regional conflicts and other instabilities, the difficult adjustment of transitional economies – each of these could endanger international stability and prosperity. For the past 40 years, the United States and Europe had maintained a very effective international partnership; could not that partnership now extend beyond the continent of Europe? Indeed, this expanded partnership might be essential, as most of the new challenges threatened both partners, and any response would require the commitment of both to be effective. There could be no solution to nuclear proliferation, no restructured relationship with Russia and the CEEC, no revitalized international economy, unless both Europe and the United States were committed to act in concert.

In addition, this seemed an especially propitious time to undertake an expanded partnership. At the beginning of the 1990s, Europe seemed poised to enhance its capacity for international policy. Through the new European Union and the relaunched Western European Union, there seemed a growing possibility that Europe would be willing and able to share the mantle of global leadership with the United States on political and security issues, just as it already did on economic matters.

In reality, of course, the fork in the road was never as clear or as obvious as described here. Since the end of the Cold War, elements of both paths have been present in the behaviour of the transatlantic partners. On the one hand, it often seems as though the first road has been taken, as the focus of activity returned to Europe, particularly with Bosnia and NATO enlargement. Even old patterns of behaviour seemed to reemerge, with US leadership as predominant as it was in the Cold War. On the other hand, the partners have successfully collaborated in dealing with some of the non-European challenges of the post-Cold War era, albeit often in modest fashion. Many of those challenges remain unresolved, leaving available the opportunity – indeed, the necessity – for further transatlantic cooperation on global issues.

COOPERATION AT A MODEST LEVEL

This volume has examined the transatlantic relationship in the years since the fall of the Soviet Union. It has focused on issues of global importance: restructuring relations with the CEEC and FSU countries; preventing the proliferation of weapons of mass destruction; coping with the so-called 'rogue regimes'; and managing the post-GATT global economy. In each case, the United States and Europe have a stake in the successful resolution of the issue, either because it affects their interests directly, or because it threatens the international order of which they are the primary protectors. In each case, as well, the basic issue is unlikely to be resolved without participation by both parties in that resolution. Sometimes an active role is required – including money and armed forces. In other cases, progress can be made by one partner as long as the other does not act the spoiler and work to obstruct the effort.

In evaluating US–European cooperation on these issues, the first question to be asked is the obvious one – to what extent did such cooperation exist? Since 1989, have the transatlantic partners been able to work together effectively to address major global issues outside of the Cold War framework? We are not asking whether these challenges have been resolved – they are much too complex for a quick solution, and, in most cases, the best that can be hoped for is that they are adequately managed. Instead, the authors of this volume ask whether the United States and Europe have worked together in addressing these problems or have they each pursued their own solution with little regard for the perspective and actions of the other. One of the most crucial challenges facing the United States and Europe has been ensuring the stability of the Central and East European countries and integrating them into the West – economically, politically and militarily. As this volume shows, transatlantic attempts at cooperation in this area have led to the reemergence of traditional patterns of interaction, including a division between economic and security issues, with the latter characterized by US leadership. As Michael Brown argues in his chapter, the breakup of the Warsaw Pact led to a debate as to the most appropriate framework for European security, with the OSCE, the WEU and NATO each representing a particular viewpoint. NATO and transatlanticism emerged predominant, with the Partnership for Peace and, later, NATO enlargement becoming the primary strategies for integrating the CEE countries into the West. Although many fundamental issues of European security remain unresolved, including reaching consensus on the nature of the threat, NATO has successfully weathered the transition into the post-Cold War era, emerging as the most successful example of transatlantic cooperation.

At the same time, and in an almost completely separate process, the economic framework of post-Cold War Europe came to centre increasingly on the European Union; a process described by Lily Gardner Feldman. The economic integration of Western Europe presented a model that explicitly linked economic development with political stability and freedom from military conflict. In the 1990s, the CEE countries were linked to that model through the signing of the Europe agreements, the development of the PHARE and other technical assistance programmes, and, perhaps most important, the prospect of EU enlargement. Although the United States has also provided foreign assistance to Central Europe, the mere possibility of EU membership has been crucial in determining the type of economic, legal and social structures established by these countries.

These two sets of institutions and processes – one focused on security, the other on economic matters – have been key to the effort to restructure relations with the countries to the East. And together they have had a fundamental effect on politics in Europe – both domestic (democratization) and

international (resolution of cross-border minority problems).
Yet, there has been remarkably little connection between the
two, as they have moved in two parallel but unconnected
processes. At first, EU enlargement seemed the dominant
strategy, as Brussels signed economic agreements with the
new CEE governments, and, with the OSCE, launched the
Stability Pact in an effort to prevent the outbreak of ethnic
clashes. But, as the EU focused more and more on internal
matters – completing the Single Market, launching the 1996
IGC, planning for monetary union, and, through it all,
attempting to cope with Europe's faltering economy – the
dates for extending membership to the CEE governments
became more and more distant. Moreover, the EU's failure
in coping with the consequences of Yugoslavia's collapse
reduced CEEC confidence in the Union's ability to meet
their political security requirements. While NATO initially
also stood on the sidelines of the Bosnia conflict, Washington's
decision to use NATO in leading Bosnia out of the morass
strengthened its claim that the Alliance was the appropriate
instrument for integrating the CEEC into the West.

While EU and NATO enlargement proceeded on separate
tracks and timetables, there were elements of transatlantic
cooperation within each process. NATO enlargement initially
met with British and French (but not German) resistance, but
the allies supported it when faced with Washington's determination to proceed and the alternative of speeding up EU
enlargement. In coping with the task of economic and political
development in Central Europe, as Feldman states, Washington
and Brussels have collaborated to a modest extent, particularly
in terms of sharing information through several consultative
mechanisms. They have also allowed a division of labour to
develop in which the US responds to more immediate needs
while the EU focuses on longer-term structural issues. Overall,
however, even this cooperation has stayed at modest levels,
hampered by a variety of obstacles.

As for Russia, even less has been accomplished and transatlantic cooperation has been even more limited, as Renée de
Nevers argues in her chapter. Aid programmes have been
criticized as inappropriate and as not living up to initial
promises, while Russian participation in PfP activities has
been limited at best. The prospect of NATO enlargement

initially caused dissension in the Alliance precisely because of Russia's hostility, although the establishment of a special security relationship between NATO and Russia quieted the opposition. One area of success has been the Western effort to counter the possibility that the breakup of the Soviet Union could lead to new nuclear threats; instructively, this effort has been dominated by the United States, with a much smaller European effort and little cooperation between the two.

If the process of building new relations with the Central European countries led to a reemergence of past transatlantic patterns, the challenges presented by global security issues have led to more varied forms and degrees of cooperation. One issue that has produced some of the noisiest transatlantic squabbles – as well as one major cooperative success story – has been that of regional conflict. In Bosnia, the disparate approaches initially taken by the United States and Europe led to much acrimony. A more cooperative framework was only achieved after the health – and perhaps even the survival – of the Alliance had been called into question. One of the strongest arguments in favour of US involvement in the former Yugoslavia was to preserve NATO's credibility, rather than to end the carnage of war. But not all regional conflicts have created such extreme transatlantic tensions. The Gulf War represents a successful example of US–European cooperation, due in large part to three factors: a clear violation of international norms; the presence of US leadership from the beginning of the crisis; and the substantial stake of the Europeans in preserving the flow of Gulf oil. Even so, transatlantic relations were not always smooth, especially in the lead-up to the use of force by the coalition.

The failure of the United States and Europe to cooperate effectively in addressing these issues of regional instability is not new – NATO has long had difficulties in achieving a consensus on out-of-area issues. It is telling that the first out-of-area involvement of troops under NATO command was in the former Yugoslavia, almost 50 years after NATO's founding. This reluctance to engage in regional issues as an Alliance is rooted in the very different perceptions and experiences of Europe and the United States. Indeed, a division on regional issues has persisted since the immediate postwar years, when Washington pressured the Europeans (who were then recovering their colonies from Japanese and German forces) to disband their empires. Differences persisted during the Cold War, when the United States and the Soviet Union battled to enlist every newly-independent state within its own camp. The Europeans tended to be much more accepting of those wishing to maintain an equidistance between the superpowers, and often retained extensive links to their former colonies. With the end of the Cold War, Washington's interest in regional conflict has grown, although its actual involvement sometimes seems random. The Europeans still retain extensive economic and political ties with former colonies, but increasingly lack the military capacity to impose order, even when asked. As a result of these very different experiences, the transatlantic allies often differ considerably in their approaches to a regional conflict.

Even when Europe and the United States agree that something must be done about a particular regional situation, they still find it almost impossible to cooperate because of fundamentally different approaches to resolving such issues, in large part because the talents and proclivities of the transatlantic allies in managing regional conflicts are distinctly different.[2] The European countries are more adept at conflict-prevention and peace-building, both of which require a focus on socio-economic issues and political reform, as well as experience with traditional peacekeeping operations. The United States, on the other hand, is much better suited when the use of force is required, even in multilateral peace-enforcement missions. In theory, this could provide opportunities for effective cooperation in the division of labour mode. In reality, it has led to many arguments, as each too often views its own talent as the sole solution, and discounts the value of the other.

The out-of-area issue that has generated the lowest degree of cooperation (in fact, almost a total lack of cooperation), has been the attempt to deal with 'rogue states', such as Iraq, Iran, Libya and Cuba. In these cases, transatlantic disputes usually focus on differences over the use of force or punitive economic sanctions. As Philip Gordon argues, while Washington often seeks to punish these regimes through economic and political isolation, and in some cases through the use of military force (the bombing of Tripoli, for instance), the

Europeans often argue that these countries are more likely to reform if integrated into the international community by way of a dialogue. As Gordon points out, these differences are derived not only from a genuine policy dispute over the 'rogue state' itself, but also from distinctive domestic require-ments, economic interests and political cultures. Nor are they dissimilar from the US and European responses to regional conflicts. Gordon points to North Korea as the exception in which the United States averted conflict in resolving the crisis occasioned by Pyongyang's withdrawal from the NPT. Ironic-ally, if instructively in this case, the United States took a more conciliatory position; in addition, the Europeans had little direct stake in the conflict and were happy to follow Washing-ton's lead.

A very different experience can be found in efforts to man-age the threat of proliferation. In this area, the extent of cooperation has differed according to the specific issue, although it has rarely been more than modest. As both Harald Müller and Brad Roberts observe, the United States and Eur-ope share a common interest in preventing the proliferation of weapons of mass destruction. Moreover, they are the only group of countries with the capacity to carry forward an effective multilateral non-proliferation effort. Because the trans-atlantic allies include three declared nuclear-weapons states, as well as major purveyors of the technical expertise and equip-ment required in any serious proliferation effort, their leader-ship will be central to any such effort.

Despite these realities, transatlantic cooperation on this issue is still far from a reliable habit. Müller also notes the very different US and European attitudes towards the use of weap-ons-grade material in civilian applications. This has led to serious disputes and for a time endangered the renewal of the US–Euratom agreement. He sees another serious dispute over IAEA safeguards. Both Müller and Roberts see widely-diver-gent transatlantic approaches towards Iran as a potential pro-liferation problem, and towards the use of sanctions as a strategy in dealing with this. Roberts also finds a significant future dispute looming on the issue of missile defense, with the Europeans skeptical at a time when the idea of some sort of defense is gaining increasing political support in the United States.

Fortunately, such differences have not been the case in all aspects of non-proliferation. Indeed, in two major areas, what began as serious rifts have recently seen the development of limited cooperation. First, tension over the US policy of counter-proliferation has gradually evolved into an uneasy cooperation aimed at reducing the likelihood that certain regimes will achieve functioning weapons systems. Roberts credits the extensive discussions in NATO's Defense Group on Proliferation with this shift, and the beneficial impact of clarifying perspectives on achieving consensus. Müller also notes a moderation of Washington's approach away from military counter-proliferation measures. Second, Europe and the United States have recently developed greater coordination over the export of proliferation-prone technologies. The transatlantic partners have been involved in a number of international arrangements – including the Nuclear Suppliers Group, the Australia Group, the Missile Technology Control Regime, and the New Forum or Wassenaar Arrangement – but the economic incentives to export such technologies led to many disputes. Following the revelations about Iraq's weapons programmes, however, coordination on this issue received a fresh impetus. Not that all disputes are settled; as Müller points out, the United States often seeks tighter restrictions, especially against particular states, while the Europeans seek to preserve the ability of each government to determine exports. The resulting cooperation, in Roberts' view, is still rather limited.

Finally, proliferation offers some examples of real cooperation, including the unconditional extension of the nuclear NPT and the denuclearization of Ukraine. During the NPT campaign, there was extensive collaboration between the United States and Europe; collaboration that was not only effective in convincing others to support extension, but that also brought the initial views of the transatlantic partners closer together. As for Ukraine, Washington focused narrowly on the nuclear issue, while the EU signed an extensive economic cooperation agreement, to come into effect only after Ukraine renounced nuclear weapons. In both cases, transatlantic cooperation took the form of a division of labour, in which the United States and Europe pursued different, but complementary, strategies towards achieving their joint objective.

The third issue area – the global economy – differs from the others in that the United States and Europe have been effective partners for many years, both building and managing the postwar international economic system. However, it is hard to term that partnership a cooperative one, for it has been subject to many squabbles, some very serious. Indeed, the shape of the global trading system has been largely determined through bilateral negotiations aimed at resolving transatlantic conflicts – not through joint coordination. This was possible because the United States and Europe represented such a large portion of the global economy that any deal between them quickly became the international standard. But as Steve Woolcock, Richard Steinberg and Beth Simmons demonstrate, the United States and Europe are no longer able simply to settle issues between themselves. They must now deal with the rise of several Asian nations, initially as trading powers, and, more recently, as financial centres. The breakup of the Soviet bloc has made it necessary to integrate many formerly command economies into the international system. Finally, economic reforms in China have made that country a potential international power, with uncertain consequences for itself and for the world economy. As a result, the transatlantic partners must work together to address the new challenges of the global economy and then convince the emerging economic powers to follow their lead. These new issues include: the launching of the World Trade Organization and the expansion of the international trading regime into new sectors; the emergence of regionalism in trading arrangements; the integration of major new economic actors (including the Asian economies and the former command economies); the increased importance of international monetary flows; and the impact of growing internationalism on sectors, such as the financial one, in which institutions and regulations used to be determined domestically.

As these chapters demonstrate, however, there is not yet much evidence that the United States and Europe have cooperated effectively in seeking to resolve these issues. As Woolcock points out, the completion of the Uruguay Round of the GATT and the establishment of the WTO led to a period of relative quiescence. Suggestions for further transatlantic trade negotiations led, not to the establishment of a Transatlantic Free Trade Area (TAFTA), but to the conclusion of the much more modest New Transatlantic Agenda (NTA) in December 1995. Thus, as Woolcock notes, the United States and Europe have focused mainly on negotiating bilateral issues, including a growing number of beyond-the-border concerns (that is, issues of domestic practice and regulation that affect imports, such as food safety and purity rules), rather than establishing a 'pathfinder' role in managing the global economy. As US and European support for multilateralism has lagged, notes Steinberg, Brussels and Washington have pursued separate arrangements with third countries. There has also been a rise in regional trade agreements. Without renewed cooperation and leadership by the United States and the EU, regionalism could erode the global economy's multilateral basis.

This need for cooperation in boosting multilateralism does not apply just to trade policy. Increasingly, regulations and practices that previously were governed by domestic factors must now adjust to international conditions and influences. The financial sector is one of the most important to be affected by this globalization, and the United States and Europe are key actors in this sector. But as Simmons argues, establishing patterns of cooperation in this issue area is complex. Governments have far less influence, while a wide array of private and NGO institutions play critical coordinating roles. As a result, transatlantic cooperation has been intense, but uneven. In general, it has succeeded where agreements are reinforced by market forces (as in the case of capital adequacy), but has been more difficult to maintain when the market encourages defection (anti-money-laundering).

As this summary indicates, transatlantic cooperation on global issues is still a modest endeavour. For 40 years, the United States and its European allies worked together closely to rebuild and protect Western Europe. With that task now accomplished, it has proven difficult for these partners to turn their focus and their efforts towards a wider arena. There have been important successes. The Gulf war and the IFOR/SFOR operations in Bosnia have demonstrated the ability of the US and European governments to cooperate when the stakes are high enough. The extension of the NPT, the negotiation of the New Transatlantic Agenda, and, to some degree, the assistance programme in the CEE countries, have shown that cooperation can exist when the agenda is specific.

But these successes also demonstrate the limits of cooperation. First, of the three forms of cooperation outlined in the introduction – parallelism, division of labour and joint coordination – the most common forms in the transatlantic relationship appear to be division of labour and parallelism. There is little evidence of the closer joint coordination, which is hardly surprising given the difficulties. However, both division of labour and parallelism carry substantial risks that the partners will lose any sense of shared purpose, and may even end up working at cross purposes. One reason that parallelism and division of labour are relatively common is that they do not require constant communication between the parties involved. At the same time, the absence of communication can be a source of dissension calling the future of cooperation into question. This is especially true if the cooperating powers do not agree that they are contributing to the resolution of the issue in an equitable manner, particularly if one supplies military forces or runs greater risks than the other.

Second, cooperation appears to exist most frequently when focused on specific issues, rather than issues of grand policy. It is not unusual, of course, for there to be a strong rhetorical commitment to transatlantic cooperation, often issued at the highest levels of policy-making. But the press of business and differing perspectives can make it easy to neglect building cooperation until a specific matter requires it. Issues such as the extension of the NPT, foreign assistance to Central Europe, and the Action Plan of the New Transatlantic Agenda, offer the type of limited, specific agenda on which cooperation can be very useful without requiring any commitment to extensive, joint policy formulation in the future. The result has been that transatlantic cooperation on global issues has occurred for the most part on a case-by-case basis, rather than systematically.

Finally, in those instances in which the US and European governments have overcome significant obstacles to cooperate in meeting a major challenge, such as in the Gulf and now Bosnia, US leadership has been critical to the success of the effort. The partnership of equals envisaged at the beginning of the 1990s has not emerged. Instead, the predominance of the United States has been acknowledged as necessary, especially on those issues involving the use of military force.

OBSTACLES TO EFFECTIVE PARTNERSHIP

Having concluded that transatlantic cooperation on the range of global issues is limited, both in occurrence and scope, and that major cooperative efforts require significant US leadership, the second question emerges – why is this so? What are the obstacles and disincentives facing those who seek to work together? Is there something intrinsic about the US–European relationship that makes effective cooperation difficult under the best of circumstances? Or, is there something peculiar about the issues examined here that limits that cooperation to modest levels?

One possible explanation for such a modest degree of cooperation, is that basic US and European interests are diverging, and, in fact, becoming quite distinct. According to this view, the United States and Europe are more rivals than partners in the international economic arena, and they are increasingly at odds in the security realm as well. Indeed, without the threat of Soviet aggression to unite the Alliance, their divergent national interests will soon lead them to drift apart. Thus, the lack of cooperation between the United States and Europe simply reflects the lack of shared interests. In fact, pushing for greater cooperation would probably only lead to greater tension as the process of identifying objectives and methods on which to work together makes their differences more explicit.

Although it is true that the United States and Europe have often acted the part of global rivals, particularly on economic matters, this volume makes clear that the transatlantic allies share a basic set of interests. It is in their interests to integrate the CEE countries and Russia into the international economic and political order. It is in their interests to prevent threats to global stability including the proliferation of weapons of mass destruction, and the use of terrorism and other outlaw behaviours by 'rogue states'. As for the international economy, it is in their fundamental interest to bolster the multilateral regimes from which their prosperity derives. Moreover, whereas the United States and Europe are frequently portrayed as rivals (and often act as such), the emergence of potentially powerful new actors has given them a fresh incentive to work together to preserve and build on the existing system.

Of course, the congruity of US and European interests can be exaggerated; those interests are not always identical, nor is it always easy to recognize the need to preserve a systemic interest when it conflicts with a more immediate short-term concern. Nevertheless, it is clear from the examples presented in this volume that conflicting interests do not offer an adequate explanation for the modest nature of transatlantic cooperation.

If basic US and European interests are similar, however, it is equally clear from these chapters that there are often clear differences over identifying a problem and deciding how (or even whether) to respond. This dichotomy of perspectives and approaches is based on three main differences:

- the United States is more likely to assume a global perspective, while the European countries primarily regard themselves as regional powers;
- the United States tends to act unilaterally, while the Europeans look for ways to act in concert, first with each other, and then with international organizations; and
- the United States tends to emphasise military solutions, while the Europeans are often slower to act, and when they do are more likely to stress political and economic options.

These dichotomies are rooted in the different histories and political experiences of the United States and the European countries. During the past hundred years, the Europeans have had to recognize the declining influence of their individual states, while the United States has gone from being a relatively isolated country to the leading international power. These are also derived from very different capabilities: the United States possesses vastly superior military power than do the Europeans, so much so that except for operations of limited size and duration, the Europeans would find it impossible to act without the airlift and logistical support of the US military. Nor is this likely to change as the Europeans face pressures to reduce their public debt in order to make European monetary union a reality, while the US Congress continues to support large defense budgets. Finally, as with all such descriptions, the dichotomies are crude, and plenty of exceptions can be found. But the patterns emerged frequently enough from the issues surveyed here that they clearly offer some guidance to transatlantic behaviour. And the differences are sharp enough that they present a significant obstacle to US–European cooperation.

The US Global Perspective vs the European Regional Focus

While Washington involves itself in issues and countries around the world, the European governments are often reluctant to act unless the issue concerns a region in close proximity to Europe: northern Africa or Central Europe, for example. The major exception is the willingness of the European governments to take an active role towards those countries with strong historical or cultural connections, primarily their former colonies. During the Cold War, this universalist perspective led Washington to categorize everyone according to their place in the bipolar struggle; now it takes the form of dividing the world into democracies and emerging democracies (with which Washington can work), and rogue states (which should be isolated). Europeans tend to take a much more particularistic view, based on their own interests or the specific circumstances in the country under question.

This US globalism vs European regionalism can be seen across many of the issues examined in this volume. When restructuring relations with the East, the West European states have given priority to their neighbours in Central and Eastern Europe, while the United States has focused more on Russia, as a former (and future) superpower. The dichotomy clearly emerges with the US emphasis on rogue states; a characterization the Europeans generally reject, while finding reasons to stay 'constructively engaged' with that particular regime. On non-proliferation, the United States has been more concerned about the potential for the spread of weapons wherever it may occur (even North Korea), while the Europeans have focused more on the former Soviet Union, the Middle East and north Africa. The dichotomy is perhaps less severe regarding the management of the global economy – the Europeans have long emphasised regional agreements (such as the EC itself), while the United States focused on global arrangements. Recently, however, as Woolcock points out, the United States has started to put greater emphasis on favouring regional arrangements, including NAFTA and APEC.

The United States Acts Unilaterally vs the Europeans Work in Concert

All too often (at least in the European view) the United States acts first and only later asks for support from its allies. Its perspective is often singular – the United States will act alone if necessary, based on its own interests, but if a few willing allies can be convinced to share the burden, so much the better. On those occasions when Washington seeks the blessing of an international organization, such as the United Nations, it usually does so only after it has decided what steps it will take. That organization, and any allies involved, will have limited influence over US strategy and actions, but will be expected to do as Washington asks. In contrast, when the Europeans are confronted with the need to act internationally, they take a multilateral approach, first conferring among them-selves in order to develop a coordinated response, and then perhaps working through an international organization. (The exceptions are situations involving former colonies, in which one European power may act alone, but usually with the acquiescence of the others.) This tendency to respond to a situation by coordinating among themselves and then with international organizations, has sometimes led the Europeans to be accused of using multilateralism to delay any effective action.

The US tendency towards unilateralism can be seen in the initial version of counter-proliferation policy, attempts to pun-ish those who deal with rogue states (for example, the Helms–

Burton and D'Amato acts), and Section 301 trade legislation. The European emphasis on multilateralism takes several forms. First, and most obvious, the members of the European Union generally consult among themselves before acting, to determine whether the issue can be addressed jointly. Second, regardless of what happens at the European level, the European governments frequently attempt to work within the UN system in dealing with regional conflict (at the very least requiring a UN mandate), or the GATT/WTO system on trade issues (as in their opposition to Helms–Burton). On control of dual-use technologies and proliferation, they have emphasised the need to develop a consensus among suppliers before enforcing restraints; an approach that is undeniably beneficial for the relevant European industries, but that also emphasizes multilateralism.

The United States Stresses Military Options vs Europe Emphasizes Political Measures

When confronted with a need to act internationally, the United States is more likely to favour military solutions, ranging from full-scale combat operations to punitive bombing raids. This approach is derived in part from US capabilities; after all, the United States is the only nation able to implement such options right now. It is also based on a sense that the military is a much more effective instrument of persuasion in the short term than are such options as economic sanctions. In contrast, the Europeans prefer to exert political pressure and encourage negotiated solutions. (Until recently, they have generally been reluctant to use economic sanctions because of the possible impact on trade.) Although individual states may use military power (especially Britain and France), when European governments seek to act jointly, the EU as a whole is more of a 'civilian' power. If Europe does decide to use military force, it tends to act under the umbrella of an international organization such as the United Nations. The Western European Union (WEU) has sponsored a few collaborative European military operations, but these have been very limited in scope and influence. This European approach is based in part on capabilities; or, more specifically, the lack of extensive military capabilities. Finally, this perspective reflects the limitations of European foreign policy decision-making, which currently emphasizes achieving a consensus rather than taking speedy action.

The US emphasis on military solutions is demonstrated by Washington's reliance on two military entities – the creation of the Partnership for Peace and the enlargement of NATO – as ways of addressing potential instability in Eastern Europe. Meanwhile, the European emphasis has been on political and economic reform, using eventual membership in the EU as a lure. As for dealing with rogue states, at most the Europeans will consider economic sanctions (and sometimes not even that), while the United States clearly considers military action to be acceptable if the transgression is serious enough. On the issue of non-proliferation, the US policy of counter-proliferation, as initially developed, included the possibility of military action – a possibility that alarmed the Europeans who found it difficult enough to agree to export restrictions.

These vastly different approaches – the United States as a global power with unilateralist tendencies that often emphasises military solutions, and Europe as a regional power that seeks to work in concert and emphasizes political instruments – do provide at least part of the explanation for why cooperation between the transatlantic partners is so limited. Even when the United States and Europe agree that a certain issue is important, these different perspectives create multiple opportunities for misunderstandings and disagreements, both in defining the problem and determining appropriate means of resolving it.[3]

But if these distinct approaches go far to explain the limited nature of transatlantic cooperation, they do not adequately explain why cooperation happens on some issues and not on others. The survey of issues presented here makes clear that this three-pronged dichotomy is present across the whole range of US–European relations. It exists in those situations where transatlantic conflict is prevalent, but also in those where cooperation has emerged. Thus, while acknowledging this dichotomy can help us understand why cooperation is difficult in general, it does not provide a reliable guide to determining when cooperation will emerge, and why.

CONDITIONS FOR EFFECTIVE PARTNERSHIP

Although there are clearly major obstacles to transatlantic cooperation, it is also clear that such cooperation does occasionally develop. This brings a third question to the fore – under what conditions is such cooperation likely to develop? At least a partial answer can be found in the complex environment in which the United States and the European governments make decisions about foreign policy. While both transatlantic partners maintain a strong rhetorical commitment to cooperation, and shared interests provide further incentives, all too often that cooperation fails to materialize in the face of distinctive approaches and competing pressures. But sometimes that cooperation does emerge and is remarkably effective. Identifying and understanding the conditions that lead to effective cooperation is the first step in strengthening and expanding that cooperation.

The first condition that affects the likelihood of transatlantic cooperation is the *degree of urgency* both partners feel about a particular issue and about transatlantic relations themselves. Although most of the issues examined in this volume are potentially extremely serious, only a few are in a recognizably critical stage. In fact, most are either resolved or in abeyance: the Uruguay Round is finished and the WTO is still in an introductory phase; the issue of Europe's post-Cold War security architecture has been resolved with NATO's reemergence as the preeminent institution; NATO enlargement has been decided for the next few years; a *modus vivendi* in Bosnia has developed despite earlier intra-alliance differences; the NPT has been extended indefinitely, the US– Euratom agreement finalized, and an understanding reached about counter-proliferation. Even transatlantic differences over rogue states have receded for the moment, due to the waiver of some provisions in Helms–Burton and ILSA. As a result, few specific issues are currently generating any urgency in US–European relations, and transatlantic relations are characterized by relative calm.

Ironically, a calm climate in transatlantic relations does not necessarily lead to closer cooperation. In fact, it appears to contribute instead to a general neglect of transatlanticism. It is tensions and even crises that seem to lead to some sort of active cooperation, as happened with the development of the Contact Group and then IFOR in Bosnia. European dismay at the US policy of counter-proliferation led to sometimes forceful discussion in NATO's Defense Group on Proliferation and a better understanding on both sides. The result was enhanced cooperation on proliferation issues. Similarly, the Gulf War created a sense of urgency and thus focused transatlantic efforts, as did the deadlines for the end of the Uruguay Round and the extension of the nuclear NPT.

An additional factor that affects the sense of urgency is the pull of domestic politics. During the 1990s, the attention of both the US and European governments has been firmly directed at domestic issues. During the first two years of the Clinton administration, little time was spent on foreign policy, with the exception of trade policy. Only as crises erupted in Haiti, North Korea, Rwanda and elsewhere did the administration turn from its focus on domestic matters. It was not until the situation in Bosnia reached a crisis in 1995 that foreign policy began to play a larger role in the administration, in part because of the credibility it afforded the President as he approached his re-election campaign. In Europe, priority was given to such intra-European issues as the unification of Germany, the Maastricht treaty and then the Amsterdam treaty, and the approach of European Monetary Union. When European governments were not focused on Brussels, they were concentrating on their own economies which were plagued by high unemployment. When they did look abroad, it was only as far as Central and Eastern Europe where the dissolution of the Warsaw Pact and the overthrow of communist governments led to serious political, economic and social instability that threatened Western Europe with a potential refugee crisis. This emphasis on the domestic situation is certainly understandable, but it has made international issues – and the necessity to cooperate in resolving them – a matter of even less urgency.

Thus one condition required for transatlantic cooperation is clear – there must be a sense of urgency, or the effort of cooperation will seem too great. That urgency can be generated by a crisis over a particular issue; a deadline for a particular negotiation, conference or summit; or by a serious malaise in transatlantic relations generally. There must be enough urgency so that top-level decision-makers on both sides of the Atlantic will escape the press of domestic issues for at least a few moments. Without these conditions, there will be general assurances of cooperation, but the actual effort of consultation and coordination is likely to be neglected. Only when an issue has become a priority, and it is clear that it cannot be resolved without concrete collaboration, does the rhetorical commitment to cooperation become reality.

The second condition that affects the likelihood of transatlantic cooperation is the existence of established and effective *mechanisms of collaboration*. These can take a variety of forms, ranging from the complex and permanent procedures of formal institutions to temporary bilateral working groups, or even simply regularly scheduled ministerial or summit meetings.[4] These mechanisms are critical to effective cooperation because they provide opportunities for regular consultations in an environment in which the incentives and pressures encourage such cooperation. By their very nature, summit meetings and working group sessions create a certain pressure to achieve an agreement. In contrast, when governments attempt to resolve differences without the presence of such mechanisms, it is easy for disincentives – lack of priority, focus on domestic politics, interest group desires – to dominate.

These mechanisms foster collaboration in three ways. First, once a decision to cooperate has been made, they provide the processes that are necessary to make that decision a reality. This can be clearly seen in the relative success of US–European cooperation in Bosnia after NATO became the predominant implementing organization. Once the issue moved into NATO's sphere of responsibilities, it was dealt with through a familiar set of procedures that reinforced US–European cooperation. Similarly, the Partnership for Peace, being based on existing NATO procedures, was much more likely to succeed than if those procedures had not already existed. Second, these mechanisms create a general climate in which it is easier for views to be exchanged in a less-formal manner. By providing opportunities for consultations they allow policies to be clarified, and may even encourage shifts in policies. This can be seen in NATO's Defense Group on Proliferation, and in the working group on proliferation established under the Transatlantic Declaration. Third, some mechanisms, especially those linked to regularly scheduled ministerials or other meetings, may encourage cooperation by establishing a series of small but regular deadlines. This can have the effect of breaking down an issue into a set of discrete, manageable steps. Thus, the presence of established mechanisms in a particular issue area may contribute greatly to the ability of the United States and Europe to work together in addressing that challenge.

A third condition – the existence of a *common external institution* – is also key to successful transatlantic cooperation. Such institutions are present in all the issues under examination here, and for the most part the United States and Europe are major participants whose support of the institution is essential to its survival. They include NATO, OSCE, GATT/WTO, the United Nations, the Wassenaar Arrangement/New Forum, the Missile Technology Control Regime and many others. Such institutions can encourage cooperation in three ways. First, a threat to the existence or effectiveness of the institution itself can raise the priority of an issue and thereby encourage cooperation. These institutions are a concrete manifestation of the transatlantic partners' stake in the existing international order; a threat to such an institution makes clear their shared interest in maintaining that order. Indeed, fears about the impact on NATO of the continuing war in Bosnia contributed greatly to the US decision to become fully engaged in finding a solution to that conflict and to cooperate with its European allies. Second, such an institution can provide effective cover for those governments that wish to cooperate internationally but first must overcome domestic opposition. The possibility that Europe would pursue a formal protest with the WTO has limited the actual imposition of US sanctions in the cases of Cuba and elsewhere, despite congressional pressure. Third, such common institutions encourage cooperation by providing fora and mechanisms for actually pursuing such collaboration, thus reinforcing the second condition outlined above.

The fourth condition that appears to affect the likelihood of transatlantic cooperation is the *nature of the issue* itself. The survey of issues here indicates that several qualities can make some issues more appropriate for cooperation than others. First, cooperation is far more likely if the topics on which collaboration is sought are specific in content rather than general. That is, cooperation is more likely if it is attempted on a narrowly-focused issue, such as a particular trade matter, rather than a broad question of general policy. In fact, even when there is a rhetorical commitment to transatlantic co-operation on a general issue (further openness in trade, for example), it is often difficult to make such cooperation a reality until specific issues are identified and addressed. Thus, the proposed Transatlantic Free Trade Area proved too large and inchoate a proposal, and the New Transatlantic Agenda (which is comprised of many very specific issues) was accepted as a roadmap for transatlantic relations. This can be taken to extremes: an agenda limited to only one difficult issue may leave insufficient room for maneuver and bargaining. But it is specificity, not generalities, that changes rhetoric into effective cooperation.

Second, cooperation is more likely to be enhanced if the issue under negotiation is focused on implementing a policy rather than on devising the policy itself. It might be argued that the United States and Europe must jointly formulate policy in order to have joint implementation, but this does not seem to be the case. Indeed, although the transatlantic partners have found it difficult to coordinate assistance to the CEE countries at the policy level (despite a basic agreement to cooperate), the actual aid providers have found ways to work together when faced with obstacles on the ground. This does not mean that the United States and Europe cannot work together on significant endeavours. But such undertakings are more difficult, especially when there is little urgency. Under those circumstances, most governments will focus on other higher-priority issues, and thus lack the determination and focus required, for example, to negotiate a TAFTA. But even under those same circumstances, they might be able to find common ground over an issue that has become merely 'technical' or a matter of implementation. The matter can then be turned over to the experts (often with an unstated, but implicit, mandate to reach agreement), while high-level policy-makers can focus on other, more urgent, issues.

Third, cooperation is more likely to be achieved if the issue is amenable to the forms of cooperation identified here as parallelism and division of labour. One consequence of the very different transatlantic approaches discussed earlier is that they make it much easier for the United States and Europe to focus on distinct aspects of a particular issue and apply their different capabilities. As Müller points out in his description of the NPT renewal effort and the denuclearization of Ukraine, it is clear that this dichotomy contributed to the development of an effective division of labour. The differing transatlantic approaches also clearly played a role in some of the coopera-tion undertaken in the CEE countries, as detailed by Feldman. Thus, although a division of labour entails significant risks, it can develop into one of the more effective – and likely – means of transatlantic cooperation.

The final factor affecting the likelihood of transatlantic cooperation is the *internal coherence of each of the partners, or if that is lacking, the willingness of at least one to undertake a leadership role.* As the Cold War ended, many believed that Western Europe was on the verge of becoming a more autonomous international actor. The original conception of an Atlantic Alliance based on two pillars – a true partnership of equals – seemed to be achievable in the near future. Yet, this did not happen. Instead, Western Europe has turned inwards to focus on institution-building. As noted above, the consequence has been that the familiar Cold War era pattern of US leadership has re-emerged. This is especially true on issues involving military force, as can be seen by the reemergence of NATO as the primary security institution in Europe, and by the greater willingness of Washington to use force in the Gulf and in Bosnia. In contrast, the revitalization of the WEU has remained in limbo, and the nascent ESDI is now lodged within NATO.

Yet, this pattern of US dominance is not inevitable. On some issues under examination in this volume there has been a more equitable pattern to US–European cooperation. In the negotiations leading to the extension of the NPT, for example, Europe was a more unitary actor and was thus a more effective partner for the United States. In such instances the European Union has either identified the issue as the subject of a joint action under the CFSP, as it did with the extension of the NPT, or the EU has legal competence over an issue because of treaty obligations, as is the case with trade policy.

Thus, cooperation does not appear to depend on whether the US leads or whether there is a coherent European actor; what it requires is that one of those conditions exist. Thus, in this survey of potential US–European cooperation, two patterns emerge as indicators for successful collaboration: first (and especially applicable to security and defense issues), the United States assumes a preeminent leadership role; or, second, the Europeans establish a unified policy process that allows them to be a cohesive international actor capable of cooperating with the United States.

CONCLUSION

This survey of US–European efforts to address several major international challenges before them reveals, above all, that transatlantic cooperation in this area has been modest. Despite the importance of these issues, and the central role the United States and Europe must play if they are to be managed effectively, successful cooperation has been limited. This is not because of conflicting or significantly differing interests across the Atlantic. Indeed, the United States and Europe share a wide range of interests in stabilizing the post-Cold War order, and transatlantic conflict is almost non-existent compared to recent decades. Ironically, the lack of cooperation can in part be explained by this relative peace in transatlantic relations. With few issues at a critical juncture, the political leadership in both the United States and Europe would prefer to focus on domestic issues. Thus, even though the rhetorical commitment to cooperation remains strong, there is little incentive to actually make it a reality, particularly when it is easier for each party to work on its own.

In addition, there is little doubt that the significantly perspectives and approaches of the United States and Europe hinder cooperation significantly. But these differences exist across all issues, even those in which cooperation is effective. Thus, by itself this dichotomy does not explain why cooperation occurs on some occasions and not on others. To understand this, we must turn to the successful examples of transatlantic cooperation, including the extension of the NPT, the enlargement of NATO, and the New Transatlantic Agenda.

These examples do reveal a set of patterns that together allow a greater understanding of when and why cooperation occurs. Cooperation is most likely to develop when five conditions are met:

- A sense of urgency exists, either about the issue itself or the transatlantic relationship generally (this urgency must be enough to overcome the natural predilection of politicians to focus on domestic politics).
- Effective mechanisms of collaboration exist.
- Shared external institutions are present (this is especially useful if these institutions are under threat).
- The issue involved is specific, and likely to be concerned with implementation rather than policy formulation.
- Coherent leadership is available and exercised.

Not all of these conditions must always be present, of course. On occasion, for example, a great degree of urgency or crisis will make it possible to cooperate on significant issues of policy, such as the commitment of military forces in Bosnia. Nor does the fact that transatlantic relations are currently quiescent mean that no movement towards cooperation can take place. On the contrary, such times can be used for establishing expert working groups on particular topics, reinforcing the routine of regularly scheduled ministerials, and otherwise strengthening the mechanisms that are so necessary to cooperation. In this way, the modest cooperation that already exists across the Atlantic can be sustained and perhaps even invigorated until it is truly effective in addressing the global issues of the post-Cold War era. It is not there yet.

Notes

1. These conclusions draw heavily not only on the previous chapters, but also on the observations of those who participated in the two

conferences associated with this project, especially Ellen Frost and Steven Miller, who drew out some general themes in our final authors' workshop. I am also indebted to my co-editor, Ivo H. Daalder, who commented extensively on earlier drafts of this paper.

2.   I am indebted to Jane M. O. Sharp for many of these observations on regional conflict, which were provided in drafts of unpublished papers and in workshops associated with this volume.

3.   For an argument that US–EU cooperation should be based on recognition of differences rather than imagined harmony, see Michael Smith and Stephen Woolcock, 'Learning to Cooperate: The Clinton Administration and the European Union', *International Affairs*, vol. 70, no. 3 (1994), pp. 459–76.

4.   For discussion of such mechanisms in the US–EU context, see Roy H. Ginsberg, 'Transatlantic Dimensions of CFSP: The Culture of Foreign Policy Cooperation', in Elfriede Regelsberger, Philippe de Schoutheete de Tervarent and Wolfgang Wessels (eds), *Foreign Policy of the European Union: From EPC to CFSP and Beyond* (Boulder, CO: Lynne Rienner, 1997), pp. 297–318; Thomas Frellesen and Roy H. Ginsberg, *EU–US Foreign Policy Cooperation in the 1990s: Elements of Partnership*, CEPS Paper no. 58 (Brussels: Centre for European Policy Studies, 1994); and Anthony Laurence Gardner, *A New Era in US–EU Relations? The Clinton Administration and the New Transatlantic Agenda* (Aldershot, UK: Avebury Press, 1997).

Index